STEPHEN FRY'S INCOMPLETE & UTTER HISTORY OF CLASSICAL MUSIC

STEPHEN FRY'S INCOMPLETE & UTTER HISTORY OF CLASSICAL MUSIC

AS TOLD TO TIM LIHOREAU

BOXTREE

First published 2004 by Boxtree

First published in paperback 2005 by Pan Books

This edition published 2015 by Boxtree
an imprint of Pan Macmillan, a division of Macmillan Publishers Limited
Pan Macmillan, 20 New Wharf Road, London N1 9RR
Basingstoke and Oxford
Associated companies throughout the world
www.panmacmillan.com

ISBN 978-0-7522-6558-2

1 3 5 7 9 8 6 4 2

A CIP catalogue record for this book is available from the British Library.

Designed and typeset by seagulls
Printed and bound by CPI Group (UK) Ltd, Croydon, CR0 4YY

This book is based on the Classic FM radio series
The Incomplete & Utter History of Classical Music with Stephen Fry
Presenter: Stephen Fry
Writer: Tim Lihoreau

Contents

Acknowledgements

I'd like to thank Classic FM's Managing Director, Roger Lewis, for the opportunity, the time and the never-ending encouragement to work on the *Incomplete & Utter History*, as well as Darren Henley for both the original idea and the generous support.

Also at Classic FM, a big thank you to Kate Juxon for all her help, as well as Giles Pearman and Jo Wilson.

A huge thank you to my commissioning editor, Emma Marriott, who, from day one, has given me nothing but support and encouragement on this project. I'd also like to express gratitude to the copy-editor Christine King and designers Sean Garrehy and Jonathan Baker.

Finally, I'd like to give a big thanks and a sloppy wet kiss to Siobhan, Millie, Daisy and Finn, for letting me have so much time in 'the den'. Love 'n' thanks.

FOREWORD

Everyday and sublime. That's what it is.

Johann Sebastian Bach is quoted as once saying, 'It's easy to play any musical instrument: all you have to do is touch the right key at the right time and the instrument will play itself.' To some extent, I agree with him. I'm pretty sure I could master the techniques necessary to be lord over, say, a recorder or a mouth organ. I could press the right buttons, probably, and who knows, maybe even manage 'Frère Jacques' before long. The part over which I almost certainly hold no dominion, though, is the part that happens both before and after you've touched the piano key or covered the recorder hole. The bit that says, 'Play this not only now, but like this.' Then says, 'And phrase it like this.' Even, 'and draw this out of the note to make people subconciously think back to that part of the tune three bars back.' That's the bit that reminds me that, yes, Bach did have his flutter tongue firmly in his cheek.

The Greeks knew this. They had their nine Muses, each shedding a light on one particular area of 'mousike' – that is the art of the Muse, covering not just music and dance but all areas of arts, science and, generally, learning. Hence, words like music and museum (even mystery) have an original connection to the works of the Muses. I sometimes wonder if it's a knowledge of this that intimidates me so much in the area of music.

At school, one of my greatest regrets was my inability to produce any two notes, in order, which could be said to resemble a tune. One note? Fine, I could produce one note with the best of them, possibly not a very nice note, admittedly, and occasionally attractive to passing wildlife, but nevertheless, a note all the same. It was only when I had to produce two or more notes, in succession, in tune, that I had any problems. Serious problems, actually, hence I tended to shut up, to not join in, to mime even. My music had charms to 'seethe' the savage breast, if you like.

So, at an early age, it was decided to leave it to the experts, let them get on with it. They seemed to be doing a good job. And besides, there was one branch of music at which I excelled. I think I'm not being unduly immodest if I were to say many thought I showed early promise in this area. Indeed, sometimes, so accomplished did I become in this particular musical discipline that I more than momentarily considered taking it up professionally. The area I'm talking about, of course, at which I consider myself of Olympic standard, no less, is... listening.

Listening to classical music. I could do it, in the words of Voltaire, '*jusqu'à ce que les vaches viennent à la maison*'. And how right he was. My favourite composers to listen to are Mozart and Wagner, but I have a quite extensive listening repertoire beyond them. *Don Giovanni*, though, is a work that I can come back to again and again and, like a favourite journey at the end of which you arrive somewhere special, I discover new things every time. Always finding something new. Similarly with Wagner. I have long since managed to separate the rather grisly man and his music. Richard Wagner was far from pleasant and his racial and political views, unpleasant to begin with, have been coloured by the cordial relations his descendants had with Hitler. But by their fruits shall ye know them, the works of Wagner are as anti-fascist as could be, espousing as they do, love over power.

This book is aimed at those who love listening to great classical music. It is, as I will remind you at various stages along the way, an incomplete book. It does not cover many of the things that it should do in order to merit the title *Stephen Fry's Complete & Utter History of Classical Music*. Hence, we decided against that moniker, ingeniously arriving at one that both suggests and hints at it, while at the same time completely bloody contradicting it. Brilliant. A stoke of genius

I'm sure you'll agree. It is also full of opinions, some of them mine, some of them not. It is full of suppositions, of flights of fancy, of musical mind trips and, indeed, of complete Tosh. In fact, where I do shamelessly resort to making it up, I've taken the liberty of inserting the symbol ☺ for Tosh, just so as not to confuse too much. Also, in order not to put you off too much, I have put some of the ephemera – explanations, asides, what have you – into footnotes, so that a reader in a hurry might be able to skip on. As a result, it is a very personal book, which, if it does nothing else at all, will convey some of the personal enthusiasm the author holds for his subject. Also, from time to time, I'll take a peek into the current affairs of the age, to see just what was going on when the great composers were, well, composing. While music is, in essence, abstract and needs no knowledge brought to it, either of music or of history, it is fascinating to see what events were shaping the world while the composers lived. Developments in history, art, philosophy and science profoundly affected composers, so during the course of this book contemporary moments, some trivial, some seismic, are mentioned.

It's not just Mozart and Wagner that rustle my bustle, though, I hasten to add. In fact, I have often stopped and wondered, while we were listening to the seemingly endless hours of live concerts and CD recordings of the works of the Great Composers in order to make this book, just exactly which one I would have liked to have been.

Beethoven is the most obvious choice after my top two. He may not have been able to hear at all, towards the end, but his capacity to *feel* was second to none. What attracts me about Beethoven is that idea of 'everyday sublime' again. Picture Beethoven, if you will for a moment, in his room in the Schwarzspanierhaus. His run-down old Graf piano is behind him, totally… well, knackered, from his attempts to beat it so hard and be able to hear it. On the shambles of a desk in front of him, next to his ear trumpet, are numerous books written and over-written with stilted notes, in which his guests had had to write their conversations. There are also sad leftovers of food, broken coffee cups, spilt candle wax – in fact it looks more like a student's bedroom than that of a man whose name would live for years through the genius of his music. Everyday, squalid even. Yet sublime.

The Brit in me can half see himself as Elgar, too, on occasion. Now that must have been a whole different ball boy. Er, I mean game – sorry, slip of the tongue. I remember seeing a picture of Elgar and his wife, Alice, standing outside their summer home, Birchwood Lodge, near Malvern. Elgar is to the right of the front door, his arms folded in a sort of 'impatient dad' manner, a flat cap on his head. Alice appears to be dawdling, head slightly cocked, at the gatepost. There's something about the photo that makes me think I would have liked the life. The idea of my father owning the local music shop appeals too. Ever since *Mork and Mindy*, the music shop had replaced the sweet shop for me as the number one in the list of Top Ten Mythically Fantastic Places to Work when I grew up. And the way he wrote the *Enigma Variations* very much appeals to my ludic tendencies – concealing not just his friends in the movements, but concealing the origin of the tune, too. Yes, Elgar. I could be him.

Tchaikovsky. How I'd love to have lived through what he lived through. The picture I try to imagine of Tchaikovsky is when he was given his honorary degree from Cambridge University in 1893. As it's a place I know well from my own student days, it's odd enough just to think of him strolling the streets, or going back to his temporary digs at West Lodge, Downing College. The man who had written the piano concerto in B Flat, the violin concerto, *Swan Lake*, the *Nutcracker* and *Sleeping Beauty* might easily have nipped off up Regent Street and watched the punts go by, humming the latest ideas he had in his head for the '*Pathétique*' *Symphony*. But there are a couple of other points that grab me about his visit. First, he wasn't the only composer being honoured at that June ceremony – he was in good company. Saint-Saëns and Bruch were also getting degrees, and the three of them got together to give a small concert the night before. Just imagine that. Also, this was the June of 1893. Within a few months of leaving Cambridge, Tchaikovsky had drunk a glass of tap water, contaminated with cholera, and he was dead.

Brahms – now there's a chap I can appreciate. Started every day at 5 a.m., in his rented lodgings, with a strong, freshly brewed coffee. In fact, he wouldn't let anyone else prepare his coffee precisely because they wouldn't make it strong enough. He would then retire to his chair where he would smoke a good cigar – at 5 a.m. – all the while sipping on his strong, dark coffee. This was his ritual of choice, every morning. Later in life, when he had been made very wealthy through his music, he still remained in his rented lodgings and he still enjoyed his 5 a.m. coffee and cigar. The everyday, you see, yielding up the sublime.

Finally, there's Handel, a fellow ardent pipesmoker (of course, his was a white, long-stemmed rune pipe whereas I personally favour a more traditional round-bowled calabash). What excites me about Handel is not his genius, or his ability to move you with some of his music – something I can find rare in a baroque composer – it's his appetite. As a man of dual nationality, it seems Handel could eat for both England and Germany at the same time. There is one famous story of him going into an English tavern and asking for a table for four. When the waiter came he ordered four hefty meals, which duly arrived. 'When will your guests be arriving?' asked the serving maid. 'What guests?' chuntered Handel. 'Now just put the food down and leave me be,' at which point he set about devouring all four meals. That's the sort of composer I want to listen to – a real one, an everyday one, and yet one capable of producing some of the most sublime music. Rossini (so popular it's easy to overlook how good he was) liked his food too. So much so that he retired from composing and devoted himself to gourmandizing. We owe the Tournedos Rossini recipe to him.

Stephen Fry's Incomplete & Utter History of Classical Music, the book, came from a project I undertook with Tim Lihoreau, Creative Director of the popular radio station, Classic FM. Long after the radio programme was a pleasantly fading memory, I was approached and asked would I like to be involved in a book based on the same project? Of course, I immediately declined, saying I had no desire whatsoever to rekindle this relationship and, furthermore, could you remind Mr Lihoreau that he still had £150 and an Abba LP of mine? The offer was, however, repeated. I turned it down again. Of course, when I had declined the offer a third time, it was pointed out that, well, they owned some photographs... and that if I didn't want them to get out, I had better agree to the book. OK, I said, so long as I don't have to cancel any work to do it. (Well, I had *Bright Young Things – The Panto* for Tasmania to work on and three jam commercials to voice. I didn't want to lose out.)

So, the ghastly chap followed me around with his tape recorder virtually everywhere I went. The Tasmanian premiere, he was there. Recording *QI*, he was there. In fact, if you watch a rerun of last year's BAFTAs, you can just see him peeping out from below the lectern. Nightmare, it was. But still. It's finished now.

To sign off, before we start, let me go back to my favourite, Mozart. There are many things about him that are everyday and ordinary. The film wasn't too inaccurate – yes, he liked to play billiards, and often composed while he played. Yes, he had a bit of a bottom fixation, which came through in his letters. But the thing that always gets me about Mozart may or may not be true. I read it a few years ago, in a music magazine. New research, it said, might shed new light on how he died. It was not, it said, poison from Salieri. It was not a fatal overdose of mercury, the fashionable cure for syphilis. It was, a new report suggested, down to the fact that some forty-four days before he died, he had enjoyed a meal of pork cutlets, and this might have been his undoing. They were, it said, possibly infected with trichinosis – little parasitic worms that live in badly stored meat, and fitted perfectly Mozart's final symptoms. So. The composer of the sublime *Clarinet Concerto*, of the sublime *Don Giovanni*, of the sublime *29th Symphony*, was eventually knobbled by a dodgy, everyday chop. Incredible.

As Tom Lehrer once said, 'It's a sobering thought that when Mozart was my age, he had already been dead for two years.'

Quite, Tom, quite.

Stephen Fry
July 2004

Preface

When *Stephen Fry's Incomplete and Utter History of Classical Music* was written, Peter Maxwell Davies had only recently signed for his case of mead and was embarking on his journey as Master of the Queen's Musick. Now, as we come to compile the 2015 edition, Judith Weir has taken on this ermine mantle, and Max is dotting the ties and crossing the high Cs on just one last musical promise. The appointment of the first ever woman to the post is just one of the signs of how healthy the world of classical music is. Indeed, a quick look back over the past eleven years only serves to prove that.

Karl Jenkins, having already staked his claim to the title of most popular living composer with a seemingly regular slot in the Hall of Fame for his oratorio, *The Armed Man*, celebrated the opening of the Wales Millennium Centre with his majestic *In These Stones Horizons Sing* (2004). Staying on home turf, Classic FM was on hand when Jon Lord was commissioned to commemorate the 175th anniversary of Durham University. I remember the tours of the splendours of the city fondly – catching the view of the grey towers from Prebends Bridge with him as he imbibed the inspiration – and hearing the resulting *Durham Concerto* (2007) premiere in the Cathedral one blustery October night, with Jon himself literally rocking his Hammond to a tumultuous climax. Just a couple of years later, sitting in Howard Goodall's kitchen, the composer explained how he wanted to reinvigorate the world of plainchant with his *Enchanted Voices* (2009). The result, and the ensuing further incarnations, was just one of the many reasons Howard was named Composer of the Year at the 2009 Classic BRIT Awards.

The Awards continue to broadcast classical music to a primetime TV audience, with the likes of Thomas Adès picking up the prestigious composer gong (2010). It may seem an age ago now, but Paul Mealor and John Rutter provided new classical music for the 2011 media event of the year: the wedding of Prince William and Kate Middleton. The mix of the intense *Ubi Caritas* and the heritage of *This is the Day* was a testament to how choral music has been at the vanguard of a healthy modern classical revival.

The opera world continues to produce its heroes too: Jonas Kaufmann won the first ever Opera Award in 2013. With record numbers wanting their say in the Classic FM Hall of Fame 2015, whether it be to beat the drum for the *Conga Del Fuego* or to provide *The Lark* with a little uplift, one thing is certain: classical music is in rude health.

Tim Lihoreau
2015

INTRODUCTION

It's both a blessing and a curse not being able to sing a note of music. A note in tune, at least. In many ways, I feel almost Palaeolithic in my inability to have my larynx form anything bearing so much as a vague resemblance to something pleasant. It saddens me. On a particularly bad day, I can barely drag my knuckles out of bed and across the floor for thinking about the similarity between my vocal talents and that of a digestive biscuit. But, on the other hand, as someone who is constantly being accused of behaving like a man from an earlier time, it does mean that I feel I have more than a smidgeon of empathy with whoever it was who first managed to utter, incomplete or not, the very first musical note. Admittedly, no one really knows who it was, his good work lost to an age where the chances of keeping hold of an original document were less than they were during Watergate. Besides, as you can imagine, it wasn't really one person, it was an entire bunch of people, working separately, working together, working for kings and queens, for pharaohs and emperors, even entire kingdoms and dynasties.

So it's almost certain that any clever chap (and, sadly, almost certainly it was a chap) who got us from grunt to note – from savage breast to soothing rest – is never going to show up in the history books. 'I thought up plainchant for Pope Gregory, you know,' might make a good story down the pub, but it's not going to get you a place in Euterpe's♬ Hall of Fame. And don't for one minute think that this book is going to shed any light on them. It's not. It isn't called the 'incomplete' and utter history for nothing, you know.

What I *will* do, however – and don't say I don't give you anything. – is take a look back at which sets of people got the whole music business moving. And to find that out, you have to go way back. And I mean *way back*. And it's not to ancient Egypt, it's not to Shang Dynasty China, it's not even to the Sumerians or Greeks. You may not believe this, but it's only France, isn't it!

FRENCH WITHOUT EARS

Typical. Not only do they make great food, great wine and great lovers, but some people also believe they got the whole music thing first, too. How best to explain this? Well, maybe you could just go with me for a minute, and imagine you are in a cave. You are not far away from Périgeaux some 30 kilometres north of the Dordogne river, once it has parted company with Bergerac. Gorgeous part of France, so possibly take in a spot of wine-tasting when we've done. It's here, in a little place called Ariège, in the Magdalanian cave of Les Trois Frères, that you come across a groovy little wall painting of a character who appears to be half-man, half-bison. (Now there's a phrase I haven't heard since my coming-out party.) In his hand is clearly some sort of bow, and many scholars who can claim to be far cleverer than me have stuck their academic necks out and said: it's almost certainly a musical bow, possibly even a dual-purpose bow – one that doubled up as half instrument, half lethal hunting weapon. I can think of any number of orchestral musicians who would relish a chance to pull one of *those* from their case.

If it is indeed a musical bow that the half-man half-bison is carrying, then he probably fixed it to his hunting mask – lining it up with his nose – and struck it with his hands. A not dissimilar practice goes on in many a city traders' toilet today, albeit of far less interest to

♬ *Euterpe, incidentally, was one of the Nine Muses, her particular area being music.*

musicologists. If you take all this as even *fairly* believable, then you do realize that we're talking at least eight and a half thousand years before the first Egyptian cat looked up from his food, cocked an eye at his master and thought, 'Something in my gut tells me that bloke's up to something'?

OK. **13,500 BC**, and you've got some sort of sketchy evidence of some sort of music going on. After that, give or take the odd 'mammoth-bone flute' turning up here and there, you have to wait another nine or so thousand years – or two and a half Wagner operas – for any real proof that music even existed. If you were to chart a musical map of, say, 4000 BC, then you really wouldn't need much in the way of different coloured crayons at all. You simply have a colour for the Egyptians, one for the Sumerians or Babylonians, and another one for the Greeks. If you happen to have a couple left over for China and India, then all well and good. Let's start with the top three first, though, and that rather uneasy cat.

CAT GUT YOUR TONGUE?

I'm presuming that the Egyptians' love of cats meant that, in actual fact, they probably looked elsewhere when they came to find strings to fit their harps. By now, somewhere around **4000** and **3000 BC**, the Egyptians appear to be putting a flag firmly in the ground and making a healthy enough claim to be the first culture to use not only harps but also flutes. If the harps were anything like the Sumerian harps from around roughly the same time, they were elliptical in shape, and probably had three strings and a rather ornate soundboard, usually carved in the shape of something important at the time. So, in Mesopotamia, you would often see your friendly, local Sumerian harp player sat there, going away at his three strings, with a lavishly carved bull resting on his thighs.

It's the time of the building of the Great Sphinx at Giza, a time when metal coins had finally replaced barley as the currency, and a time when musicians fought over the best gigs in town – playing for the religious ceremonies that celebrated the day's chief deities: the

Mother Goddess Innin and her son Tammuz. Of course, it's always made me think that double-bookings must have been very common, partly because musicians have always been a scatty bunch at the best of times, and partly because the Sumerians and the Egyptians were operating on different calendars. Egypt had adjusted its calendar to 365 days by now, whereas the Mesopotamian cities were operating on the good old-fashioned 'twelve months of thirty days each', making 360. Decidedly confusing and, if your birthday fell in the wrong five days, very disappointing for presents.

'SUMER' IS ICUMEN IN

By the time you get to the Sumer of **2600 BC** and the period known to its friends as Early Dynastic III, the latest, must-have limestone reliefs seem to show the harps have now got six or seven strings. There's even a pot found somewhere near Bismaya that shows the harps slung round the neck – either things are coming on, or this lot had worked out what to do with all that left-over barley and were as drunk as skunks. The Egyptians, meanwhile, had taken to using a rounded, bowed harp called a 'bint' – presumably because it was curvy and everyone wanted to pluck it – as well as long flutes and a double-pipe, often referred to as an 'aulos'. Some one hundred years later, when the tomb of the recently deceased Queen Pu-abi was being prepared at Ur – a good four hundred years before Abraham was ready to leave – she was provided with a fetching eleven-stringed, straight-necked harp. Clearly, by now, the harp has become the 'electric guitar' of its day – utterly ubiquitous and open to numerous stylistic interpretations.

There even appears to have been a niche for the 'glam-rock' harp, one with not just a bull-shaped soundboard but an entire bull. Honest. The whole harp was one big... *thing* which sat on the wooden bull's legs. Sadly, reliefs do not show whether it was customary to pick it up at the end of a concert and bash it into your amp and speaker.

'GANG' OF FIVE

Let me momentarily flit away from Egypt and Mesopotamia for a moment. I know it must be hard to think snow amidst all this but it is true that it was around about now that paintings were made in Rodoy, in southern Norway, of what appears to be people skiing. No doubt they were less concerned with the 'I say, let's go for a jolly glühwein after the piste, what?' aspect of it, preferring to concentrate on the 'RUN FOR YOUR LIFE THERE'S A MAMMOTH!' feel of things. Seems fair. Of course, it has nothing to do with music, you understand. I just wanted to fill in a little detail for you, as it were. Anyway, while I am flitting, then, let me go the scenic route back to neolithic Babylonia, that is to say via China.

China was – and still is – a bit of a genius when it came to the maths stakes, so it is probably no surprise to find that, by now, they had put two and two together to make... five. Or at least, a five-note scale, which appeared to be in use, big-time. It went something like this:

gang | shang | jiao | ji | yu

which I think loosely translates as Dave, Dozy, Beaky, Mick and Titch.

That is, more or less, the first five degrees of the scale, early Chinese style. Had Dame Julie of Andrews been around at the time, it's just minutely possible that the big song of the day would have been not 'Do, a deer' but 'Gang, a fang'... Would have gone something like:

Gang, a fang, a big wolf fang,
Shang, a drop of golden rain,
Jiao, a name I call myself,
Ji... I shout when I'm in pain,
Yu, the one who isn't me... (etc, sorry, not all of the lyrics still survive)

THAT'S MY GAL

Actually, talking of one-time famous singers, try this name for size. Pa-Pab-Bi-gaggir gal. It's a corker of a name, isn't it? And, no word of a lie, he – or it could have been she, it's very hard to tell, much like today – was the big musical star of the period 'Early Dynastic III'. The 'gal' bit in the name simply means GREAT and he/she is referred to in several texts or reliefs. He/she could have been a royal servant or a temple tunesmith, or simply could even have been a gigging musician, booked for special events and rituals. Whoever he/she/it was, they would almost certainly, by their time, be familiar with a battery of instruments that is really beginning to take shape. Harps, lyres, and the odd bit of percussion.

The singers, judging again from reliefs found in Old Kingdom Egypt♬, usually had their left hands held to their ears. Singers today insist this is to hear your 'inner tuning', although some say it is so that you don't hear the guy next to you. With their other hands, they appear to be 'signing', for want of a better word. This, I imagine, was either something similar to what a cantor does in a church to indicate roughly which note he's going to sing next, or it's a signal to the barman to bring another tray of pints across. Other pictures show the singers playing a set of clappers or rattles (sistra) with one hand, the other being used to pinch their larynx. Again, singers today will tell you that pinching your own throat alters both the pitch and timbre of the note, but most musicologists put it down to a desire to 'get in first, before anybody else does'.

LYRE, LYRE, PANTS ON FIRE

Incidentally, do you know how to spot a lyre? No? Well, in that case, lend me a tenner and I'll give it back to you tomorrow. Actually, as bad as that joke was, it was marginally less boring than me telling you that a harp looks like this:

♬ Old Kingdom' is the period in Egypt from around 2850 to 2052 BC*; it was preceded by the period of 'the Two Kingdoms' and followed by the 'Middle Kingdom' period. So you see – the history of music at this time is very much an unwritten Tolkien novel.*

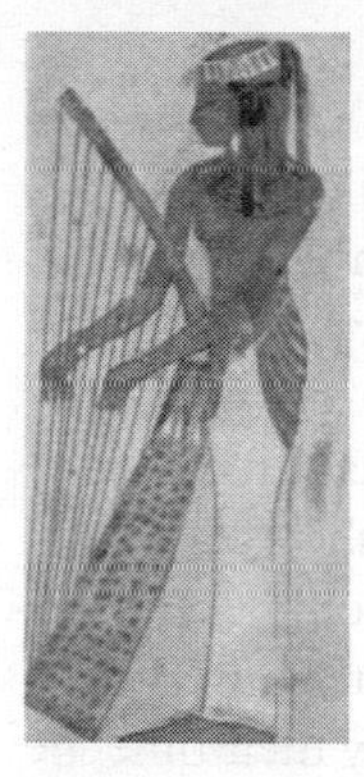

whereas a lyre looks like this:

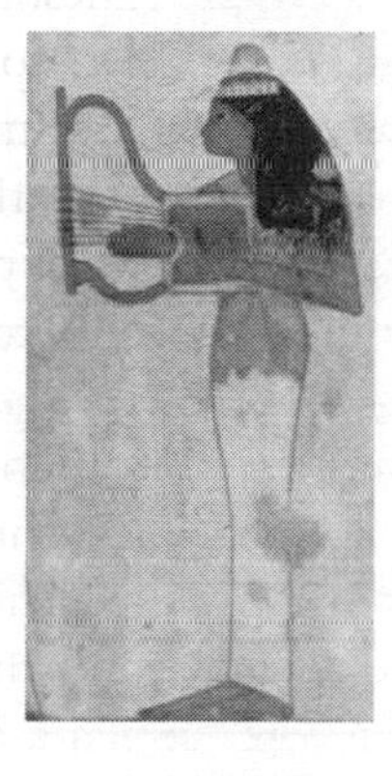

Got that? Good. Well, maybe write it down, alongside the name of the Early Dynastic III period's leading pop star – Pa-Pab-Bi-gaggir gal, remember? The minute you've written it down, fold up the piece of paper, carefully, and place in the bin. Hopefully you'll never need the information ever again. If you do find yourself using this information again, then... well, I think I've sat next to you at a dinner party from hell once.

THE GUTI CALL

So. Lyres, harps, flutes and rattles. My word, things were really flying. The Sumerians, though, were having a bit of a torrid time of it. From **2370 BC** onwards, they were conquered by just about anyone with a few hundred pounds and a good line in swords. Probably the most noteworthy conquerors were the Guti – which, although I have not an ounce of etymological evidence, I like to think was pronounced Gooti, to rhyme with 'booty'. The Guti were a band of mountain barbarians. It's always the way, isn't it? Everything is blamed on 'the barbarians'.

The other 'wave of incoming', as far as the Sumerians were concerned, were the Semitic Akkadians who, probably because of their rather complicated and ill-conceived branding – well, I mean, Guti on one side and Semitic Akkadians on the other: I know which would test better in *my* focus group! – decided to adopt the Sumerian culture they had overthrown, rather than destroy it. Despite its brevity, this Guti/Akkadian period was great for music. Temples were built and, as the saying goes, where there's temples, there's music. In this instance, pipes were almost certainly 'in', as were bull's-horn trumpets which look, from contemporary carvings, extravagantly striking and impressive. Particularly if you are a bull.

After this point, the Sumerians hosted the biggest 'bring and die' party seen for some time. They were conquered, surmounted, reconquered, overcome, defeated, re-reconquered, multi-conquered, triumphed over and generally given a jolly good seeing-to. I think I've made my point. As I'm here, it might be worth just stopping off briefly to put the Babylonian kings under the spotlight and, in particular, one of the most famous of their number, Hammurabi.

Two things have often occurred to me, on more than one occasion, and I think I should share them both with you. They both concern 'the afterlife'. You see, I've often thought that, if there were to turn out to be such a place, then, firstly, it's going to feel something like a motorway service station. Don't know why: just think it would. I imagine it to have distinctive red-and-white branding, with a cute if slightly disembodied-looking mascot resembling a Fury, who gently beckons you to pull in and sample the plastic and largely overpriced post-death environment. I realize this is probably not everybody's view of the afterlife, but, well, you're never going to be able to prove me wrong, so SUE ME! The second, and let's face it more important, aspect of post-mortem existence that has always struck me is that, despite the promise of infinity, I can't for the life-after-death of me see how I'm going to find time to get round to speaking to everyone with whom I'd want to have a jolly good chinwag. And this brings me back to Hammurabi.

Apart from the obvious list of people and questions that you would have in any afterlife – you know, 'Ahh, Mr Einstein, can I interrupt your brunch a minute? I just wondered if I could go through this "$E=mc^2$" thing again. Sorry – haven't quite got it. By the way, don't forget, you get a free refill with that coffee.' Well, apart from all the obvious ones, there's all the ones who you just didn't realize would be quite so interesting. And I think old Hammurabi falls into this bracket.

IF I HAD A HAMMURABI

I say old. Hammurabi almost certainly died young but, nevertheless, he presided over a period which saw huge leaps forward in all walks of life: he put laws in order, as it were, establishing what is almost certainly the first structured legal system, and with it, the first crack-down on 'drink-charioteering'. He did similarly well with the medical system, too. But his successes in the music business are what concern us here. In Hammurabi's time, music really came on. Good things happened to it. New things. This 'West Semitic' period, as it's often known, saw existing instruments become much more portable – a great deal smaller and almost certainly lighter. No doubt the fashion concept of being 'so last dynasty' was introduced, as were brand-new ways of playing instruments. Hammurabi's time introduced a new lyre, again smaller and lighter, which you held with the soundboard against your body and which you plucked with... wait for it... a plectrum! Jeepers creepers. I mean, although it would have been originally just a little piece of quill, you can imagine the scene when that little puppy was introduced into the temple.

Hammurabi: What's this?
Musician: It's a plectrum, your suspended floraness.
Hammurabi: A what?
Musician: A plectrum, O Euphratic one.
Hammurabi: And what do you do with it?
Musician: You pluck the lyre strings with it, sire. It stops your

fingers getting all hard and calloused, and means the lyre player can play for longer…

Hammurabi: I'm not sure that's any real use to me…

Musician: … er, which means shorter drum solos.

Hammurabi: Order me a thousand. ♬

Just in case you don't consider the plectrum to be musically significant enough to justify Hammurabi's inclusion – and let's face it, these days some rock stars get by very well using their teeth – he did also oversee the time which appeared to give birth to the kettle drum (timpani) and the cymbals. So, whenever you sit through a performance of 'Rule Britannia', just think: that drum roll and cymbal crash that comes on

'Ruuuuule…[roll]… Britann-ya… [CRASH]…
Britannya rule the waves…'

… remember: we owe it all to Hammurabi and his ilk. Ironic, really, to think that the scoring of 'Rule Britannia' owes its existence to what is now a small, desolate place nearly 90 kilometres south of Baghdad, central Iraq.

SUMERIA 1, EGYPT 0

Over in Egypt, things were not half as good. The Semitic Hyksos kings, having driven the Egyptians south and set up their own regime around the Nile Delta, appear to have been the exact antithesis of their more or less contemporaneous Babylonian next-door-but- one neighbours. When it comes to music, culture and the arts in general, their tenure of this precious region, roughly from around **1650 to 1550 BC**, produced the following things: nihilum, οὐδέν and

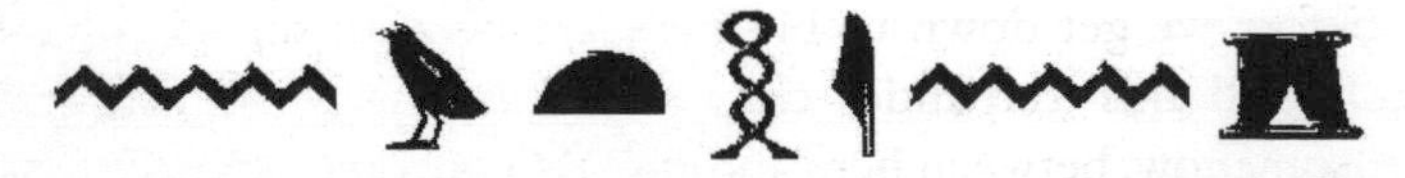

♬ *Although there is no surviving relief depicting this encounter, the conversation has been handed down through the centuries.*

Or, to expand, nothing, nothing and nothing, in Latin, Greek and cod Egyptian. Yes, a bit of a don't-hold-your-breath period for Egyptian arts. No new instruments, no new music and the charts full of sad cover versions.

Let me round up a little, then. **1500 BC** already, and we're doing pretty well. We have a 'version' of music, as it were: very little harmony, though, and mostly one-note stuff, with rather weird instrumentation. So, something that we in the UK today might not recognize too much, unless you happen to be a Phil Collins fan. The Hittites of northern Syria were doing very well, thank you very much, with a whole host of instruments, among them the guitar, trumpet, tambourine and lyre. Later still, around **1000 BC** onwards, there's also evidence of professional singers and musicians being connected with religious ceremonies in Israel, using many of the same instruments. But to get to the first actual recorded piece of music, you have to skip a full two hundred or so years, back to the Sumerians. They had got their five-note scale, too, some time after **800 BC** and left the first ever piece of music not long after. It was a hymn and, obviously, when I say recorded, I mean it was carved on what is known as a cuneiform tablet, a wedge-shaped piece of clay, which would be inscribed with a stylus when wet. Now, if I simply ignore the best part of a hundred years or so – and believe me, I am more than prepared to do that – then I can get on to the Greeks, in earnest. And who better to start with than Terpander of Lesbos? Er, that's a rhetorical question, by the way.

MAYBE IT'S BECAUSE I'M A LESBIAN...

Well, who knows, it could have been the title of a song. But before we get down to business, we need to see what sort of artistic world this Terpander chap was born into. You see, somewhere, somehow, between here and the old court musicians in Egypt, music had gone from being pretty much nothing to pretty much everything. Music, the Greeks now believed, was the bringer of all things good. It shaped morals. It educated. The 'aural' pleasure of music was but the tiny tip of the iceberg. Music was much more important than just the smile it raised. It was, also, not just about music. Music to the Greeks – *mousike* – meant three things: dancing and poetry, as well as music itself.

Terpander of Lesbos lived from **712 to 645 BC**, and was probably born in Antissa on the north-western side of the island. He is credited with inventing the seven-stringed lyre and, whether he did or not, he certainly made a big enough noise with it at the 26th ancient Olympiad, held in Sparta, to become a bit of a national hero. If this wasn't enough to win him fame and fortune, he also allegedly started the first music schools in Sparta.

Around the same time, a more legendary character was also making a bit of a splash in the music world. Arion was a native of Samos, a famous musician working at the court of Periander, the king of Corinth. These days, he is largely remembered for two things: first, that he introduced the idea of 'strophes' and, thus, 'antistrophes' – that is, the alternating parts of a stanza. Secondly, though, and slightly more interestingly, he is also remembered for what happened to him at sea. On the way back from a music competition in Sicily, his boat was stormed by pirates, who robbed him and were about to throw him overboard when Arion asked that he be allowed to sing one last song. He took up his lyre and sang so beautifully that dolphins gathered around the boat. When he was finally made to walk the plank, he got a lift on the back of a dolphin and was ferried safely to the shore. I do love a happy ending.

The next major character in the incomplete and utter history of Greek music is the multi-talented Pythagoras. No, there weren't two people named Pythagoras – this is the very same person who lived from 580 BC and came up with the theorem for right-angled triangles. If you think about it, though, music was at much the same point in its development as mathematics and science, so it's not surprising that a philosopher/mathematician would, at some point, focus his attentions on music. Pythagoras more or less came up with the scale we have today. Legend has it that he got some of his inspiration from watching and listening to a blacksmith at work hammering. Noticing that the hammers all produced different sounds, he discovered that they weighed 12, 9, 8 and 6 pounds each. It's said that, from this, he derived the intervals of an octave, a fifth, a fourth and a tone. If true, it wouldn't be the last time that making music and getting hammered had gone hand in hand.

Pythagoras died in around **475 BC**. He was overlapped, so to speak, by a guy called Pindar, a great Greek lyric poet, possibly the greatest. He was a 'Boeotian' – that is, both a resident of central Greece *and* a particularly nasty turn of the letters from Carol in *Countdown*. Pindar was a well-travelled nobleman and enough fragments of his work survive to make it clear that he more or less invented the ode. He was also a bit of a wiz on the aulos, the cithara, and the lyre. Clever clogs, no doubt, but a bit B-list when you compare him to the chap who came along just eleven years after he died – Mr Lato: Mr P. Lato.

PLATONIC SOLFA

OK, OK, I hear you read, just what is another philosopher doing in the *Incomplete & Utter*? Well, I'll tell you. Not only did Plato give us most of our info on Pythagoras, he also laid down a few 'philosophical' ideas about music, too, both in his *Republic* and *Laws*. Music consists of three aspects, he said: the word, the harmony and the rhythm. Instrumental music was out. Words were integral. He also had a few things to say about the nature of the different modes. The different modes were, more or less, the different scales that each piece was played in – not exactly scales, and not exactly keys, to be precise, but the groups of notes used to play any given piece. Plato believed he could define many of the characters of the modes, and, going one step further, could prescribe and recommend different modes for different things. The 'Mixolydian' mode, he said, was full of wailing and lamenting, while the 'Lydian' and even 'Ionian' modes were effeminate and relaxing – and therefore unsuitable for fighting men. Pieces composed in the 'Dorian' mode were heroic, while the 'Phrygian' character was persuasive. I wonder if anyone ever took his advice to heart and faced a marauding enemy of barbarians, armed only with a Lydian ode, hoping to relax them to death?

INSTRUMENTAL INSTITUTION

Just as Plato was a pupil of Socrates, so Aristotle was a pupil of Plato. Born in Stagirus, Macedonia, in **384 BC**, Aristotle studied with Mr P. at his Academy in Athens. Aristotle (wouldn't it be lovely if we could find evidence to suggest he was known as Ari to his friends?) was not a great musician, as such, but, like Plato before him, he applied his thinking to many areas of life, one of them being music. He, too, thought that music was MUCH more important than the simple aural pleasure that it gave. It had real ethical power, and it was vitally important in the process of education. He disagreed with Plato, though, on the subject of words. He *was* prepared to accept instrumental music, because, he thought, it spoke directly to the listener's emotions, unhindered by a poet's words. To him, music was almost homeopathic and certainly cathartic. If he were in charge today, you'd probably be able to get a prescription at the chemist's for string quartets, to be taken two or three times a day, with food.

His pupil, Aristoxenus, a generation later, took his thoughts and, ignoring almost all other areas of philosophy except music, came up with 'Elements of Harmonics' and 'Elements of Rhythm'. One of *his* principal theories was that the soul is to the body what harmony is to the musical instrument. He also moved away from the ideas of his former teachers, the Pythagoreans, by saying that you shouldn't work out notes of a scale by mathematical ratio alone, but also by ear.

Aristoxenus' dates are not known, exactly, but presuming, as most do, that he was dead and curried by, at the latest, **300 BC**, then what we are left with is what Greek scholars call '*megalos trypa aimatodis*', or, to translate, a bloody big gap. Nothing much happened until around **50 BC**.

GETTING ORGANIZED

To be fair, 'The Bloody Big Gap of 300 BC' – as it's known in our house – did contain the early stirrings of the organ. At some stage in this period, some clever sausage decided that the aulos, or pipe, had one fatal flaw and that was the aulos players. They were always running out of breath. So, a 'pumped aulos' was born, on much the same principle as the uilleann pipes, where a player would squeeze an air bladder with one arm, while playing the pipes with both hands. Then, in the third century BC, an engineer called Ctesibus, working in Alexandria, was said to have gone one step further with the '*organon hydraulikon*' or water aulos, which used air compressed by the weight of water. Came complete with galoshes.

Ctesibus was the son of a barber and very popular with the emperors of Rome. As an engineer, he had worked on the restoration of the aqueducts. In fact, he had even designed machines of war for the emperor, intended to inflict maximum pain on those with whom they came into contact. So I suppose it was only natural that he turn his hand to the organ.

It was probably he who more or less invented it. Contemporaneous accounts tell of his '*mechanike syntaxis*', a pan pipe 'which is played with the hands and is known as the hydraulis' in which 'the wind mechanism forces the air into a pnigeus of brass placed in the water'. Got that? I think it's basically saying that he almost certainly developed the first organ, of sorts, and with it, presumably the first bandy-legged musician, with slightly staring eyes, a somewhat mad smile and a tendency to invade your personal space. Or should I say, 'the organist'.

The organ was to prove a big hit at Delphi in 90 BC when Antipatros won a big competition playing it. It was followed by the next big thing, some forty years later, just as Gaius Julius Caesar and Pompey were fighting it out for the laurel wreath, namely the oboe. In fact, although he is now almost always considered first and foremost a violinist, the Emperor Nero was almost certainly an oboe player. Sadly, when I think of the words 'Emperor Nero' now, I immediately see 'Emperor Christopher Biggins', swimming in a not-quite-voluminous enough toga in front of a set that's only just this side of shaky. *I, Claudius* has a lot to answer for.

Skipping blithely over the fact that the Chinese reordered their octave into sixty parts in 38 BC – quite how or why, I've no idea – we get to another *megalos trypa aimatodis*. Although, in this instance, I should probably say '*grandis cavus sanguineus*'.

JC. AND I DON'T MEAN BACH

This was a *grandis cavus sanguineus* with a difference, though. This was a *grandis cavus sanguineus ET CHRISTIANUS*. Of course! AD is all the rage, now, and absolutely *everybody* is accessorizing with a fish. Music would prove useful in spreading what was at first no more than a sect. Statement and response psalms were a fantastic tool in the spread of Christianity, as was the soon-to-be-ubiquitous 'hymn'. Saints Augustine and Jerome were quick to see the benefit of being able to keep a message at the front of the mind with a catchy tune, although they did, at the same time, worry about the 'sensual pleasure' that the music gave and whether there was damage being done. Because of the essentially 'word of mouth' nature of the medium, too, it was frequently the case that incorrect or even deliberately false info was getting through in these hymns. This is where the first big saviour of music stepped in. He was big, he was bold, he was brash – he was Bishop, to be fair, of Milan. And he went by the seductively sexy name of...

AMBROSE!

OK, not that sexy, I admit, but still, eh? Don't shoot Melinda Messenger, as it were.

I THINK THEREFORE I AMBROSE

It's fair enough, really. Ambrose was, indeed, the Bishop of Milan, elected in a bizarre manner when he was thirty-five. It's said during a gathering to find a new bishop, at which Ambrose was present but not actually a contender, a child from the crowd began to chant the words: 'Ambrose... bishop... Ambrose... bishop'. Taking this as divine intervention, of course, rather than, say, just plain odd, a rather reluctant Ambrose was given the office.

The reason a reluctant bishop makes it into the *SFI&UHoCM* is because his big claim to fame was not theological or liturgical, at all, but musical. Up to Ambrose's time, music in church was generally performed by professional chanters, who would more or less monopolize all the best tunes. Ambrose opened up the singing to the people, with antiphonal chanting, which was enough to move St Augustine, for one, to tears.

It's known now as 'Ambrosian Chant' and is still practised today in the northern part of Italy, favoured over the now almost wall-to-wall Gregorian chant (after Pope Gregory IX – more on him in a minute). To put it into context, this was around the time that the Roman legions started the mass exodus from the inclement little outpost they called Britain – something to do with muttered complaints of 'It's always raining…' and 'You can't get a good latte…'.

Ambrosian chant, Gregorian chant – it all comes under the banner headline 'plainsong': generally sung by monks in monasteries, on one note, with occasional organ accompaniment. I always think it is an unfortunate phrase because it's often far from 'plain' at all. It's beautiful stuff.

This whole period of Ambrose and Gregory is, to be fair, considered by many to be more or less the start of classical music, as we know it today, mainly because it is the first period where we really got anything like a sizeable chunk of the stuff written down. Of course, as we've seen, there had been music around long, long before this. The Sumerians playing from their wedge-shaped tablets, the Greeks on their aulos, and even the Egyptians on their flutes. See? Clever chaps, the Egyptians – even had James Galway before everyone else.

NON UNUS BOTULUS

But then, quite suddenly and dramatically, and, it's got to be said, wholly without warning…

…nothing happened.

In fact, immediately after this, it happened again.

Nothing, I mean.

To be fair, it went on happening for a good two centuries.

Nothing. Happening for two whole centuries! If you want to get any idea what that must have been like, try ringing a computer helpline.

All the while, though, the world just kept on turning.

Just.

The years fairly creaked by.

Tum ti tum.

In fact, before you knew it, it was already, ooh, later the same afternoon.

Eventually, though, the last Roman out of Britain had said '*Bonum ridensum*' and now turned off the light, a rather angry young man name of Attila the Hun came and went, and the Ostrogoth navy, now split from the Visigoths, was defeated by the Byzantines.

There you are, see. Less 'the history of this period' and more a role-playing game.

Then, all of a sudden, before you could say 'bring out your dead', it was **600**.

I'D LIKE TO TEACH THE WORLD TO SING... IN PERFECT MONODY

Year **600**, that is, and up pops another Pope. Step forward... Gregory I. He, as well as despatching St Augustine to Thanet with the words, 'Mmm, Gus, baby, I've got a cute little job for you... go get your brolly...', he it is who decides to get together a school, the Schola Cantorum, in Rome, to have another go at sorting the whole music business out.

Allegedly, it was also around now that a new breed was formed, the *managerius brandius* or 'brand manager', as they came to be known. Or at least, it was the first known time that anyone used the phrase 'Let's make sure we're all singing from the same hymnsheet.' Greg One, as the numberplate on his horse and cart read, also published

The Anitphonar, a collection of church chants. To be fair, it's almost certain, now, that he was just one of a bunch of mainly religious figures who tried to move music on, generally, but, through a mixture of legend and personal influence, it's he who is remembered for it. The personal influence is obvious – he was Pope (from 590 to 604) and, back then, you probably couldn't have a safer bet for making sure you got your 'plus one' on a bouncer's guest list. The legend is more difficult to fathom. It appears that, despite being just one of a bunch of important people in music, the passing of the years – and possibly the desire to blame someone – meant that he was seen as the person who not only gathered together plainchant, but also the one credited with writing most of it, which is almost certainly untrue. Still, it does give us a very convenient pivot point.

Gregorian chant had arrived and the last echoing spoonful of Ambrosian had faded away to nothing.

BIRTH

So. We're officially off the mark. PLAINSONG. Beautiful, generally single-note stuff. Music has arrived, thanks to a mixture of Saints Ambrose and Gregory. The next chap who gets a look-in with regards to the 'Important people in Music History' *Stars in Their Eyes Special* is a man called Guido. No, not Fawkes.

Sorry to rush but I do have rather a lot of centuries to cover. I've taken the liberty of moving on a few hundred years, if that's OK? King Canute is now boss of Britain Plc, and paddling is in. Bigtime. And just as Mr and Mrs Khayyám put a small ad in the *Persian Post* announcing the birth of little Omar, the musical world was getting to grips with a new system invented by a man called Guido d'Arezzo. He it was who laid the groundwork for another mythically talented musician, the great aforementioned 'Julie of Andrews'.

As his name suggests, Guido spent a lot of his life in the Italian city of Arezzo, some 30 kilometres north of Lake Trasimeno. He was a Benedictine monk who had moved from his native Paris.

Guido's method invented a series of words to go with the notes, or in the words of Queen Julie herself, 'One shalt commence at the very outset, indeed a goodly place wherein to begin. When one dost peruse, one surely inaugurates the process by means of the initial three symbols, ABC, when thou singest, thou leadest with "Do re mi"'. Er, etcetera.

But, to be fair… it more or less sums it up. So next time you're talking about *The Sound of Music*, maybe drop into the conversation,

'Ah, yes, the old tonic solfa system, as pioneered by Guido d'Arezzo in the eleventh century. Or was it Steps?'

In fact, old Guido was a busy little sausage. In this same year, just as the Chinese were putting the finishing touches to their pleasant albeit lethal mix of charcoal, sulphur and potassium nitrate – aka gunpowder – and the weird sounding poem on everyone's lips was *Beowulf* (well, either that, or they were all drunk), our man in the music world was also developing that cute little five-line thing that all music is now written on, called 'the stave', also known as the staff. This thing.

With this little thing, musicians need never get lost again. Unless they were male and driving with their girlfriends, of course. Anyway, the stave was from year **1000**.

It was left to sad music students hundreds of years later to make up mnemonics like 'All Cows Eat Grass', 'Every Good Boy Deserves Favour', and my personal favourite, 'Guinevere Eats Cordelia's Aardvaark for Dinner'♬, to remember the notes. Guido needed someone to work on his PR though, because most people have never heard of him. Maybe add a power initial to his name... let's see, Guido G. d'Arezzo. That would have done it. That would have made them sit up and take notice. No doubt had he been living today, he would have been called something like the Guid-o-stave, just to make sure his name survived the years.

Guido d'Arezzo died in **1050**. Just forty-eight years later, there came another musician working in a similar world – days spent in prayer and thought. This person, too, would make a significant contribution to music – maybe not in quite the same tangible and enduring way as Guido and his five famous lines, but important all the same. This person, born in **1098**, really did move music on to new heights, made sure it got noticed. But the truly shocking thing about this particular composer, arranger, poet and dreamer is... she was a woman!

♬ *Which is, of course, the spaces downwards on the treble clef. 'All Cows Eat Grass' is the spaces upwards on the bass clef, and 'Every Good Boy Deserves Favour' is the mnemonic for the lines upwards on the table. Glad to have cleared that up.*

FROM 'STAFF' TO DISTAFF

One of the things I've always found curious about the abbess, composer, 'see-er of dreams' and general all round eccentric Hildegard of Bingen is that, well, she wasn't. From Bingen, I mean. She wasn't *born* in Bingen, she didn't *live* in Bingen, and she didn't *die* in Bingen. If, at this point, you're thinking you may as well, just as accurately, from now on, refer to her as Hildegard of Basingstoke, or Hildegard Von Symonds Yat, then, well, sorry. No, although she was born in Rheinhessen and died in Rupertsberg, at least Rupertsberg – which is around sixty kilometres south-west of Stuttgart – is *near* Bingen. Good. Glad to clear that up.

Hildegard was clearly a remarkable woman, someone just as happy doling out advice to bishops – popes even – as she was preparing a soothing poultice of plant extracts, mixed to her own recipe. She had visions from an early age, and was sent off to become an 'anchor' very early on. An 'anchor' was a sort of cross between a nun and an SAS survival expert – Ray Mears meets Sister Wendy – and Hildegard would have experienced a last rites ceremony before being shut off in solitary confinement.

When she was forty-two, she had a vision which she said gave her total understanding of religious texts, and, from this point on, she wrote down everything she saw in her dreams and visitations. Today, her major contribution is considered her musical one. She left behind her a large number of plainchants, often to her own texts, rather than the existing settings so common at the time. I still find it sad that Hildegard is famous now not only because she was one of the first important composers of whom we have any record, but also because she was one of the ONLY female ones. Still. As Mr Brown said, it's a man's world.

Verily, be it the globe of a gentleman.
But, moreover, he would amounteth to little...
...NAUGHT, indeed,.... minus a woman or a nun.

At least I think that's what he said. Hard to tell, when he shouts so much.

Her story is all the more remarkable when you stop for a moment and think how hard it must have been not just to be a female composer in those days – jeepers, that's hard enough now – but, well, how hard it must have been to be a female ANYTHING! 'Yes, I am a woman. Yes, I am a composer. Yes, as it happens, I *do* have visions, which I write down as soon as I can. Er, no, actually, I'm not a witch, thank you very much!'

I say we clasp a picture of her in one hand, a full goblet of wine in the other, and zoom on to **1179** to toast her non-witchly, eccentric musical-ness. Or whatever.

Actually, is that a wart on her left cheek?

THE FIRST MUSICAL JOKE (BUT NOT MOZART'S)

So. 1179, the year of the death of Hildegard of Bingen, or Rupertsberg, depending on how much of a control freak you pride yourself on being. It was also the year, in fact, that the world's first musical joke started doing the rounds. It lives on now as a Bing Crosby/Walt Disney joke, but the original, as you can see below, was about Hildegard herself. It went something like this.

> *Interrogatio: 'Quod differentum est trans Hildegard von Bingen et Waltus Disnius?'*
> *Repondatum: 'Bingen singen, sed Waltus Disnius!'*

Mmmm... Maybe you had to be there. The twelth century, I mean. It was probably around this time that early jokes about drummers and percussionists were born. Jokes such as, 'What's the range of your average drum? About ten feet with a good throwing arm.'

If you think I'm being a little hard on drummers, then let me tell you: this is no more than my job. I'm told there is a long-standing musical tradition, going back centuries – as you can see – which is behaviourally requisite for all musicians, and always has been. It runs alongside the virtue of 'always keeping an eye on where your next job is coming from' and it's known, in the business, as 'always being rude about drummers'. It is up there alongside 'always taking the piss out of viola players' and, to a lesser extent – albeit just as important – 'always dragging your knuckles along the floor of the pub if you play a brass instrument'. The drummer must always expect to be the butt of 'musical jokes'.♬ To this end, I have enclosed a simple list of the best 'drummer' jokes, except the one that's so rude it can't be published.

1. *Q: How do you know when there's a drummer at the door?*
   A: The knocking speeds up.
2. *Q: What do you call someone who hangs around with musicians?*
   A: A drummer.
3. *The one that can't be published.*

Anyway let's get on. We've got to get to 1225, for 'the next big thing' in music, as they say. Along the way let me try and fill you in on anything you need to know. Modena Cathedral is consecrated in **1184**, and, not to be outdone, three years later, the good burghers of Verona complete theirs. In fact, cathedrals are huge at the moment. Not just literally. Everybody wants one. Bamberg start theirs, Chartres theirs and the ochre-topped buildings of Sienna look forward to being ever in the warm shade of theirs. I tell you this for a reason, obviously, not just to pass the time of day, but more of that in a moment.

CARMA-CARMA-CARMA-CARMA-CARMINA BURANA... YOU COME AND GO...

Don't let me forget to tell you about the *carmina burana*, now, either. It was around the year **1200** that the *carmina burana* were written. These were a set of monastic songs, many of them with

♬ *With the possible exception of Mozart's work entitled* Musical Joke, *it is my theory that there is no such thing as a good musical joke. A 'musical joke' is an oxymoron, put about by slightly nerdy music students to get them out of the spotlight and have it shone back on the IT mob.*

somewhat racy lyrics in Latin and German, which were found in Benediktbeuren in what is now Bavaria but back then was Bohemia.

Despite their origins within a monastery – or, more likely, because of their origins in a monastery – they concern themselves with subjects like love, and… drinking and… well, how shall I put it… lust! These bawdy ballads were written around the same time as Cambridge University was being founded, but were relatively unknown for a good eight centuries or so, until the Munich-born composer and educationalist Carl Orff put them to use in his piece of 1937, which he called simply *Carmina Burana*. I've made a note to mention this nearer the time so, for now, let's get on.

Stand-up comedians. They started around now too. Probably to give the musicians a break, chance to nip to the bar, that sort of thing. Of course, they were called court jesters and they started to gain in popularity following the turn of the thirteenth century. Apart from that there were a bunch♫ more cathedrals: work started on Reims, Salisbury, Toledo, Brussels and Burgos, as well as a new one for Amiens (old one burnt down – careless!), and a façade for Notre Dame. All in all, if your business card read 'Keith Groat – Cathedral Builder' then my guess is, despite the name setback, you were going to be a rich man. Which brings me neatly, if idiosyncratically, to **1225** and 'the next big thing'.

SPIRES INSPIRE

First up, a brief overview of and foothold in 1225. Well, the Magna Carta is on its third reprint. Not bad for something with a dull ending and no real plot. In terms of the big names around at the time, on the one hand there's Francis of Assisi, who has a year left to live. On the other hand – definitely on the other hand – there's Mr Khan, or Genghis, to his friends. It's the time of the later

♫ *Anyone know the collective noun for cathedrals? If not, can I venture 'floon'? A floon of cathedrals. Sounds fab to me and makes about as much sense as most other collective nouns. I figure collective nouns are much like mountains and polar regions – whoever gets there first can claim them and name them. So. Cathedrals. A floon. Thank you, and I'll brook no arguments.*

Crusades, the Mongol invasion of Russia and papal excommunications galore. In fact, you couldn't move for being excommunicated. You had to so much as invade Scotland and that was it – VUMH! – excommunication.

So, that's just some of the detail of 1225, if you were to run up the highest mountain and look around. But what of 'the time'? How must it have felt and smelt, if you know what I mean. And how *was* it, musically speaking? Well, that's why I was banging on about the cathedrals going up all over the place. Let's put ourselves in medieval shoes for a minute.

Cathedrals – two things need to be understood about cathedrals. They're not cheap and they take a bugger of a long time to build. You can't buy them flat-packed with inadequate instructions and one bolt missing. These things are raised across generations. And that gives you a big clue as to who had all the money in 1225. It also gives us a clue as to the state of the music business in 1224. Because cathedrals needed filling not just with people but with music. In 1225, MUSIC was basically a *six*-letter word spelt like this: C.H.U.R.C.H – music. Also, to the peasant in the street, it was oral, not unlike herpes simplex, in that it was passed from mouth to mouth. OK, doesn't quite bear up but you know what I mean. True, some written music was creeping in, in places, if you were rich enough. But generally, the norm was still a bunch of blokes, with faces like cows' bottoms, in draughty buildings singing one-note stuff. A bit like folk music today.

And now 'the next big thing'. Well, again, if you were rich enough, you could say the next big thing was 'cotton', which the Spanish had, just this year, started manufacturing. If you weren't rich enough, though – and let's face it, most folk weren't – then 'the next big thing'♬ was almost certainly a piece of music called 'Sumer is icumen in'.

♬ *Stephen Fry breaks the world record for highest number of print mentions EVER of the phrase 'the next big thing'. Official.*

SUMER L'UV IN. ADME A BLAS

Ignore that title and try this:

Sumer is icumen in,
Lhude sing, cuccu
Groweth sed and bloweth med
And springeth the wude nu
Sing cuccu♫

or to translate:

Spring has come in
Loudly sing, cuckoo
Grows the seed and blooms the meadow
And the woods spring now,
Sing, cuckoo.

'Sumer is icumen in' – beautiful words, aren't they? – is an important piece in the great musical scheme of things, in no small part due to the simple fact that it even exists – quite a rare feat for *any* piece of music from this period. In fact, come to think of it, quite rare for anything written down at all. I imagine there are historians the world over who would scream with orgasmic delight if they were to unearth a piece of notepaper saying 'Gone to mother's – chops for tea' if it came from 1225. So the fact that we *have* it is great. But also, 'Sumer', if it doesn't mind me calling it by its first name, is important because it is so advanced. It's a round – a song where everybody sings more or less the same tune but at different times, a bit like 'Frère Jacques' – and it was written in six parts, four tenor and two bass, and was very complicated for the time. It dates from the mid-thirteenth century and its language is the beautiful and slightly unkempt Middle English. If you don't speak

♫ *Every time I read those words, I can virtually hear the birds singing, almost feel the sun shining, practically touch the disfigured heads as they're lovingly spiked on to sticks. Ahh… to be in 1225 again, now that 'Sumer' is here (or at least icumen in). OK, so 'sumer' means spring, so what: what's a season between friends?*

Middle English – and to be fair there can't be many who do who aren't called Gandalf – then just try reading some in a Cornish accent. Works for me. It was almost certainly quilled by a monk of Reading Abbey, who is remembered now simply as John of Fornsete. It was meant to be a springtime song, heralding the approaching summer – figures – and is very folksong-like in style. There are some Latin words available to sing to it, but they don't fit anywhere near as well as the 'folk' type words and were almost certainly a later afterthought, just to show willing. It gains its 'next big thing' status by being so pioneering for its time. People just weren't meant to be singing this sort of thing in 1225. Indeed, some scholars think they weren't. In fact, when a very learned sort by the name of Doc Manfred Bukofzer looked into it in 1945, he decided it was almost certainly from a much later time. Still. Despite his concerns, it has managed to keep its place in the music history books as being written around 1225. So good old 'Sumer', that's what I say.

ARS IS NOT TO REASON WHY

Over the next seventy years or so, some important things gathered momentum in the world of music. This was a period when what was known as the '*ars antiqua*' was still the in thing. Meaning, literally, the old art, it was a term used only retrospectively for what was going on about now. It didn't really get its name until someone coined the term '*ars nova*' – new art – which was generally a freeing up from all the styles and some of the rules of the *ars antiqua*.

The big three in the world of *ars antiqua* would have to be Léonin, Pérotin and Robert de Sabilon. Léonin was often referred to as an '*optimus organista*' – or 'very good when it comes to writing those lovely medieval-sounding harmonies' – and lots of his stuff still survives to this day. Pérotin was the top man at Notre Dame in Paris for a time. De Sabilon also worked out of Paris, doing things you wouldn't believe with independent melodies. In fact, Paris was pretty big, generally, around now, and Notre Dame particularly. There were lots of troubadours, and minstrels all gathered in the city alongside monks and men of learning. It strikes me that it might have been not dissimilar to the turn of twentieth-century Paris, where artists, musicians and thinkers all gathered to form a steamy, Bohemian café-culture. This went on to leave its own heady mark on the arts in general, both then and now. One thing is certain, though, and that's that, in both periods, the cappuccinos were almost certainly cheaper.

FRANCO IN GENERAL

Other luminaries giving off the dying light of the *ars antiqua* were chaps like Franco de Cologne.♫ Franco de Cologne – I know, unfortunate, isn't it, but at least he resisted the urge to spell it Franceau – was the guy generally credited with sorting out how long notes lasted. Sounds odd to say that now, I guess, but back then – well, someone had to get it all together. Just like Gregory the Gorgeous had sorted out plainchant, so Franco got to grips with notes and how you wrote down how long each note lasted. He set his stall out in a little book called *De musica mensurabilis* or, if you like, 'Of Music and Measures', which sounds a little like a lost manuscript by John Steinbeck.

Up until now, there had been no agreed system for showing how long a note lasted. He it was who standardized the 'breve' as the unit of musical measure.

A semibreve is this 𝅝 and is four beats long.

This 𝅗𝅥 is a minim, and lasts two.

And so on, down through to 𝅘𝅥 the crochet (one beat) and the cute but ridiculously named hemi-demi-semiquaver 𝅘𝅥𝅱, the sort of Tinkerbell of notes: you have to believe that it exists or it won't.

♫ *You know, it seems to me that being around back then meant you could pick your name rather like newly ennobled lords pick their provenance today. So, today, you have Lady Thatcher of Kesteven and Lord Wilson of Rievaulx or whatever, back then you had more or less the same, but you didn't have to wait to get into the Upper Chamber to do it. Everybody was at it. Personally, I think I'd go for Fry of Soho. Maybe even... Fry of the Route of the 77 Bus – give me a bit of leeway.*

MACHAUT MUST GO ON

Now on to three of the leading names in music after **1300**. De Machaut, Dunstable and Dufay. First up is the romantically titled Gaul, poet and composer: Guillaume de Machaut. Again, sorry to digress once more, but what a beautiful name. Just say it to yourself – Guillaume de Machaut. Gorgeous name. De Machaut was born in 1300 and soon realized he had a talent not only for poetry but also for music. By the year **1364**, with still a good fourteen years left to live, he would have been forgiven for sitting back, resting on his *ars nova*, and enjoying himself a little. I mean, to be fair, simply *being* sixty-four in those days was a bit of an achievement, considering the new black was... well, the Black Death. ('Darling, MWAH, oh you look drop-dead gorgeous... Oh... you've dropped dead.)

De Machaut was one of the last great composers living in the age of the trouvères or troubadours, the particularly French version of what we in England called 'minstrels' or the Germans called '*minnesingers*', literally 'love singers'. A minstrel was effectively a paid, freelance musician, descended from the 'mimes' of ancient Greece and Rome, who were cast out during the barbarian invasions. They were originally actors who took up instruments to pay their way, at a time when this was considered very much a dubious thing to do (no change there, then). If this were the Bible, then the line would probably go something like this:

Mimes begat joculatores; joculatores begat jongleurs: jongleurs begat troubadours: troubadours begat trouvères: trouvères begat menestriers; and menestriers begat minstrels. See?

If, in this world of troubadours, trouvères and menestriers, you are having trouble spotting a minstrel, then here's a useful rule: troubadours sing and rhyme, menestriers play for dances, and minstrels melt in your mouth but not in your hand.

And de Machaut, in the trouvères tradition, was as famous in his lifetime for his words as for his music. A more or less exact contemporary of Boccaccio, the man of the *Decameron*, he was born in the Ardennes but, having become both learned and a priest – and I'm sure it's possible – he enjoyed lengthy stays in the courts of John of

Luxembourg and the Duchess of Normandy. But it was around the time of Navarre that he put all his efforts into achieving the as yet unachieved, pulling off the as yet unpulled, and doing the as yet... undone. The four-part Mass. No one had, as yet, come up with a Mass that moved according to the 'laws' of harmony, but that sounded... well, good. Rules can be obeyed to the letter, to make a perfectly 'correct' four-part Mass, but as to making it sound great – that was a whole different ballgame.

MASS HYSTERIA

A four-part Mass, that is the issue. Could any composer manage to get four separate 'voices' (i.e. sopranos, altos, tenors and basses, for example) to sing separate tunes and yet cleverly make it all sound like perfect harmony?

Imagine it this way, if you would. It's a still, muggy evening in Reims and de Machaut's 'Roger Bannister' moment is not far off. He and his team had been competing against the Italians to be the first to produce the musical holy grail of the time – the four-parter – but the journey had been cruel. What looked like early successes were hastily rehearsed, only to reveal several chunks of the Mass that were not in four at all – some were periods of three parts, some two. There was even an early prototype which had all the manuscript appearance of a four-part Mass, but, when sung, sounded almost totally monotonous and in unison.♬

The setbacks had taken their toll, not just in terms of morale – two of the team had left with larynx problems, another had set up on his own, and de Machaut had lost a fourth in a tragic tongue accident sustained during a particularly fast bar of hemi-demi-semiquavers. But he was not deterred. He knew he could do it. No composer in history had yet done it, and the spoils to the victor would be great. Well, ish! In a moment which will forever go down in the annals of history as 'that time when Guillaume de Machaut finished his Mass', he, quite

♬ *This was thought to have been lost until it resurfaced some 720 years later as 'The Lady in Red'.*

brilliantly and with a single flourish of his quill, put the finishing bar line to his masterpiece. Inside, he knew this was it. He didn't need a rehearsal. He didn't need to sing it through to his mother. He knew. This was the first four-part Mass in history! As legend has it, he leant across to his chief-of-staff and uttered the now immortal line, '*Bof! J'ai besoin d'une tasse de thé. Ou peut-être quelque-chose plus fort. Allons! Au tête du cheval.*' Or, to translate: 'Ooh, I couldn't half do with a cuppa. Or maybe something stronger. Let's nip down the Nag's Head.'

Great moment. Truly great moment. *Ars nova* at its best. And the Mass itself? Well, romantic reports would have it that it was used that night in the coronation of Charles V and, in that respect, signalled the start of a small but perfectly formed golden period in French music.♫

Charles was one of those monarchs who don't come along very often, who loved music. Under his reign, France enjoyed a period as the shining light in world music. From the very year of Charles's coronation until the first twenty years or so of the fifteenth century, France was the centre of the musical universe – its capital city, if you like – a glory mirrored in the separate but corresponding worlds of French Gothic architecture and the learning symbolized by the University of Paris.

If that was France, then what of good old Blighty? Who was raising the standard for rising standards in the world of music? Well, for that we have to look to Dunstable, both the place and the man.

THE FIRST RHYTHM METHOD

John Dunstable was almost certainly born *in* Dunstable, and his name is probably a derivation of John of Dunstable. He produced some of the most beautiful music of the period, albeit not all of it in England. Lots of his work was eventually found in places like Trent, Modena and Bologna, suggesting that the English presence in Italian music of the time was a very real one. Dunstable eventually died in London, though, but not before having dedicated much of

♫ *Although many think it dates from much later.*

his life to gaining approval for one of his lifelong *causes célèbres* – natural rhythms.

Up until now, it was very much the done thing that you set words to tunes, and not the other way round. What I mean is, the words were not as important, therefore you found yourself a great tune and simply fitted the words in. As a result, the natural way of saying the words was often completely lost, along with a lot of their meaning. To get what I'm on about, imagine the way a song sounds when a gramophone is running down. All the words get contorted and pulled about, eventually becoming so slow and tortuous that their original meaning is somewhat lost. Well, Dunstable hated that. Couldn't stand it. So he devoted a lot of his time to fighting the fight for 'natural rhythms', music with words that are sung with the everyday metres as you would say them.

Yes, there is a case for saying he needed to get out more. But, to be fair, it's people like him who, as we'll see, were the crucial cogs you needed if the wheels of music were ever going to turn.

Dunstable was also big in the world of counterpoint. Mmm, dodgy one, this. Counterpoint may not mean much to you now but, back then, it was one of the most contentious subjects in music. And, remember, if it was contentious in music, then it was, at this point anyway, contentious in the Church, and that could spell trouble for anyone who decided to rock the boat. Way back in 1309, one Marchettus of Padua pleaded with the powers-that-be to allow counterpoint into music, but, in a response matched only by Directory Enquiries in its speed, Pope John XXII forbade its use in 1322. Well, no one could say he hadn't had time to think about it. But what was so wrong with counterpoint? Why did the Church hate it so much? And, more to the point, what the hell *is* counterpoint? OK. Here we go.

WHAT'S THE COUNTERPOINT?

Last things first. Counterpoint is the bits in music where composers get bored with writing just one tune and write a few, instead. Of course, that's fine for them – they probably write them all at different times, one in the morning, one after lunch, polish another off before the tea interval, that sort of thing. Fine and dandy. Problem starts when they put them all together, because we then have to listen to them all at once. Lots of different parts of the music playing different tunes ALL AT THE SAME TIME. It's a bit like jazz, but without the farty trombone. So this might explain why Pope John XXII thundered at composers in his *Docta Sanctorum*: 'they cut up melodies with hoquets,♫ smoothe them with descants, sometimes force upon them vulgar tripla and moteti...' Well, if he had any point at all, he's probably ruined it by spelling smooth wrong. Damn – must have been cursing himself for that. Incidentally, the 'tripla' and 'moteti' in this case would translate as soprano and alto, respectively, with the full four parts at the time going 'triplum, motetus, tenor, contratenor' downwards. Don't say I never tell you anything.

John XXII and his '*doctas*' didn't appear to bother John of Dunstable, though. Up until his death in 1453, counterpoint was, it's fair to say, his bag. He continued to write his Masses and his isorhythmic motets – ones where he repeated the same rhythms even though the music was changing – and was probably even the first to write instrumental accompaniments to church Masses.

Dunstable's period was that of Donatello in Italy, as well as Fra Angelico and the Medicis. In Portugal, they had Gonzalo Cabral and Joao Diaz, the great explorers. And in England? Well, in England, they had the plague again, and a rather unpleasant period of country-wide quarantine. As for Dunstable, his influence was still being recognized some two or three centuries later. And it's said that the person he influenced most was another Guillaume.

Guillaume Dufay was originally from Hainaut in what was then the Low Countries, now the Netherlands (Londoners, try and put the Central Line out of your head), but spent a lot of his time in service with the papal choir. This was quite a cute job around this time, mainly because the papal court was constantly shifting, and hence Dufay got to see a lot more of the world than just Rome. He spent

♫ *Hoquets – rather like musical hiccups, this is when a composer leaves gaps in one voice, which he fills with another voice. The resulting effect is of a 'to and fro', a tennis rally, in the music.*

some time in Cambrai, near the French town of Lille, too, where it is said the Pope himself was very taken with the choir and also the Netherlands. So much so, that when the court shifted back to Rome, he embarked on a programme of importing Netherlands talent. Indeed, at one point, almost the entire papal choir was made up of singers from the Low Countries (did they ever call them Lowlifes?) with just one native Italian singer.

In his day, Dufay was considered the finest composer in the Netherlands, and one of his lasting achievements was in precursing the standard choral setting of today, that of soprano, alto, tenor and bass, with his use of a bass below the tenor and counter-tenor. Try a quick listen to something like 'Ecce ancilla domini', one of his last Masses, and you get the whole glorious idea.

Dufay was effectively both the end of a period known as 'medieval' and the early stirrings of the brand-new – well, almost – all singing, all dancing Renaissance. Born the same year that Chaucer died, **1400**, his generation would play host to the Battle of Agincourt, the emergence of the first ever printed books, and the burning of Joan of Arc at the stake in Rouen. Dufay would eventually settle in Cambrai, which he helped make into one of the most talked-about things since the Rouen executioner uttered the unforgettable words, '*Zut! J'ai perdu mes alumettes!*' But by the time Guillaume returned to the small town of Cambrai, Dunstable was dead, and the Byzantine Empire was gone, with the death of Constantine XI. Interestingly enough, though, and perhaps more important for caffeine addicts the world over, the south-west Arabian port of Mocha had become the centre of the coffee-exporting universe.

For now, close your eyes and imagine: cue the noise of small children playing, the sound of water splashing, and the fuzzy barking of a megaphone. 'OK, everybody, it's **1450**. New era please. All those with a red, medieval wristband on, please leave the genepool. I repeat, it is now **1450**, can anyone with a red, medieval wristband please leave the genepool. It is now the Renaissance era. Thank you.' Aside to his assistant: 'OK, let the Renaissance lot in.' OK, it didn't happen quite like that – but at least we're off the starting blocks.

REBIRTH

Around ten years before the medievalists got thrown out of the pool in 1450, the local paper in Conde, in Hainaut may have announced the birth of one Josquin des Pres. JDP was possibly the biggest talent of his age, and, in an era when very few were actually fêted while they were still alive, he was hailed as a bit of a genius, with even Martin Luther being moved to comment: 'He is master of the notes: others... are mastered by them.' Bit dramatic, Martin, but still, I get your point. In his day, he was often known not by his full name, but simply by the one word Josse, or even Joseph. No doubt had he been around today, he may have gone one step further and done away with the name altogether in favour of a strange squiggle. Something like:

ξ – the artist formally known as Josquin

There. Quite preposterous, isn't it? And no doubt, as a result, it would catch on. In Josquin's day, though, it would, hopefully, have been frowned upon. And when was Josquin's day? Well, to put him into context, he was born some twelve years after Leonardo da Vinci, and was probably much more famous than the *Mona Lisa*. Certainly, he died ten times as happy, by all accounts, having made himself quite well off and become the Canon of Conde. He died a couple of years after Magellan left his house in Seville with the words, 'I'm just popping down the shops.' In Josquin's lifetime, Michelangelo started work on the Sistine Chapel, while in England the Tudors came to power, and the finishing touches were put to the palace at Hampton Court.

There's one thing that's always bothered me about Josquin. Or should I say Josquin des Pres? Or should I say, Mr Pres? Or Mr Des Pres? And that is... well, those last two lines. Where does he come in a music dictionary? Nobody can seem to agree. I know, I know, it may seem a tiny point, but it really annoys me to look him up in one book under Pres, only to be told in rather curt fashion 'See Josquin'. Well, why, for goodness' sake? You don't look under Beethoven and find the words 'Bugger off and look under Ludwig.' Then you check a different book under J and you're told 'See Des Pres.' And then 'See Pres.' Ooh, it really gets my goat. Tiny point, I know, but, well, the devil is in the detail, as they said when Beelzebub went to do his National Service.

JDP, Mr des Pres, Josquin, ξ – whatever you want to call him – strikes me as quite a sorted individual. While he was young, he travelled a lot, eventually entering the Pope's service for about thirteen years till about **1499**. During that time, and even over the next twenty or so years, till his death in **1521**, he was a big influence on music generally. His Masses are important because they began to break free from an absolute strict adherence to rules. In his settings, Masses began to express the spirit of the words. This might seem like nothing at all, now, but music then was as much a discipline as a pleasure. JDP freed himself from an almost pedantic obedience to the rules and, well, let his hair down a little. And, as a big influence, he was lucky enough to be at the beating heart of music at the time. This wasn't the court of Louis XII in France, although he was there. It wasn't the court of Emperor Maximillian I, either, although he was there for a time, too. And it wasn't really the diocese of Conde where he spent his final years as Canon. No. The beating heart of music at this time was, quite simply, the Church.

JOS YOU, JOS ME...

Let me skip on a few years from Josquin's death in 1521. Rather like a submarine, I'll submerge for a few years and come up in

1551. Let me try and briefly fill you in on what was going on at sea level. Henry VIII has been through all six wives, and finally shuffled off himself. If you believe his PR man, he also left us the song 'Greensleeves', although this is open to doubt. Edward VI is now the boss. Over in France, Nostradamus has issued his first set of predictions. In his lifetime, he was said to have predicted that Hitler would come to power, that Ronald Reagan was the devil, and – one that I found myself only the other day when I was leafing through – the fact that David Beckham would break his second metatarsal just before the 2002 World Cup.♬

What else? Well, court jesters – the sixteenth-century version of stand-up♬♬ – are the new rock and roll across Europe. Titian is the favoured artist of those in the know, and, perhaps most importantly, the pocket handkerchief has come into common use in a big way. So far, I have been unable to determine whether deckchairs and rolled-up trouser legs came into vogue at the same time.

But to 1551, and there is big news. A man called Palestrina has been made the director of music at St Peter's in Rome. It was a quite fortuitous turn of events for the twenty-five-year-old composer. Palestrina had been organist and choirmaster of his local cathedral for the last seven years. Then, in 1551, the bishop whom he had been supplying with cute little Masses every week suddenly wasn't a bishop any more. He was a Pope. Totally different. Within days, Palestrina was installed as choirmaster of the Julian Chapel at the Vatican, under the new pope, Julius III, and Palestrina was busy telling eveyone 'we go *way* back.' Now, today this may not seem particularly important in the scheme of things, you might say. On paper, after all, it's only 'man gets Church job'. But in 1551, music *was* the Church, and virtually everyone wrote not just *for* it but also *by order of* it. A lot of them considered it their duty – thoughtful, well-educated men (because it almost always *was* men) who often decided that God had given them this gift of music, therefore they had to repay him, by dedicating their work and often their life to him. Add to this the fact that the Church's motto at

♬ *Pretty sure that's what he meant by 'a prince with a club foot'.*

♬♬ *Most popular joke of the day: 'I wouldn't say my wife was fat... but when they put her on the ducking stool, there was a tidal wave in Shrewsbury... nay, verily, but seriously, good people...'*

this time appeared to be something like 'Scium Quo Habitas' – 'We Know Where You Live' – and, well, it's not surprising to find that '*ad majorem dei gloriam*' appeared on many a front page.

And here's another thing: not only does MUSIC = CHURCH at this point, but also, MUSIC = SINGING. Now why is that? Why was more or less all music composed by these Church-loving composers at this time vocal?

I'm glad you asked me that, as politicians are prone to saying, because I'm not going to answer it. I will in a moment, but first back to Palestrina.

FILL THE SPACE

Sadly for Palestrina, within a few years of being given the top job in Rome, he was out on his ear, kicked out by the incoming new top doge, Pope Paul IV, who clearly didn't like the cut of his cassock. Happily for Palestrina, though, his time would come again, a few years later, reinstated by yet another different Pope. I don't know. How did they cope with all this coming and going? Maybe this was the model for Italy's political system. Anyway, regardless, Palestrina enjoys his new period of favour, and immediately starts doing what everyone around him was doing too. Lassus♬ was doing it, Byrd was doing it in England – everybody was doing it – and that was writing music for the amazing spaces that were these huge cathedrals. Yes, I know, this might sound obvious, but it needs saying. These cathedrals, in their own way, changed the face of music for a time, because everyone wrote in order to sound good in them. And just the smallest knowledge of acoustics will tell you that writing music for, say, a concert in your local village hall and writing music to fill the enormous caverns of St Peter's in Rome are two very different exercises.

The cathedrals had gone up as huge, unmissable symbols of how great it was to be a Christian, and the Church went around throwing

♬ *Orlande de Lassus, a well-travelled and much favoured composer. Worked all over – Naples, Sicily, Antwerp, Bavaria, Munich – the boy done well. Wrote some 1,200 works in all, including some of the most important Masses of his day.*

money at the sweet problem of getting the best people possible to fill them with beautiful sounds. Palestrina no doubt felt like the cat who'd got the cream, the cream being St Peter's. And this is important, because Palestrina (whose real name, by the way, wasn't Palestrina at all – Palestrina was the small Italian town he came from; all we know of his name is that he was called Giovanni Pierluigi) was NOT an innovator. He was NOT a pioneer. Admittedly, throughout this book, we will celebrate many people who *were* innovators and pioneers, but Palestrina was *not* one of them. He was more concerned with writing sheer, beautiful noises that would sound fantastic in the Pope's local church. Music like his glorious *Missa Papae Marcelli* – the Mass for Pope Marcellus, a gorgeous piece of polyphony written specifically not to advance music into the next century, not to shock people into the next era, but simply to sound unutterably gorgeous as it bounced off the walls of the Vatican, taking, no doubt, minutes to fade as it did so. Divine.

Onward, now, to the Lennon and McCartney of the sixteenth century. Who were they? How did they manage to run the biggest musical monopoly since the last dodo learnt to whistle? Well, get your Renaissance head on, I'm going in. Cover me.

RENAISSANCE MAN

Imagine, if you will, it is **1572** – just over twenty years since Palestrina landed the top job in Rome. In Inghilterra, Elizabeth I has been on the throne for some thirteen years. In fact, speaking of the two in more or less the same breath, only a couple of years earlier, Pope Pius V had issued a jolly little excommunication 'bull', as they're called, which went by the cute little name of 'Regnans in Excelsis'. It's quite a lengthy document, but if I might summarize it for you, it would be to say, 'We're not going to talk to you any more.' The Pope, that is, isn't going to talk to Elizabeth. Sad, really. I imagine Elizabeth would miss their little chats.

However, it was a good year for other forms of communication. In literature, we'd witnessed the births of John Donne and Ben Jonson, and in pigeonry – well, it was pretty high tech, back then – we had witnessed the first use of Nelson's favourite birds to send messages. It was from the Dutch town of Haarlem, which was under siege from the Spanish.

So: are you there yet? In the sixteenth century, I mean. Because it was against that background that things were really starting to bubble. In the Italy we've just left behind, the Gabrieli family were quite big noises now. Andrea Gabrieli, composer and organist at St Mark's Venice for the last six years, was busy adding all sorts of brass parts to his vocal music. More importantly, perhaps, was his nephew Giovanni, who took over from him at St Mark's, and who could be said to have preceded Dolby by some 400 years.

Giovanni Gabrieli was another organist/composer (I suppose you would say 'singer/songwriter' these days) who started to do the first experiments

in stereo, effectively,
writing music that had choirs and voices
pitted against each other at either side of
the huge St Mark's, making for some glorious
antiphonal effects
which must
have really
surprised his
audience at
the time.
It must
have been
less like
being at
a concert
and more
like being
at a
tennis match.

Stiff necks all round at St Mark's, maybe.

But back to good old England, and the Lennon and McCartney of the time. For it was in 1572 that the composer William Byrd was sent to work alongside fellow composer Thomas Tallis, forty years his senior and operating out of the Chapel Royal. Tallis had already been there some thirty years before the two joined forces, and, together, they became one of the biggest things in music since Pope Gregory first started to hum in the bathroom of a morning.

JOHN, PAUL, GEORGE, RINGO, WILL AND TOM

Byrd was from Lincoln, Tallis possibly from Waltham Abbey. Apart, they were good musicians in their field – Tallis, particularly, respected as one of the grand old men of English music. But it was Queen Elizabeth who was to make their names still legendary today. She it was who, some three years after they joined forces, gave them the sole right to print music in England. Imagine it. Every note issued across the land belongs to them.

How could you fail? Their first venture was the 'Cantiones Sacrae' of 1575, a collection of motets♫ written by the two composers themselves. Of course, I wouldn't want you to think that they took the opportunity of having cornered the market in the world of music printing to release only their *own* stuff. No, no, no! I mean, it's true, of course, but I just wouldn't want you to think it. The good thing was that at least it was in the hands of masters. I mean, the 'Cantiones Sacrae' was some of the most exquisite published music of 1575, albeit, to be fair, some of the ONLY published music of 1575.

What would happen now, then? I mean now that music was going to be printed on a regular basis? Well, despite the fact that it was still expensive and rare, it *was,* at least, getting out there. People with money *could* read it and get together and sing it, because, after all, it is

♫ *A motet is a short church choral piece, or mini canal encircling a castle.*

still almost all vocal, remember. And here's where a lovely, serendipitously head-on collision of events and fashions comes together.

PRESS ON

Printing. We take it for granted now. We take it for granted that it's our inalienable right to arrive at work with thumbs covered in rubbed-off black ink, and eyes like Ching Ching the giant panda. But just imagine what it did to music! Music was suddenly… available.

It was 'in print'. Scores were available. Musicians and singers were available. And, against that backdrop, the next 'chance fashion' that came along would certainly find that the land was lying differently. Everything had changed. Everything was to play for.

And what was the next big thing?

Greek and Roman style and culture was the NEXT BIG THING. And not just the styles, but the forms and features as well. So, some folk got into Greek drama again in a big way – the intellectuals, mainly. Only now, because this time around they had more than rocks and drums for accompaniment, the music became a much more important part. The writing had always been there. But the music? Well, the music relied, as it always did, on the technology of the day – the instruments, which had been somewhat primitive when the Greeks tried it first time around. The new versions of Greek dramas saw much more emphasis on the music – '*dramma per musica*', plays through music, as they were called, and they would become big hits. Where, first time round, you had dramas, this time round you had something completely different. In fact, it would only take someone, in the right place, at the right time to think… 'Hang on a minute …this could be big' and PING!

You've got OPERA!

Who would be the first? Who would be the one to write the first ever opera? Who would be the one to go down in the annals of music history alongside the man in the iron mask, the man who broke the bank at Monte Carlo and the man from Delmontehesayyes. Who would be …

'The Man Who Invented Opera!'

Well, whoever it was, was sure to become a household name. The first ever opera.

Just think of it.

You'd be famous the world over.

You'd be fêted for years to come.

You could write your own cheques.

People would name their children after you.

You'd be guaranteed an upgrade to business class, even if you weren't wearing a suit.

You'd be remembered throughout all history.

So how come it was...

...Jacopo Peri?

THE FIRST EVER OPERA (BUT ONE)

Mmm. I know what you're thinking. Who he? Ed? Quite, quite. You see, the world has decided, somewhat dubiously, that the first opera ever written was Monteverdi's *L'Orfeo*, which is only fair in so far as... well, in so far as it wasn't. Monteverdi's *L'Orfeo* was, in fact, the *second* opera ever written. Peri's *Dafne* was the first. So, where did it all go wrong for Peri? Because it's a bit like, well... imagine Neil Armstrong setting foot on the moon, the first man ever to do so, and yet the world decides to remember Buzz Aldrin as the hero. So, where did it all go wrong for Peri?

Well, it seems that giddy fortune's furious fickle wheel is really the culprit, here. True, Monteverdi, it seems, was probably by far the more skilful of the two composers, with an oeuvre richer in harmonic invention and melody. Peri was more or less his contemporary, born in Rome and one of the great musicians of his day, as well as friend of the Medicis. He was also one of the in-crowd, as it were, and, as such, probably there at the sharp end when *dramma per musica* came back in. Indeed, he almost certainly had a hand in reviving it, alongside some of his fellow writers. Where fortune seems to have favoured Monteverdi, though, is in the simple but crucial matter of survival. The score of Monteverdi's *L'Orfeo* survived; the score of Peri's *Dafne* didn't. To add further insult to injury, Peri's second opera, *Eurydice*, was written some seven years before the first performance of Monteverdi's *L'Orfeo*, and is, technically speaking – with full surviving score, etc – the first opera in existence. And yet, despite all that, the ground-breaking nature of Monteverdi's opera still leads many to describe it today as the first 'real' opera ever written. I don't know, what is a man to do? It reminds me of the story of Edison and his telephone and the dodgy dealings which led to the failure of rival designs.

Still. What's done is done: Monteverdi is remembered some 450 years after his birth, while Peri is no more than a piece of trivia in the classical music section of a pub quiz. Isn't life a bastard?

IF IT'S NOT BAROQUE...

Now, sorry to make this book nigh on interactive, but would you just help me a moment. Close your eyes, again, and imagine if you will a huge 1950s post-war British factory.

Are you there?

Bugger. Actually you can't read this if you close your eyes, can you? OK, open them again, and I'll do the imagining.

I'm seeing a aircraft hangar-sized factory in the fifties. Lots of people are working – only not on anything vaguely mechanical. They are writing... with quill pens and parchment manuscript. Suddenly, a huge, almost air-raid-siren-like hooter goes off, and, immediately, many of them down quills. Then a voice booms over the loudspeaker: 'Ladies and gentlemen, it is now **1600**. It is now **1600**. The Renaissance shift is now at an end. Will composers please remember to take all their belongings with them when leaving, so that the baroque shift can get to work immediately, and we won't have any complaints. I repeat, the Renaissance shift is now finished. Anyone who's working a double shift and staying on for baroque is entitled to five minutes to stretch their legs. Thank you.' BING BONG.

OK, OK, so it never happened like that, I know. Why do you think I did it? It just shows, in a way, how useless these labels are... Renaissance, baroque, etc. People just... composed. True, music evolved over time, but not in one year. So maybe that's why many scholars have even had difficulty in agreeing where one period ends and another one begins. Most plump for baroque as starting around 1600, but then this becomes meaningless when you see that composers such as Dowland, Gibbons and Monteverdi – all of them hardly contenders for the title 'Mr Baroque of Morecambe Bay, 2004' – were working long into the seventeenth century. Still, as politicians are wont to say, where do you draw the line? Well, here, as it happens, so I guess we've got to lump it.

Now, let me take you by the hand and lead you through the streets of the early seventeenth century – I'll show you something that'll make you change your pants.

1607. Good year? Bad year? Well, bad year if you were Guy Fawkes, I suppose. Bad in that you were dead, I mean, your head satayed with peanut sauce just a year earlier, after you'd been caught in the House of Lords, walking backwards with a carelessly leaking keg of gunpowder. 1607 means the new play from everybody's favourite bard, William Shakespeare, namely *Antony and Cleopatra*. It means the new gadget from Galileo, a compass, so now you could see your way through the stench and fog of south London to go and see Mr Shakespeare's play. And what else have we got? Let's see... Oh yes, we've got opera, as I said earlier. Opera. What more could you want?

Well, opera singers, I suppose: we haven't got them yet. Well, that's not fair, actually. We have got opera singers, we just haven't got *women* opera singers. Not yet, anyway. It's still all blokes. Ever since St Paul, no less, said that women should stay silent in church, they've become as rare as a witch at a diocesan coffee morning. So, if we don't have women, who is going to sing the high bits? Who is going to hit the top Cs? Well, looks like someone will be going to the ball, after all. If you get my drift. Well, OK, someone is going to the ball, but it turns out it's going to be your personal surgeon – now remove your trousers, please! Yes, along with opera came the meanest men in all Italy – and you can't deny they've got good reason to be – THE CASTRATOS. Mmm, could be a great series on Channel 4, produced by HBO.

I would seriously have loved to hear a good castrato, just to see how different they were from today's counter tenors. The idea, most common in Italy, it's got to be said, was to castrate a boy soprano, thus preserving the boy's voice, and combining it with the chest, lungs and therefore range of an adult. One of the most famous castrati who ever lived was a man called Farinelli (1705–82) who, it is said, was employed by Philip V of Spain to sing him the same four songs every evening. Check out the film about him – very good.

GOODBYE, LOVE. HELLO, LUVVIES!

Yes, OK, I know. It's not my fault. Don't blame me. Yes, we have opera. It's a big fat hit with virtually everyone who goes to see it. And you can see why – it was so starkly different to anything that had come before it. As beautiful as a four-part Mass is, especially when delivered in the glorious settings of a visually stunning cathedral, just think how ALIVE an opera must have seemed in comparison. It must have been a bit like when Special FX first started to take off in films. Audiences had, literally, seen nothing like it before. Well, opera must have been like that – different from anything they'd ever seen before.

But how did I know they'd go and invent opera long before they had proper sopranos? Amazing, really, when you think. But nevertheless, opera was here to stay, and, with opera, came egomaniac primadonnas. But, as we've said, not female ones. In fact, arguably, much worse: egomaniac primadonnas *with a grudge*. In fact, with a grudge and no balls. What an awful combination.

What's the most amazing thing about the revolution that was opera, though, is that, despite being the biggest thing in vocal music in years, centuries even, it, more than any other innovation, led to a dramatic improvement in another, seemingly completely different, area, namely instrumental music. Why? Well, because the accompanying orchestra in the pit was called on to play more and more dramatic music. Very often, this dramatic music would mean playing new things, new sounds which had never been tried before when instruments were simply for accompaniment. Now that ever new sounds and textures and effect were called for, composers needed ever better players who could pull off the more technically demanding music they were writing for their operas. This would eventually lead to the orchestra leaving the pit altogether, and going up on to the stage, on their own, much to the outrage of the Church.

The Church, you see, HATED instrumental music. And why? Well, because of the very fact that it was instrumental, and therefore NOT VOCAL. If there were no voices, there could be no words, and if there were no words, there could be no praising God. But, well, it's post-Reformation, now, and the Church's influence is very much on the wane. Even it could not stop something as fundamental as instrumental music from taking root. And so it would grow and grow. And we'll follow it as it does, but for now, let's to♬ the court of Louis XIV.

I say, witch? Could you hold up both hands and tell me the time? What's that you say, **1656**? Thank you!

Well, I've checked and the hands on my witch tell me it's 1656. Time for an update. 1656. Where are we? Well, it's thirty-six years since Miles Standish and the Pilgrim Fathers landed at New Plymouth, which is an astonishing coincidence, when you think – all that way round the globe in a souped-up junk boat and they land somewhere with almost the same name as the place they left. Also, the English Less-Than-Civil War had been and gone, and Charles I had had his headache cured in rather dramatic fashion by the men with the Beatles haircuts, Cromwell and Co.

BATON CHARGE

Over in Paris, however, the French King is having an altogether nicer time of it. In fact, if you had dropped in any time around 1656, you might have come across a rather remarkable piece of entertainment. Remarkable not only for the fact that the reigning monarch of France is about to dress up in a golden solar costume and prance around like a wazzock, but also because, by the time he's finished, the development of the orchestra would be on a different planet. The

♬ *Did you like the way I left the verb out, there? Very post-Ref, don't you think?*

occasion was a little ballet, cooked up by the King's composer in residence, Lully.

Jean-Baptiste Lully was an Italian working in Paris, who was born not only with a musical ear but also with dancing feet. He and the King were about to dance a duet, with Louis Quatorze dressed as the Sun – hence the title *The Sun King*, which stuck. I guess as titles given to you for prancing around like an idiot go, the Sun King isn't bad. I imagine Uranus King would have been much harder to explain to the vicar.

Such a success was the ballet that Lully was promoted from a lowly 'violon' player to Director of the King's Music, eventually going on to set up a revolutionary orchestra of twenty-five violins as well as flutes, oboes, bassoons, trumpets and timpani. In fact, if you ever get the chance to listen to anything by Lully performed live, try to remember that half of the instruments you are hearing were, at that time, brand, spanking NEW. They were gadgets, gizmos, the new toys, only just developed. You see, Lully was experimenting with music and the sounds of the orchestra. More importantly, he was experimenting with the sounds of the orchestra and getting it right. He was changing the face and sound of the orchestra for good.

LULLY. FALSY SENSY SECURITY

Sadly, nowadays, not much Lully is ever really played or heard. He is, to be fair, best remembered these days for the manner of his end which, despite being well chronicled, deserves to be recounted. It's said he was in the middle of a performance of his *Te Deum*, a piece which, irony of ironies, he had written to mark his beloved King's recovery from some illness or other. No doubt one of those particularly unpleasant seventeenth-century ones. Er, probably involving pox. Whatever.

Anyway, back then, when you conducted an orchestra, you didn't just wave a baton in front of them. Oh no, back then, they made you earn your money. You had a big stick, roughly the size of a broom handle, sometimes with bells on, sometimes not, and what you did was you held this stick vertically and banged it on the floor, every first beat of the bar, or howsoever took your fancy. In this tragic performance of the *Te Deum*, though, there was Lully, banging the floor with gay abandon, when he suddenly whacked himself in the foot – I don't know, maybe some particularly attractive 'bit-of-wig'♬ walked past. Whatever happened, a few days later an abscess is said to have developed, whereupon he contracted gangrene and died some time after. Dead at the age of fifty-five, and forever consigned, alongside Alkan,♬ ♬ to that section of music books entitled 'Composers who met sticky ends' Poor sod.

PASS THE PURCELL

England. **1689**. (Cue that sort of stirring yet scene-setting music that you get in a classic black-and-white, Sunday afternoon movie. The music dies.)

There's been a bit of a reshuffle, as it were.

Cromwell, the Lord Protector, as he ended up, is long buried. Let's hope he was dead. All in all, though, thank goodness – I mean, *ghastly* haircuts.

Charles II also came and went. A bit like when we went from the 1960s to the 1970s: out went the roundheads, and in came the long, flowing locks. (Wonder if they wore flares?) The capital has more or less fully recovered from both the Great Plague – which killed off some 70,000 people, give or take a stiff – and the Great Fire. And so to music, where there is now a bunch of great composers, carrying on the good work in the current big thing, opera, and none more so than England's finest, Henry Purcell.

Much like Lully in France, Purcell was composer to the King's private band, as well as being organist at Westminster Abbey. In historical terms, Purcell is a bit of a mystery man. Very little is known

♬ *This genuine Louis XIV piece of original slang has been authenticated from the only surviving manuscript of* Thesée et ses gateaux de fer *–'Thesée and his buns of steel'* ☺.

♬ ♬ *Charles-Valentin Alkan, a couple of centuries later, allegedly reached up to retrieve a book from a top shelf and was killed by his falling bookcase.*

about him. In fact, so little that I've had to make some of the next bit up, see if you can tell which.

Now some thirty years old, his rise to musical stardom had been more or less meteoric.

He was merely the bellows pumper on the organ at fifteen and yet composer to the King at eighteen. By the time he was twenty, he was the best-known composer in England.

And his favourite colour was purple.☺

Well, sorry, but there's not much else we know about him. Let's see.

He wrote a variety of different music, from lascivious rugby songs to music for Royal State occasions. (See, that bit's true.)

What else? Well, he wrote music for three different monarchs: Charles II, James II and Queen Mary.

Mm, right, well, he once wrote a fantasy based on a single note.

And he had a pet rabbit called Keith.☺

Damn, sorry. Anyway, as I say, there's very little of his real life that we know anything about.

Back to 1689, and the thirty-year-old Purcell unveils his latest creation – *Dido and Aeneas.* It's a superb addition to the blossoming opera genre, and it shows Purcell's ability to set words as being second to none. It contains one particular lament that is not just the high and low point of the opera, musically and emotionally, it is also all set over the same repeated set of notes in the low parts. It's called a 'ground bass', and is intended to be repeated, over and over again, with the tune and occasionally the harmony changing above it. Purcell's use of this is inspired. In comes this gorgeous, painfully sad aria sung by one of the opera's leads, Dido. She is sort of saying... 'I want to thank you, for giving me the best years of my life – remember me.' Now that's what I call a case of history repeating itself.

If you ever see it on the bill, then go see it. What can I say? It's just fab. It might have been written some 313 years ago, but it's still one of the most moving pieces of music ever. And, of course, beloved, particularly, of schoolchildren, because Purcell sets the words so that they pause just at the right point to embarrass the music teacher: 'When I am laid... am laid in earth.' Cue fits of giggles from the back. 'OK, stop that, stop that, everyone, or I'm keeping you *all* back.'

Anyway, can't stay here, musing over Purcell's *Dido and Aeneas.* I've got people to meet, music to hear, wars to watch people being dismembered in.

Here's a bracing thought. Despite the fact that we've only just gone past Purcell's 'When I am laid in earth', let me tell you: Bach is already four years of age, as is Handel. Despite their genius, though, we're not going to hear much out of them both for a good while yet. Lully has, by now, popped his clogs – almost literally, sadly for him. But what of the 'age', as it were. What is it 'the age' of?

CiD

Well, how about 'The Age of Wren'? Christopher Wren is around and still building. Remember, it's only just over twenty years since the Great Fire, and, although the powers-that-be didn't go for his plan for a complete rebuild, he has nevertheless enjoyed a bit of a boom time. His legacy, as it were, will all have been built over the next thirty years or so – St Michael's, Cornhill; St Bride's, Fleet Street; the Sheldonian Theatre; the Ashmolean Museum; and, of course, due to be finished in a mere... twenty-one years, the big one: St Paul's itself. Running the country now are William and Mary, and the full list of their subjects runs to some 5 million names, compared to say about 58 million today.

But, if you wanted to, you could focus in for a moment. It's also the age of a man called Johann Pachelbel. Now Pachelbel, despite sounding like the cheese from a child's lunchbox, was a composer from Nuremberg. He had a few minor jobs as... well, you know, organist of St Stephen's, Vienna, court composer to the Duchy of Wigan☺, that sort of thing. But he merits his place in the history books for three reasons. First, Bach liked him. Well, to be fair, Bach would, wouldn't he? He's only four right now, and could no doubt do little more than smile and dribble on him. But give him time and Bach would draw a great deal of influence from Mr Pachelbel.

Secondly, Pachelbel pioneered some musical stuff that we now more or less take for granted. Symbolism, for example, he invented that. Well, more or less, with a prevailing wind, he did. He started doing things like minor key music means sad. (If you want to think of something minor key, think, say, the theme from *Schindler's List*.) And, consequently, major key music (try, say, Peter's theme from *Peter and the Wolf*) means happy. Sounds more or less obvious, now, of course, but, just like Everest, somebody had to get there first. Pachelbel even paved the way for Vincent Price, by deciding that the diminished seventh chord (think... well, Vincent Price, really) means evil. So, next time you watch the classic *Masque of the Red Death*, why not flick the mute on the remote control with your toe and lovingly whisper in your loved one's ear, 'Ah, yes, the broken diminished seventh, as pioneered by the seventeenth-century Teutonic music of the great Johann Pachelbel. Pass the Doritos, will you, love?'

But I did say he was in the history books for three reasons and here comes the third. For some inexplicable reason, despite the no-doubt hundreds of chorales, fugues and motets he wrote, he is, sadly, a one-hit wonder. The Joe Dolce 'What'sa-matter-you, HEY' of Nuremberg, the seventeenth-century St Winifred's School Choir. His one hit takes the form of a canon in the key of D. After years of research, scholars have proven, too, that it's for this reason that he gave it the name of 'Canon in D'. It is still a favourite today and is frequently given a rebirth in some TV commercial or other, making it the biggest thing that was going to happen to Nuremberg till someone at the back of a rally in 1938 shouted, 'Speak up!' Now, a brief round-up, if I may. TAXI!

B & H

Of course, you couldn't actually get a black cab back then, but, to be fair, sedan chairs *were* all the rage. They still wouldn't take you south of the river, but they did at least make you a little more mobile and they didn't cost too much. I could do with one right now, in fact, to take me to the... C18. Let's see, where is C18 on my map... Ah. Here. C18...the eighteenth century, here it is, just past Fulham.

What else is popular in the brand, spanking new, 'should auld acquaintance be forgot', crisp, shiny eighteenth century? Well, sad to say, war hasn't gone out of fashion. Never will, I suppose. The current one is the War of the Spanish Succession. I guess who succeeded in Spain was a fairly crucial point because you got some major heavy-weights battling it out. In the blue corner, you've got Britain, Austria, the Netherlands and Denmark. In the red corner, there's France, Bavaria and, not surprisingly, Spain. It was Louis XIV who started it, when he was looking round for a present for his grandson. Presumably they'd sold out of Beanie Babies, because Louis decided to give him Spain. To be fair, it might not have been totally Louis's fault – maybe they'd positioned it far too temptingly at the checkout, and it was an impulse buy. Who knows? Anyway, it all caused a bit of a hoohah, I can tell you – fisticuffs, name calling, the lot. By the end of it – and I'm talking, what, **1714** here – Britain was better off to the tune of Gibraltar, Minorca and Nova Scotia, while Austria had ended up with Belgium, Milan and Naples. Was it all worth it? I wonder. Personally, I'd have made them just spud for it. You know... 'Five potato, six potato, seven potato, MORE. Yeah... I get Spain!'

Other stuff of interest? Well, Captain Kidd has been hanged for piracy, back in 1701. What else? Oh yes, TAXES. Taxes, yes. If you thought we were bedevilled with taxes now, then just imagine what it was like back then. Taxes were the new rock and roll. So popular, it seemed as if there was a prize for the silliest thing you could introduce a tax on and still get away with it. There's the Salt Tax in England, obviously, as well as the Window Tax, which I think they should bring back for modern architects only. In Berlin, they came up with an Unmarried Woman's Tax. Nice! But the winner, and my personal favourite, has got to be Russia, which in around 1750 introduced a Beard Tax. What a great idea. Never did like getting too close to a man with a beard. Unless, of course, it was long and white and attached to a red man with knee-length black boots, as he hands over a Gameboy or an Action Man. But less about my parties.

Other news. The Mary, of William and Mary, has now died, and so, as Richmal Crompton would have said, it was just William, who no doubt went through not only a period of mourning, but also a period of handing out cards saying 'William' with the 'and Mary' crossed out, while his new ones came from the printers. Queen Anne, she of the unfortunately shaped legs, has also been and gone, and now we have George I. The recently created Bank of England seems to be doing well, as is the Duke of Marlborough, or... The Butcher, as they call him. Pleasant. But for now, let's get on to some of the music of this time, and, in fact, to the big two, who really did dominate the age. Bach and Handel.

Johann Sebastian Bach and Georg Frideric Handel were both born in 1685 – the year Judge Jeffries' Bloody Assizes dealt a gory blow for James II after the Monmouth Rebellion. Bach was born in a small place called Eisenach some 200 kilometres north-east of Frankfurt. His was a musical family and at an early age he would obsessively transcribe music scores for his own personal education. After a spell in a youth choir, he got the first of various organ jobs, at Arnstadt. From then on, in a career that lasted till he was sixty-five at Mulhausen, Weimar and Leipzig, Bach wrote acres of superb music. Despite most of it being devoted to the greater glory of God, he did have a few small weaknesses. Coffee was one. At that time, coffee was seen as almost a dangerous narcotic, but Bach indulged his caffeine passion to such an extent that he even wrote a piece of music about it.♪

Another was numerology. Bach was convinced certain numbers were significant. If you give all the letters a numerical value pertaining to their position in the alphabet (so A = 1, B = 2, etc) then, as far as Bach was concerned, his second name added up to 14 (i.e. B2 + A1 + C3 + H8 = 14). And so 14 became very significant for him, and he would write cantatas where the main tune had just 14 notes. One choral prelude, 'Wenn wir in hochsten Nöten sein', has exactly 166 notes, which, if you care to add it up, is the numerical value of his full name. Look:

J + O + H + A + N + N = **62** 10 15 8 1 14 14	
S + E + B + A + S + T + I + A + N = **90** 19 5 2 1 19 20 9 1 14	**total 166**
B + A + C + H = **14** 2 1 3 8	

♪ The Coffee Cantata, *'Schweiget stille, plaudert nicht' from 1732.*

Handel was born not a million miles from Bach, some 60 kilometres west of Leipzig. His family was an entirely different kettle of fish. His dad was a barber-surgeon – the very mention of the phrase 'barber-surgeon' makes me wince: apparently it was a 'jack of all trades' mini-doctor who would pull your teeth one minute then amputate your arm the next (and you'd only come in to say hello) – and Handel had to go against his dad's wishes in order not to follow him in the grisly family business. Ironically, he eventually went to university to read law, but became an organist on the side, at the Domkirche in Halle, before eventually leaving for Hamburg and a job playing violin and harpsichord in the Hamburg Opera. Gradually he began to get more and more of his operas staged, and set off round Europe to play, compose and take in the music of the continent's greatest living composers.

I think it's fair to say that, yes, although they did dominate the age – the age of baroque, that is – it was in very different ways. Despite the fact that they lived at exactly the same time, they were really like chalk and cheese. Handel was a great traveller who went all over Europe. Bach stayed at home. Maybe washing his hair. Handel was opera mad – in fact, set up the Royal Academy of Music specifically to promote opera and wrote operas till they were coming out of his ears. Bach wrote none.

Handel was a shrewd cookie, a clever entrepreneur who always knew which side his bread was buttered when it came to the next commission, or concert series or cushy job – very much the smooth operator. Bach? Well, Bach was a bit hopeless with money. He never really felt comfortable in 'building his part up' as it were, and even went to gaol because he couldn't always bite his tongue when confronted by someone dangling a state job in front of his nose. And having a family the size of Bournemouth didn't exactly help much, either. I always had the image of the Bach family home as a bit like the one in the Monty Python film, *The Meaning of Life* – kids leaping out of cupboards and cries of 'Ooh, get that for us, will you, Deirdre?' as another sibling comes into the world.

Also, I imagine, and, true, I'm just surmising here, but I get the feeling Handel was a bit of a goer – liked to party, eat for both England and Germany at the same time, and generally live a little. Bach was more the pious, totally dedicated and strictly Lutheran artist, who worked to express the profound musical thoughts that were in his head, for the glory of God. It's said he once walked a round trip of some 426 miles and several pairs of boots, just to hear a recital by fellow composer Buxtehude. To be fair, that could be down to commitment, but it could also be just general 'organist madness'. Organists, see! Take my word for it – they're not normal.

Bach's output, despite his dishevelled life, was staggering. The job of collecting and publishing all his music took some forty-six years.

To get some idea of the similarities of Bach and Handel, and yet, at the same time, the amazing differences, you could do worse than listen to the *Water Music* back to back with the *Brandenburg Concertos*. Bach's *Brandenburg Concertos* are simply DIVINE, absolutely fantastic – I couldn't rave about them enough. And yet they have a general... seriousness about them. Alongside them, Handel's *Water Music* is overwhelmingly joyous and, dare I say it, almost light. In fact, even the genesis of the two pieces is typical of both composers. Bach's were a slightly desperate gift to the Margrave of Brandenburg, given to him in the hope of eliciting some much needed money – money which never came, sadly. Handel's, on the other hand, were light and fun – twenty short pieces written to accompany George I on a boat trip up the Thames. Indeed, their first performance was on a boat, rocking like nobody's business, with musicians desperately trying to keep their music on the stands.♬ Somehow I couldn't see Bach in the same role. That said, both pieces are brilliant and gorgeous, and I couldn't live without either.

ANT AND HIS SISTERS

Quick update, if I may. Technology, first. Technology is coming on in leaps and bounds. Someone, for example, makes a bid to be forever remembered in the history of music by inventing the piano. The guy's name was Cristofori. I repeat... Cristofori. You see, I can't

♬ *Mmmm, I can see the school essay subject now: 'Handel was not so much a composer as a Royal Ghetto Blaster – discuss. Not more than 1,000 words.'*

help thinking that he missed a trick, really – more or less blew the 'history' bit. He should have taken a leaf out of, say, Biro or Hoover's book, and called it the Cristofori. That way, today we would be quickly nipping over and playing scales on the 'Cristofori', or listening to Cristofori concertos. Even watching tea commercials on TV where performing chimps said, 'Eh, Dad. Do you know the Cristofori's on my foot?' 'No, but you hum it, son, and I'll play it.' As it is, he called it a 'piano', and, so nobody knows his name.

What else? Well, Handel and another of the big, young composers, Domenico Scarlatti, have had a piano duel. That's just like a real duel, only you're expected to kill your opponent by throwing a piano at them. Not surprisingly, it was declared a draw, and they both lived.♬☺ Elsewhere, we've had the first cricket match – Londoners versus Kentish men – and also in England banknotes are now in. Only a matter of time, I suppose, in that snuff had been around since 1558, so… well, sooner or later you were going to need a banknote, weren't you? All this AND the Prussian army introduce pigtails as their standard haircut, beating the corporate Britain of the 1980s by some 270 years.

Now, I want to introduce you to Antonio Vivaldi, the man who wrote 400 concertos. Or, as Stravinsky said, wrote one then copied it out a further 399 times. (Saucer of milk for the Russian – he was expressing the not uncommon view, it has to be said, that many of Vivaldi's concertos can sound a little… well, samey. At least after the first 200.)

Vivaldi was born in Venice just three years after B & H and was lucky enough to have a rather musical dad – a fiddler at St Mark's. At the age of fifteen he entered the priesthood, and was ordained fully some ten years later. The combination of his holy orders and his mop of Chris Evans ginger hair led to him being nicknamed '*il prete rosso*', the red priest, although having a special dispensation that allowed him not to say Mass, I'm not sure quite how much of a priest he could have been. It's a bit like being a rugby player, but not actually playing any matches. (So, Jonny Wilkinson at the moment, then.) Vivaldi spent most of his professional life as music director of a girls'

♬☺OK, that's not what a piano duel is at all, I know. But it does sound more fun. The real duel saw Handel playing organ and Scarlatti playing keyboard, and each was adjudged to be the best on their respective instruments.

orphanage in Venice, the Conservatorio dell'Ospedale della Pietà – or, often, the Pietà, for short.

His priesthood was called into question, again, when he was rumoured to be more than just good friends with not just one soprano but two: sisters, Anna and Paolina. Eventually he, too, like Handel, travelled all over Europe, but precious little is known about what he got up to. He spent the last couple of years of his life in Vienna, where, sadly, he pulled off the Composer's End No 207 – the so-called 'Death in Poverty' position – perfectly. He was sixty-three. Thankfully, he left behind him some fifty operas and 400 or so concertos (or just one if you agree with Stravinsky), the most well known, now – almost to the point of distraction – being part of 'Il cimento dell'Armonia e dell'inventione' Opus 8. That is, *The Four Seasons*: not just a beautiful series of concertos, but also not a bad hotel and a fine pizza.

THE PACKAGE HOLIDAY

Well, it's **1725** already. My word, doesn't time fly when you roll it up and throw it at somebody. 1725. The year of *The Four Seasons*. The year that Peter the Great became less so, in that he died. The year that Bach, in a breathtaking display of foresight, wrote the music for a mobile telephone incoming call alert, although he called it the *Anna Magdalena Notebook*.

The year the Italian adventurer and author Casanova was born and, very soon, became the next big thing. But where exactly ARE we? What age is it now? Who's in, who's out, who's up, who's down? And why DO birds suddenly appear every time YOU are near? Well, let me try and answer some of those questions, starting with the easiest first.

It's no longer the age of Wren – Sir Christopher is now a two-year-old tourist attraction in his beloved St Paul's. It is, though, still the age of one of the greatest double acts in science – Isaac ('gravity') Newton and Edmond ('comet') Halley. It is also, arguably, the time of Congreve, the man who put the 'oration' into 'Restoration comedy', with his deft prose and elegant construction.

It was, too, the age of the Grand Tour. Now I could have coped with this. Ever since the delightfully named French painter, Hyacinth Rigaud, had written a sort of eighteenth-century version of the 'rough guide' to the Grand Tour, everyone had been at it. Composers, artists, even Tsars – Peter the Great had tried it before he croaked, under a pseudonym.♬ Anyhow, with the Grand Tour came the grand tacky souvenir, naturally. In fact, a whole school of artists grew up, the '*vedutisti*' or panoramists, who fulfilled the demand for memories of Italy by positioning themselves in the major tour resorts and coming up with huge, horizontal horizons of Venice and other places. No doubt each one bore the legend '*Mia Mamma e andata a Veneziana, e tutto questo que mia apportato e questa bruta maglietta!*'♬♬ Canaletto is the man remembered now for this sort of stuff, although at the time Francesco Guardi was perhaps more popular.

So, if it was the age of the Grand Tour, what music might have beguiled you had you ventured to Italy? Well, one man you might have come across if you'd got the right room with the right view was Albinoni.

SO THE OLD ADAGIO GOES

The Venetian Tomaso Albinoni, despite his many good works, was destined to become not even a one-hit wonder. Like many composers, he would often be working on several pieces at once – whether operas with Metastasio, the Tim Rice of his day, or symphonies, a form in which he was reputed to have been quite a pioneer. Sometimes, he would simply write down an idea, or part of an idea, with maybe only the odd part sketched in, the intention being that he would leave it aside to return to another day. It was one such 'sketch', a mere fragment of manuscript, which the Italian scholar Remo Giazotto found in 1945, lining his wastepaper basket. It had

♬ *That is, 'before he croaked',* and *'under a pseudonym'. Not 'before he croaked under a pseudonym', if you understand me? Just wanted to make that clear. In fact, as far as I'm concerned, Tsar Peter never, to the best of my knowledge, croaked under a pseudonym. Good. Glad to clear that up.*

♬♬ *Translation: 'My mum went to Venice and all I got was this lousy painting.'*

only a handful of notes scribbled in on the violin part, and some but not all of the bass part. With a little bit of guesswork and a prevailing wind, he came up with what is now known as 'the Albinoni Adagio' – despite the fact that Albinoni hadn't actually written it.

Being an 'adagio' – the Italian word meaning 'at a slow pace' – it is an unhurried and simple string tune, punctuated by a soft, often reedy organ sound. As a result of its hybrid composition, it is more romantic than most baroque pieces of its type. So when you listen to it next time, think of Albinoni and his sketches; think of Remo Giazotto, going largely unremembered; but most of all, think of Canaletto, painting the sun setting over Venice, the lap, lap, lapping of the weedy canals, the cumbersome clunk of paint-peeling gondolas. Beautiful. Deliquescent. And, before we go any further, let me answer the question I posed earlier, on page 61. Simple. Just like me, they long to be ... close to you. There. I think that's covered everything.

DON'T FORGET NATHAN THE PROPHET!

Right. Where are Bach and Handel? Well, they're still dominant, to be fair. Bach was coming up with stuff like the *St John Passion* and the *St Matthew Passion* – more of which later – whereas Handel, well, he managed the opera *Rodelinda* (from which we get the gorgeous aria 'Dove sei') and even *Zadok the Priest* (not forgetting Nathan the Prophet – more on this later too). Each a sort of separate leg of the... compositional Colossus, bestriding the... harbour that is... well, that is music. As it were. OK, needs work. But where is music at, as they would have said in the '70s? Where is it *all* at? Where is it all *going*? Well, it's more or less doing what everyone else is doing – it's going on a Grand Tour. Let me try and explain, before you send someone to sit with me.

Here's what I mean. Imagine you are music in general, right? Well, behind you... is home – that is, Church music. Like home, it will always be there, but for now, well... we're off exploring. The journey has already taken in opera, which has reached its first peak and is already on the wane. Its time *will* come again, but not for years. For now, instrumental music is King, and its kingdom is Italy.

In terms of instrumental music, overtures came first – a band playing as one. Then the band split – two separate sections of the same band, almost like teams, playing against each other. This 'two-team' formation was called the concerto. Then, one of the groups became smaller. So now it's a small bunch of soloists versus the rest of the band – or the concerto grosso – the great concerto.

Try and look at it like this. Imagine each is a player in the orchestra.

In an overture, the orchestra was like this:

All together, see?
Then the orchestra split:

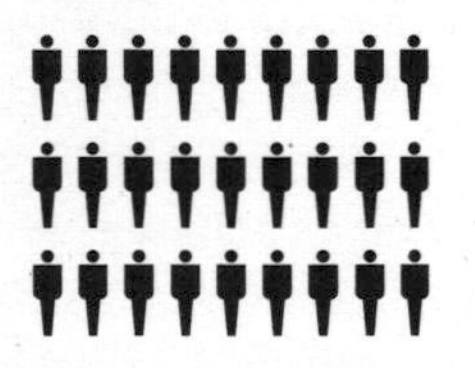

... to play a concerto.
Then, one side became smaller than the other:

... to play the concerto grosso.

The Italian Corelli was big on these 'concerti grossi', as were lesser-known names like Geminiani and Torelli, as well as Handel himself. From here, it's not a huge leap to the 'solo concerto':

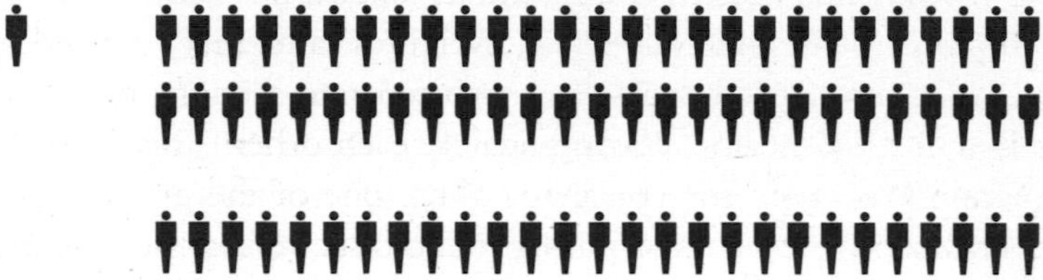

...just one player versus all the rest, and by far the most popular version. The one we're most familiar with now, to be honest. Vivaldi did virtually all he could with this format – one or 400, depending whether you agree with Stravinsky or not.

With the concerto, came – rather obvious, really, but it has to be said – The Soloist. And, presumably, with the soloist came, what... luvvie fits and outrageous dressing room demands. Good. Just what we need. 'I want a bowl of M&Ms with all the blue ones taken out... oh, and a music stand.'

Technology-wise, the organ is the big thing, but other new instruments are coming online all the time – not just the piano I mentioned earlier, but the piccolo (the funny sort of dwarf castrato flute, as it were), the clarinet too, and, oddly enough, the tuning fork.♫

TOCCATA AND FEUD

So what's bubbling in **1729**? Who is damned? Who is faintly praised? The South Sea Bubble is well and truly burst, Catherine the Great has succeeded Peter the Great – nice to see she took his name – and *Moll Flanders* is still one of the public's favourite books, some seven years after its release. You can possibly see why. Handel, himself, has relinquished his right to be first to the deckchairs by becoming a British citizen. Bach, of course, still hasn't left Germany, although he has now moved pretty far afield for him: down the road

♫ *The tuning fork, incidentally, was invented by a brass player. If anyone was going to feel the need for an implement to keep you in tune, it's not surprising that it was a brass player.*

to Leipzig.

Johann Sebastian is in a bit of a feud situation with the Church authorities, not helped, no doubt, by the fact that he was the last choice for the Leipzig job. He was less preferred than the exceedingly dull Telemann, and even less preferred to the exceedingly unknown Graupner. Who he? Ed. (In fact, who Ed?) Bach found himself in trouble with his employers on more than one occasion, and I think, to look at it fairly, there was right and wrong on both sides. Bach's jobs were ridiculously labour-intensive, with music to write and arrange for so many different places and events. But, equally, he could, by all accounts, be a bit tough to get on with. On one occasion, he applied for a new job and got it, neglecting to tell his new employer only one vital fact – he already had a job, and they didn't want to let him go. He ended up being placed under house arrest to prevent him skipping to his next gig.

The good thing, though, is that all Bach's wrangling with the powers-that-be does not appear to have affected his writing. A stream of great works just seem to pour forth from him like sweat from a mere mortal. One of them is the marvellous *St Matthew Passion*, in which Bach used not only the St Matthew version of the Passion but also the odd extra verse written by a man writing under the name of Picander, who was in fact a postman from Leipzig. As you can imagine, a man as committed to the Church as Bach would have put all his resources into a dramatic setting of the crucifixion and resurrection of Christ. The 'oratorio Passion' was a particularly German affair, having grown out of the liturgical Lutheran Passion music, pioneered by early musical settlers such as Schütz.♫

Bach, though, tailored the Passion to his own needs. He increased the amount of non-biblical texts, putting increasing demands on poets such as Picander – Postman Pic, to his friends – to provide him with original but no less fitting words. In the *St Matthew Passion*, or, to give it the name Bach gave it, the *Passio Domini nostri J.C. secundum Evangelistam Mattaeum*, the great man had increased the new

♫ *German composer, born in Saxony, who worked mainly out of Dresden. He loved his Passions as well as his opera. His 'The Seven Words of Christ' – not to be confused with a Haydn piece of a similar name – sets words from all four gospels beautifully.*

bits from twelve to twenty-seven biblical verses. It was to be the last of his great Passions, and was performed at St Thomas's Church, Leipzig, on Good Friday, 1729. That was its first performance. Sadly, it had to wait another hundred years for its second performance, conducted by one Felix Mendelssohn in Berlin, but that's another story. It's a big piece, if you ever come to take it in, but more or less every bit is gorgeous, particularly if you are a Bach junkie, and none more so than the glorious 'O sacred head, sore wounded'.

As for Georg Frideric, he'd had a minor opera out the year before – *Tolomeo*, which contains the yummy 'Silent Worship' – but he was more likely than not basking in the glow afforded to the four anthems he'd written just two years earlier for the coronation of George II. In fact, basking in the glow afforded one of them in particular, the first, which went by the now almost household name of *Zadok the Priest* (but don't forget Nathan the Prophet!♬). In fact, they're so popular, they've been performed at more or less every coronation since. If only he could collect the royalties♬♬ on it.

WAR AND PEACE MORE WAR

So that was 1729. More or less, give or take a couple of years. To get to the next major landmark, you have to traverse the opening of the Covent Garden Opera House, the birth of Haydn, and the founding of the Academie of Ancient Music. That's just in music. Elsewhere you also had the building of 10 Downing Street; the rise of the game Ninepins; the advice of Dr John Arbuthnot to watch what you ate; the founding of the Seventh Day Baptists by Conrad Beissel; the coronation of Christian VI of Denmark; the succession of Tsar Ivan V's daughter, Anne – who apparently gets expenses and a company cart; the beginning of the four-course system of husbandry by Viscount 'Turnip' Townsend – no, don't ask me, either; the death

♬ *The opening line of* Zadok the Priest *continues 'Zadok the Priest and Nathan the Prophet annointed Solomon King.' I always feel sorry for good, reliable Nathan the Prophet. He got equal billing in the original story but it is only Zadok who gets remembered.*

♬♬ *No pun intended.*

of three of the great English literati – Daniel Defoe, Elijah Fenton and John Gay; the birth of Stanislaus II, the last independent King of Poland; and the first ever subscription library started by Benjamin Franklin in Philadelphia. My word, glad that's over.

In addition to that, there's a war on. Well, to be fair, there usually is, somewhere or other. I mean, I don't want to belittle these things in the slightest, but I do often think it was a case of 'Look, whose turn is it?' A bit like planning the office holiday rota:

> *'Erm, right, well, the Spanish Succession boys would rather take the last two weeks in August. Apparently that allows them July to violate the Partition Treaty. Fiona, pass me my coffee, can you, love? Now, that means the Thirty Years will have to go in June, the Hundred Years in the front half of July, and... now who are you?'*
>
> *'The Seven Years!'*
>
> *'Damn, forgot about you. Erm... right, Seven Years... Seven Years... oh, look! You guys can have the back half of July... when the schools break up. Everybody happy? Right, let's have a look at that stationery order...'*

Well... possibly. Possibly not. In actual fact, the war that's just started is the Polish Succession. Nice name. Good branding. Next year there'll be one with Turkey and Persia, but it'll only last twelve months or so. Huh! ONLY! The year after that, it's Russia and Turkey, then Prussia meet Austria in the quarter-finals in 1740, before Turkey and Persia come back to battle it out in the play-offs. Result: Turkey win on the away dead rule. I don't know. Millions of lives, millions of pounds and all for a handful of disputed borders and dodgy marriages. These days, government central office would simply rearrange the boundaries without anyone noticing. Which reminds me: BACH!

How does that remind me? Well, you see in **1733**, Bach was having a minor war himself. Not quite on the same scale, it's true, but still, a war no less. JSB's war is with the church authorities – again! – this time the ones at St Thomas's in Leipzig, and, of course, the problem is over money. Or, according to Bach, the lack of it. His job of

Cantor means he plays the organ, writes new music – every week, mind! – for two churches and all their services. He rehearses, directs and trains people at a *further* two churches, and also, in his – wait for this – *spare time*, he has to teach Latin and music at the local school. Added to this is the fact that the living quarters that go with the job are a tad squalid, and the salary mere peanuts. So, you can imagine, it's a virtual running battle. And what does it do to his 'muse', as it were? Does the music dry up? Is he writer's-blocked, and unable to pen a note? Well, no, actually. Quite the opposite, oddly enough. The Leipzig years will turn out to be one of his most prolific times.

Great pieces were to come from this period. The *Art of Fugue*, albeit unfinished, was a huge undertaking, using almost every feature of the current music thinking at the time. It is one HUGE piece of showing off, really. In it, Bach wrote himself one single tune. He then set about showing you how many times and in how many different ways he could change and vary and re-present this tune. It's a bit like a jazz musician being given a small tune and then improvising on it for hours, just to show how clever he is. Then there's The *Musical Offering*, the *Goldberg Variations* and, of course, started in this very year, 1733, the mere trifle that is...The *Mass in B Minor.*

CRITICAL MASS

The *B Minor Mass* – or to give it its German title *Die Messe in H Moll* – is considered by many to be the greatest achievement of a great composer. It's massive. A full Latin Mass in twenty-four sections, with monumental versions of the Gloria, the Crucifixus and the Credo. What's even more interesting is that it's a Catholic Mass, which is odd for Bach, the foremost Protestant composer of his day. It seems he was probably touting for business, and would send the Kyrie and Gloria to the Catholic King of Saxony, to see if he could get the job of court composer. Again, and I know I've said this before, but go and see a live performance. It's a BIG piece, and even the best recording on CD can't do it justice.

By **1736**, the muse Euterpe is still putting all his eggs in just two baskets, namely B and H. With both now at their absolute peak, though, just how does it feel? I mean, how does it smell, to be in 1736? What does 1736 taste like? Well, let me see if I can't take your index finger and rub it across the grain of the year.

Well, baroque is well and truly, incompletely and utterly king. If you're a baroque star, it doesn't get any better than this, so enjoy it while you can. The Classical period is only just around the corner. Opera, though, is past its first peak. It is still being written – in fact it's being written like mad. And as they only finished the Covent Garden Opera House in 1732 – four years ago – then someone obviously believes in it enough to throw pots of money at it. But in the form that the crowds of the time knew it, opera had had its first day. Oratorio was gaining on it, and would give it a good run for its money in the pop stakes, before it was finished.

To be fair, despite it being at its most popular, the writing is nevertheless on the wall for the fiddly, florid-sounding music that is baroque. But not yet. Not quite yet. For now, Bach and Handel continue to dominate. Others do get a look in, though.

BAROQUE STARS

Jean-Philippe Rameau, for example, the man from Dijon. He was incredibly popular in his day, which was around now, to be fair. He knocked out some thirty or so operas and ballets, and generally helped to move things on a bit, particularly opera-wise. He'd had a big hit only last year – 1735 – with *Les Indes Galantes*, the hit ballet of the season. It wasn't *just* a crowd pleaser, either. It was pushing back the boundaries of what was then considered the done thing. He it was who was very big on putting musical descriptions into his works. Up to now, music was largely just... well, music – either for its own sake, or for the glory of God. Rameau decided that there should be the odd description of worldly things in there, too. So, in something like *Les Indes Galantes*, there are musical earthquakes, storms, volcanic eruptions, clay-pigeon shooting☺, all depicted by Rameau in his music.

Then there was Pergolesi. Again, forgive me this moment while I wax on about his name. Beautiful name, I've always thought – Giovanni Battista Pergolesi. From Jesi. Mmm. Lovely. Anyway, as I say, he was from Jesi, in Italy. He led a tragically short life, dying at the age of twenty-six – but he filled those years with some fifteen operas and twelve cantatas. One of his operas, *La Serva Padrona* – 'The Servant as Mistress' – was so important in its day, particularly around the time of its Paris performances, that it was said to have influenced the path of French music significantly. He also found time to come up with a bunch of pieces of sacred music, one of which has stayed in the repertoire for one simple reason – it's gorgeous. It's a setting of the *Stabat Mater*, the words from Passion Week which describe the mother of Jesus standing at the foot of the cross.

Now, if I were to tell you that 1736 was but a dim and distant memory, would you believe me? Well, obviously you would, because it was hundreds of years ago. What I mean is, let's move on from there, six years, to **1742**. Things have changed. Music has changed. The world has changed. My underpants have changed.

Vivaldi, of the 400 Concertos and the Two Women, has died. So, probably, died happy, one might presume. But, as they say in show business, as one door closes, another swings back in your face. Or, if you prefer, opens. And in this case, it opened. The music world has gained the composer who is a good contender for the 'Best name not just in music but in all history'. He goes by the name of:

Carl Ditters von Dittersdorf

I mean, I don't know why his parents didn't save on valuable ink and call him:

Carl Snigger Now Please

Actually, doesn't save them much ink, does it, but still, you get my drift. Carl was Viennese, a one-time fiddler who had toured all Italy captivating audiences, and who would go on to live to the grand old age of sixty. As such, he is what is now termed a lesser contemporary of Haydn and Mozart. Sad thing to declare at the Pearly Gates, I imagine. Name: Carl Ditters von Dittersdorf (cue hails of laughter). Occupation: Er, lesser contemporary of Haydn and Mozart. Favourite colour: Well, I'm not really sure, I mean, there's so many to choose from.

Other wins, as it were, in the musical world at the time? Well, baby Haydn is now young choirboy Haydn and he has just started at St Stephen's Cathedral in Vienna. He's a bit of a rising star, clearly, and he could do well if he can only shake off the cutsie reputation. What else? Well, there's the music from the Last Night of the Proms – that was written about now. 'Rule Britannia', the flag-wavers' favourite (although, whatever you think of it, it's at least a bit livelier than 'God Save the Queen').

ARNE STORMING!

Thomas Arne was only thirty years old when he produced the one tune that has become one half of what he is remembered for today. This Eton-educated would-be lawyer had been forced to practise on a muffled harpsichord, in order that his dad didn't discover him pursuing his music.

Eventually, though, he came out of the composers' closet – jeepers, it must have been crowded in there – and, with his father's blessing, became a successful composer. It was in 1740 that he produced his stage play with music, *Alfred*, from which comes the now evergreen 'Rule Britannia'. The other half of his claim to fame is that he's part of a sort of musician's slang, alongside Edward Elgar, used in order to suggest that someone doesn't know their stuff. As in… 'He doesn't know his Arne from his Elgar'.

Thomas Arne premiered 'Rule B.' in front of the Prince of Wales at Cliveden. Which leads me on to a useful question: who *does* rule the waves, as it were, in 1742?

'IN DUBLIN'S FAIR CITY, HANDEL MEETS THE COMMITTEE…'

Let's zoom out and go global, then zoom back in again.

Global first. Frederick the Great♬ of Prussia has got his cue for his fifteen minutes of fame, or, to be more precise, forty-six years of fame. And before we zoom back in, what else has happened? Well, the Pope has got all hot under the collar about Freemasonry. Doesn't like it. Doesn't like it one bit. In fact, he's issued a papal bull about it along the lines of 'What's with all this closed shop practices, silly costumes and odd ceremonies!' Well, you can see why he feels threatened.

Zooming back in, slowly, there's the Swiss astronomer, Anders Celcius, who, just this year, has invented the 'centigrade' thermometer, just some six years after Gabriel Fahrenheit had died.♫♫ Closer to home, Britain has gained censorship on the stage, with all new work having to go before the Lord Chamberlain. This doesn't stop David Garrick from having a much-acclaimed London debut as Richard III, though. Dick Turpin, the man who demanded outrageous amounts of money while people were in the middle of their journeys, has been and gone, although, today, numerous cafés alongside the A1 do their best to keep his memory alive.

Musically, though, Handel is about to offer up an oratorio form of the words, 'You ain't seen nothing, yet' while on a trip to Dublin. He'd been invited to the Irish capital by the Duke of Devonshire, for a charity gig, and had accepted readily. He'd recently lost around ten grand in an Italian opera company that had gone pits-up, so he was very keen to do well as a 'continental star' in Ireland.

He'd gone there with the intention of just doing a few concerts, making some good money, and leaving. In the end, though, his reception was so favourable that he stayed nine months, in a rented house in Abbey Street, and doubled the planned number of concerts from

♫ *If I could digress at this point, it would be to say: the naming committee. Who are they? I mean the people who come up with the descriptions to go with world leaders. Frederick... THE GREAT. Ivan... THE TERRIBLE. I mean, who says Ivan was terrible? Surely that's a matter of opinion? Granted, there are some that are more or less indisputable. Like Attila... THE HUN. Robert... THE BRUCE. St James... THE DISMEMBERED. (Poor guy, I imagine he pretty much had to earn that name. Eww!) But... THE TERRIBLE. Who says so? I've never seen an ad in the paper recruiting for members on the world leaders' naming committee! I've never seen a laminated sign pinned to a tree, like planning permission, inviting comments of proposed future names. SO WHO SAYS? And why not Ivan... THE LOUSY. Or Peter... THE OBJECTIONABLE. Frederick... the WELL HE WAS OK BUT NOTHING SPECIAL! And, while I'm on the subject, poor old Ethelred. Just because he came down to answer the door in his jim-jams. Very unfair. Anyway, I digress, sorry. But at least I told you I would.*

♫♫ *Gabriel Fahrenheit died aged fifty, but nothing could dissuade him from his belief that he was actually 122.*

six to twelve. During his stay, Handel grew increasingly respectful of the local musicians. This changed his preconceived idea that they would not be able to pull off the new oratorio that he'd been working on. So he put an ad in the *Dublin Journal* on 27 March that year.

> For the relief of the prisoners in the several gaols, and for the support of Mercer's Hospital in Stephen's St, and of the Charitable Infirmary on the Inn's Quay, on Monday the 12th of April, will be performed at the Musick Hall in Fishamble St, Mr Handel's new Grand Oratorio, call'd the MESSIAH, in which Gentlemen of the Choirs of both Cathedrals will assist, with some Concertoes on the Organ, by Mr Handel.

Seven hundred people attended the premiere, in a hall made for 600. Paper reviews were effusive. 'In the opinion of the best judges, the work far surpasses anything of that nature which has been performed in this or any other kingdom.'

And so was born one of the great legends of music. Some say he wrote it in twenty-five days, some say less – eighteen, even. All that is certain is that he had a huge hit on his hands in Dublin that year. He went on to try and clone the success of the *Messiah* with a string of others: *Semele*, *Judas Maccabaeus*, *Joshua*, *Solomon*, *Ernest meets the Tickle-Monsters*☺... sorry, mixed up my notes.

TIME OUT 1749

You'll have to go with me on this one. If you were to buy a copy of *Time Out* in **1749**, what do you think you'd be able to read when you opened it? Well, chances are, you wouldn't. Be able to read, I mean. But just presuming you were literate, what then?

Well, there might be a double-page interview with Henry Fielding, who has a new book to plug, *Tom Jones*, and rather saucy it is too. There might be a review of the travelling theatre company that has brought over the latest offering from the Italian comic playwright, Goldoni, called *The Liar*. Great title, don't you think? There might even be a piece on the recent retrospective of the painter, Canaletto, who is currently enjoying a near ten-year-long stay in England; or possibly a *Groundforce*-style garden makeover, with the hot prospect on the flora and fauna front, Capability Brown. Er, no doubt, with pictures by Gainsborough.

Somewhere on the letters page there's probably a 'What will they think of next?' piece, talking about Pereire's new thing, sign language for the deaf. In the news columns, there's a small 'Where are they now?' feature on Bonnie Prince Charlie, and little paragraphs on Philip, the No 5 shirt for Spain, who has been sent off and replaced by Ferdinand in the No 6 shirt. There might even be a *Hello*-style 'The Holy Roman Emperor, Francis I, invites us to spend some peaceful time with him at Aix-la-Chapelle'.

Musically, though, *Time Out* of 1749 should be reporting that we really are on the brink. To paraphrase Bob Dylan, ye times, they are y-changin'. Or whatever. Just as in architecture, where the finicky, twiddly bits of the rococo and baroque stuff have had their day, well, so, in music, the finicky, twiddly bits of the baroque with all its counterpoint stuff – that's out any minute, too. In architecture, by way of replacement, they got neo-classicism, inspired by things like Stuart and Revett's *Classical Antiquities of Athens*, and all that sort of stuff. In music, they got... well, more or less the same. Only, as it hadn't actually happened before – or at least, not on paper – they simply called it classical. Or at least, they *would* call it classical. It hasn't happened yet. But it soon will.

People will start to pare music down, to strip away Bach's counterpoints and fugues, and so on, to rely less and less on the more academic and mathematical side of music, only to push things on in other ways. But, as I say, it hasn't happened yet. It's only 1749 and baroque has gone to extra time. It's got a good... let's see, twelve months left on the clock. It's playing itself out with Domenico Scarlatti in Spain, Rameau in France and Handel more or less all over the place. In fact, to be honest, when Bach stops, so will baroque. Seems fair really. But, till the hooter goes, Handel just keeps on turning out the hits.

Indeed, the Queen now arriving at Platform 1 is the 1749 from Sheba, calling at Cairo and Addis Ababa. Actually, that reminds me of a scene from the bible of classical music, *Fry's Classical Lives*, subtitled *An Eye-witness's Diary of the Classical Period as it Happened*. Allow me to quote a substantial but important passage.

> As I was leaving the courtyard, I couldn't help but notice a tall, dark-haired gentleman, rushing to catch the Classical coach.
>
> 'I say, wait on,' he cried, but to no avail. The coachman was by now muffled against the potentially treacherous weather and, in any case, had gathered up such a head of speed on the courtyard's rain-soaked cobbles that he fair shot past him like a bullet, spraying his cloak as he went.
>
> 'Dash,' scowled the stranger, then, realising I was in earshot, 'I'm sorry.'
>
> I nodded my head, all the better not to retrieve my hands from their now cosy, southerly home in my pockets. He stepped towards me.
>
> 'Excuse me, fine sir,' he said, 'which coach was that I have missed?'
>
> I frowned slightly, betraying my imminent bad news.
>
> 'That was the 1750 – Classical Period. Er, change at Slough.'
>
> 'Dash,' he said again. And again, 'Sorry.'
>
> He paused. 'And the next one?'
>
> I looked at my pocket watch.
>
> 'The next? Not until 1820... or thereabouts. That's the Romantic Period.'
>
> At this, the tall stranger looked crestfallen.
>
> 'Seventy years? Seventy years till the next one?'
>
> As sure as I was of my facts, I proffered some last hope.

'Let me just check,' I said, fruitlessly. 'Yes, the 1820, Romantic. There is something leaving at 1800, but that's if you've paid in advance. You haven't paid in advance, have you?'

His gaze fell to his galoshes.

'Er, no. No, I haven't.'

'Then your best bet is the 1820. Come, let me buy you a hot whisky and bitters. You can let your troubles float off in the vapours!' It was all the comfort I could offer.

'Thank you,' said the would-be traveller, and we both transferred inside.

Lovely moment, isn't it? A real-life, eye-witness account of one man's missing the start of the Classical period. Touching, if a little surreal.

Could someone bring me a blanket for my legs?

...DON'T FIX IT

So. It's classical, Jim, but not as we know it. Well, not really. Not yet, anyway. And why not? Well, mainly because not enough people knew it was classical yet, just in the same way they didn't know it was baroque until it came up and bit them in the head. The '1750, start of the Classical period' nonsense is exactly that. Nonsense. It's a very convenient and very general label put on things to show that, from roughly around this time, the first pieces of what we now recognize as classical music began to be written.

But still, we are now 'officially' classical. The period from which all classical music gets its name. And why? Why did this one period from around 1750 to 1820 or so give its name to ALL this type of music, from year dot to the present day? Baroque, romantic, even modern music... why do we call it all 'classical' music? The answer?

Haven't a clue. You'll have to read another book if you want to know the answer to that one.♪

Of course, it's early days, yet. And just like at the end of an exam, when the bell goes, very few people immediately just put their pens down. So, very few people just stopped writing baroque, just like that. Well, OK, Bach did, but that was more down to a personal request from the Grim Reaper than a change to classical. Most others carried

---

♪ *May I suggest* Why We Call All Classical Music Classical, Including Baroque, Romantic and Even Some Modern, *by Stephen Fry, price £40, discounts for orders over 30. If I get enough orders, I may even write the book.*

on a bit, writing baroque, until the teacher physically wrested the pen from their hands. Metaphorically speaking, of course. A couple, however, were beginning to show many of the hallmarks of the classical period, particularly CPE Bach. Also, many of the younger lot, the new guys just graduating straight into the classical era, found it natural, of course, to write nothing else. And there was one Bavarian who was quick to see the point of this new 'classical thing' – what the marketing men today would call 'an early adopter'. And what's more, not only was he about to write his best work EVER, but, more to the point, he also had *a mildly amusing middle name*. FAN-TASTIC! Step forward...

Christoph Willibald von Gluck

Yes, I know. As Frankie Howerd would have said, 'Ooh-er, no, dear, don't titter. No... titter ye not!' Anyway, before we come to him, let me quickly set the scene for you. Imagine it's **1762**. Yes, I know – doesn't tempus fugit, especially when you want to cover thirty-two years in the next ten pages. Still. Can't have everything, as it were.

DANDY

So, what's happened since our last little chat? Well, let's see. Johnson's Dictionary has been out seven years now, taking its place on all good bibliophiles' shelves, alongside, perhaps, Laurence Sterne's *Tristram Shandy*, Voltaire's *Candide* and, just this year, Rousseau's *Social Contract*.

Not so much of a bedtime read, that last one. The same house that had a burgeoning bookshelf also might have had one of Thomas Chippendale's cabinets – very 'This Year' – or even a painting by George Stubbs. George Stubbs was more or less like Damien Hirst in his time, except that he left his subjects *whole* and favoured oil over formaldehyde. Josiah Wedgwood had, only a couple of years ago, started a pottery in Etruria, Staffordshire, and, more recently, Beau Nash had... well, been busy being Beau Nash – dandy and bon-viveur. Great title, isn't it, Dandy? I can just imagine him down the job centre. In fact, I think there's mention of such an incident in Fry's *Classical Lives.* Gosh, that book is useful.

> I had been a guest of the government before, and found their weekly gatherings at the 'Maison de Travail' to be not unpleasant. On this occasion, I found myself next in the queue to the great bon-viveur, raconteur and general dandy, Mr Beau Nash. Indeed, at one point it appeared that he had been 'viveur-ing' rather too 'bon-ly' the previous night, and his right cheek made a more than passing acquaintance with my shoulder. When it came to his turn to demonstrate his government artistry, I woke him from his slumbers and prompted him to play his part. He requested that I accompany him to his desk, as he had a touch of gout that might make his walking a little less stable than normal. This I was glad to do, and, as a result, I was by his side for the entire encounter, which passed in something like this manner.
>
> 'Name?'
>
> 'Nash, Beau.'
>
> 'Occupation?'
>
> 'Dandy.'
>
> 'Sorry?'
>
> 'Dandy,' I say.
>
> 'Dandy?'
>
> 'Yes sir, dandy. I am a dandy. I... I... I dand. And frequently. Now, pray tell me, my good man... I am present primarily to solicit travails and labours wherein I might, by their subsequent execution, seek to procure, for my own part, a modest pecuniary – some might say nummular – advantage. What say you?'
>
> The representative of good King George raised his head. 'Come again?' he said, somewhat nonplussed.
>
> Nash stared at him, sniffed once and said, 'Gizza job!'

What a beautiful extract. How lucky we are to have such a fine account of the times. Thank goodness for my forefathers, that's all I can say.

BEANO

To return to 1762, what of sport? Well, sport, it would appear, is thriving. St Andrews has been founded, as has the Jockey Club, and, thank goodness, someone's even laid down the rules of whist. In other areas, a couple of important factories have gone up, too, notably the world's first porcelain factory and the world's first chocolate factory. One, clearly, far more important than the other. On a more 'world' stage, George II has died and George III is here. Things are beginning to rumble in America, with everyone talking independence, and, just to keep the tally going, we are currently six years in to a seven years' war. And I think that's more or less it. Oh, no... someone has invented the harmonica. The thoughtless bastard.

Musically speaking, though, there has been a shift taking place. The centre of the music universe is moving. It was Italy, having previously been Holland and Flanders, but now it was shifting again to Vienna, principally because of the Hapsburgs, the all-powerful family currently enjoying a spell as Holy Roman Emperors. Handel is now gone, just three years ago, and with him, the last great champion of the baroque art. Classical music, as we know it, is getting a firm foothold, mainly because the baroque composers have all but died off. It's in among all this that the man with the mildly amusing middle name, Gluck, decides to write a new opera.

WHIZZER AND CHIPS

Now, bearing in mind that opera has been seen by some as having had its day, Gluck's move is interpreted by some as a kind of 'so what?' move. But not by Gluck. And, to be fair, Gluck had the advantage over some in that he was a traveller. He'd been around, got ideas, nicked ideas: heard styles, nicked styles. He'd also married the daughter of one of the wealthiest bankers in Vienna – for love, you understand – and so could more or less sit back and write what he liked, anyway. And what did he like? Well, he liked realism. He wanted there to be more realism in music – less 'music for music's sake' and more 'this bit of music is meant to sound like this', or 'this section of music is meant to be imitating that'. He'd tried it in a ballet already, based on Molière's *Don Juan*, and he'd rather liked it. So he did it again, this time in an opera.

He got his mate, who ran the local lottery, to provide the libretto♪ and, well, Robert be thine uncle, as they said back then. He had a hit. Audiences had heard nothing quite like it before. It was *real* humanity on stage, *real* truth. And it all sounded much more dramatic than anything they'd heard before, mainly because Gluck of the Mildly Amusing Middle Name was trying out new sound effects, if you like, using the full orchestra. The audiences felt they could actually *hear* the thunder in the music, *touch* the wrath of the Furies, and almost *see* the beauty of the Elysian fields. Could opera be a hit, once again? Well, Gluck of the Mildly Amusing Middle Name certainly thought so. And what was this work that made the difference again for opera? Well, would you credit it, it was a reworking of the story that had become more or less the first ever opera hit, back in 1607. It was *Orfeo and Euridice*.

ORPHEUS IN HIS UNDERPANTS

Orfeo and Euridice – Gluck. *La Favola d'Orfeo* – Monteverdi. *Orphée aux Enfers* – Offenbach. Even *Orpheus and Eurydyke* – Krenek. It's amazing to see how this story has been constantly recycled. As an opera libretto, it has been used more frequently than any other and, on at least two occasions, was right there at the forefront of innovation in music. Unsurprising, then, to hear that the story is, of course, all about the 'inventor of music', Orpheus, who recovers his beloved Eurydice from Hades, only to lose her again in the moment

♪ *Hence the now famous tenor love song 'It could be you!'*

of reunion. Gluck, interestingly, gave it a happy ending – Amor appears and restores Eurydice to life – in sharp contrast to Monteverdi's tragic denouement, where Orpheus loses Eurydice but, by way of recompense, is transferred to the stars by Apollo. A classic story, making at least three classic operas, in their own ways. In fact, as we're talking about the inventor of music, let's just sit back and take stock a moment.

YOUR NAME NOT BACH?

Bach has now got the job he'd finally been expecting – Kapellmeister to the Heavenly Host: which he would eventually job share with Handel. I imagine Big George would probably have been content to sit out rehearsals as long as there was roast chicken provided – liked his food, our Handel. In their place, Haydn was just beginning to make a name for himself,♪ Gluck's doing his bit for opera. But what of the time? What of the year? It's 1763. What's going on?

1763, and the generals in the Seven Years War looked at the fourth official and, with no stoppage time to fight, blew the final whistle – the Peace of Paris, as it was called. In England we'd already had Pitt the Elder, we'd just got Pitt the Younger, but the latest thing to hit the news was Pit – the pony. 1763 saw the first use of these sad creatures down the mines.

The travelling music man, Charles Burney♪♪, was thirty-seven and was making Michael Palin look like a couch potato. In France, Rameau has just one year left in him. In Austria, Mozart is seven – no doubt about to retire already. You have to remember that Mozart years are rather like the inverse of dog years. So 'seven' is actually about twenty-one or so, as far as a mere mortal is concerned. Hence,

♪ *Knowing Haydn, if he were to make a name for himself, it would be out of macramé... not the most exciting man in the world, Haydn. Of course, you didn't hear it from me, OK?*

♪♪ *Charles Burney was actually a doctor from Shrewsbury, who travelled extensively throughout Europe, writing up his musical experiences into a book,* The History of Music. *A case of 'right place, right time' made an otherwise minor doctor and music lover a must for anyone with more than a passing interest in the music of the time.*

he was chucking out music like it was going out of fashion and making a mint with concerts all over Europe.

Elsewhere – and as they say in some very strange places where you have to know Otto to get in – 'Bach is dead, long live the Bachs!' OK, no one actually said that. I made it up. All I mean is that 'Bach' Bach – Johann Sebastian, the big one – is dead. But there are still two other Bachs knocking around, somewhere, keeping the brand name going, as it were. Operating out of England, there's JC Bach – known accurately, if somewhat unspectacularly, as 'The English Bach', while in Germany, there's Carl Phillip Emmanuel, CPE Bach, known as... well, known as CPE Bach, actually. The English Bach is said to have visited London and loved it so much, he bought the company – that is, stayed. He became friends with Gainsborough, went to posh parties, everything. In fact while I'm about it, let me round up that list of the Bachs in full.

JS Bach – Daddy Bach
JC Bach – The English Bach (youngest son of above)
CPE Bach – The No Nickname Bach (second son of above)
LBW Bach – The Cricketing Bach ☺
SAS Bach – The Daring Bach ☺
TCP Bach – The Gargling Bach ☺
NCP Bach – The 'Oi you can't park there' Bach ☺
HSBC Bach – The Listening Bach ☺

You see: 1763 – positively dripping with Bachs. But as for the rest of classical music, if I were to step back for a moment, to have a sort of musical 'out of body' experience, what would I see? Well, classical music as we now know it is more or less 'in'. Baroque and rococo are still around, but very 'last year' – or very 'week one', as they say in *Big Brother*. Going, going, gone is the 'diddle-iddle-iddle-iddle' contrapuntal stuff, and coming up now is a more pared-down sound, albeit with much more intricate forms. Of course, they didn't just happen – 'Yawn... mmm, I think I'd like to invent... a symphony.' 'And so you shall!' said the Fairy Godmother, with a PING! and a whoosh – no, they sort of evolved, all Darwinesque. As the Bible would have said: Opera begat the opera overture, opera overture begat the stand-alone overture, the stand-alone overture begat the sinfonia and the sinfonia begat the symphony. After that, well, it was a bit like teams of Arctic explorers all working separately to conquer the pole – all the composers working in different camps, each tweaking a little here, or sticking an idea in there. And not just with regards to the symphony, but about all music. Music as a whole is getting go-faster stripes.

You've got a Bach in England, a Bach in Germany, a Haydn in Austria, and of course, a Gossec in Belgium.

I say, 'You've got a Gossec in Belgium!' Tell you what, nip to the top drawer of the sideboard, get yourself that pen that doesn't really work and leaves inky blotches yet you still keep putting it back in the drawer, and write down the name Gossec. Keep it handy in the kitchen, perhaps on one of those magnet sets based on Michelangelo's *David*. Then next time you're playing Ten Famous Belgians and you've reached Jean-Claude Van Damme and stopped, run to the fridge, memorize the name between the kitchen and the living room and coolly lob in the grenade 'François Joseph Gossec'. Nice.

GOT ANY GOSSEC?

François Joseph Gossec was a Walloon – what a lovely word: Waaaaallllloooonnnnn. Lovely. And even nicer when spoken like you are winding down. To be precise, Gossec was a Walloon who moved away from Antwerp, where he was a boy soprano, and went to work in France. If you were 'the Music Business' in 1763, then he was 'our man in Paris', developing, in his own special way, his symphonies, his string quartets, and all manner of other stuff. In fact, he was the first *real* symphony man in France, and he wrote hundreds and hundreds of different and, at the time, important works. But now? Well, now he's remembered pretty much for one work. It's not a symphony, sadly, considering that he was a bit of a pioneer in this area; it's not a string quartet. It's a piddly little piece of flute music called *Tambourin*, the favourite of novice flautists the world over, because it's not too hard and it makes them sound like James Galway for just a few minutes, instead of the soundtrack to the Clangers.

It's a tough one, this. What can you do about the fact that numerous composers have written masses and masses of great work – or at least, totally pleasant work – and yet for some reason, history has chosen, in some instances, to remember them for only one work in particular. They're often called 'one-hit wonders', but this isn't quite fair. A one-hit wonder is literally that – someone who wrote or sang one hit, and then couldn't repeat the success. As we mentioned before, Joe Dolce 'What'sa-matter-you, HEY', Renee and Renato, those guys who sang that bloody awful 'Matchstalk Men and Matchstalk Cats and Dogs'. But the classical guys, well, they *did* write lots of other hits. It's just that cruel fate has decided that the others won't get a look in. Having said that, at least they get one piece remembered, I guess. There are those who wrote some of the most popular pieces of their day, only to be totally erased from the history books. People like Paisiello, for example, who was massive when he was alive. Now? Well, lucky to get a rare aria included as a filler track on the latest Cecilia Bartoli album.

It's **1764**. Here is the news. Buildings are going up like there's no tomorrow. Just finished last year in Paris was La Madeleine, and, this year, Adam's finest, Kenwood House in Hampstead – lovely tea rooms. Talking of all things London, the chattering classes are all abuzz about the latest wheeze – house numbers. Anyone who's anyone has got one, and, indeed, many people who aren't anyone have one too. And what a good idea they are. I mean, London has had post boxes for 120 years, now, and the 'penny post' system for over eighty years, so why not house numbers?

Actually, wait a minute, that doesn't make sense. Why did they have post boxes forty years before they had the penny post? What did they have to collect in the post boxes? Just imagine, forty years of unlocking post boxes – 'Oh, empty again… that's odd.' Still. Mine is not to reason why. Anyway, they've got house numbers now, so somewhere to stick their penny post, as it were. Next year, too, they even get pavements, so the guy delivering the mail looks more like a postman and less like Swampy the Eco-Warrior. But I digress a little. Over in

America, they are just coming to grips with the taxes on the colonies and it's not looking good, if you ask me. As Foghorn Leghorn might have said, 'There's troub – ah say, there's trouble a-brewin', boy, and it's git – ah say, it's gitting worse bah the cotton pickin' minute.'

Sorry. I'm OK now.

THE PRODIGY

The big thing in 1764, musically speaking, was the little thing, as it were. The first offerings of the eight-year-old Mozart. You can just imagine him being patronized by people who didn't quite realize the genius they had in front of them. 'Awwww, little Wibbly-Wobbly Amipoopot Mozart... aww... have you got some music for the nice people... have you?... have you?... Oh, it's a full symphony, right. In, er, four movements. Good. For full orchestra. Right. Good. Well. Let's hear it then.' Then, quietly, under their breath, 'Clever little sod.'

I don't know if you've ever heard Mozart's *First Symphony*, from 1764, written when he was all of eight years old. By his standards, it's quite a simple thing, certainly compared to the majesty of the 'Jupiter', the originality of the 40th and, my own personal favourite, the brown-ness♬ of the 29th. And yet, despite it being simple, small even, it is perfectly formed. And it is easy to just pay lip service to the fact that it is by an eight-year-old boy. EIGHT YEARS OLD! Mums and dads, just think – that's only Year 3. If your Year 3 infant came home one day with a picture of the sky made from cotton-wool, a papier-mâché Hallowe'en mask and a four-movement symphony, just think how you would feel! Exactly. You'd be shocked, wouldn't you? And you'd have every right to be – making cottonwool collages of the sky is for nursery school – what the hell are they doing sending your eight-year-old home with it? And, of

♬ *If you haven't listened to the 29th, then try and hunt down a recording. The first movement is, quite simply, brown! Gloriously brown. I don't know why, it just is. This is probably one area where I'm up there in agreement with Scriabin or Bliss – I think certain sounds suggest certain colours. Don't know how they could, but they do. And the* 29th Symphony *by Mozart is most definitely BROWN. Good. Just wanted to get that off my chest.*

course, in addition to that, you'd think, 'Jeepers, she's written a symphony!!' I'm only labouring this point because I think, to some extent, the notion of a child prodigy has lost its impact today. The Charlotte Churches, the Hayley Westernras, even, to some extent, the Ruth Lawrences – they don't mean 'child prodigy' in quite the same way that Mozart was a child prodigy. A fully scored symphony in four movements at eight years of age was even astounding then, in the eighteenth century, the very era of child prodigies. It certainly makes me put things into perspective.

We'll get on to Mozart properly soon, but, for now, I want you to forget about 1764. It's dead. It's gone. It's history. Well, obviously it is, but you know what I mean. It's a mere memory. Instead, now, I want you to think the season of **1772–73**.

Are you there yet? If not, let me help you place it. It's a bright, sparkly new time. Captain Cook has just discovered Botany Bay, and, as his diaries from the time show, it was not quite as they had expected:

> Day 13. Sighted land. After weighing anchor, I led an initial party of brave men in a rowing boat in an attempt to befriend the natives. Once on shore, we gave them gifts – gold, silver, the pennant bearing the coat of arms of our good King George III, and some mirrors. They, in turn, gave us fresh water, some much needed food and a barbecue.
>
> (Not sure what to do with the last item. Have given it to Mr Banks.)

In addition to Cook discovering Down Under, the *Encyclopaedia Britannica* had been published for the first time and things are generally starting to feel a little exciting – new worlds, new learning, better understanding of the old learning. And, of course, the old guard die off and get replaced. So, Canaletto is gone – or should I say gondola?... no, OK, gone, then – and Gainsborough is gone too. The frisky Frenchman, Fragonard, is still putting out the eighteenth-century version of the saucy postcard, and the French nobility are lapping it up. Just a few years ago, he painted a suggestive little number called

The Swing, and found he had quite a hit on his hands. In fact, France is a swinging place in 1773, all in all. Choderlos de Laclos, another little goer, has just published his *Les Liaisons Dangereuses*, and very steamy it is too. I can't say the words, myself, without thinking of John Malkovich writing on Michelle Pfeiffer's back. Best say no more. In fact, when all's said and done, life in France couldn't have been better –

if

you were on the right side of the tracks, that is. (And that's a pretty big if.) Quite. Yes. Indeed. It's a case of 'Réveille et sentir le café' – wake up and smell the coffee.

HAYDN – ESTERHAZY DOING?

Haydn isn't having too bad a time of it, either. In fact, to be fair, he had it cush! None of the starving artist, garret flat and pauper's grave for him, thank you very much. Oh no. He ran his composing less as an artist's life and more as... well, an insurance firm, or something. He got himself a nice little deal as composer-in-residence for Prince Esterhazy at his residence in Eisenstadt not far from the Austrian capital, and then, well... simply kept it. *All his life.* True, he did work hard and he had to churn out music at a rate of knots. But as far as living on the edge was concerned, well... lion-taming wasn't for him.

He did, though, once write a symphony where he instructed all the orchestra members to walk off the stage at the end, one by one, after their bit had ended. So you had the effect of, one by one, a gradually emptying stage, with the music being played by just the last person remaining – he wrote them a special 'staggered' ending to do it. Eventually, the last person left the stage and stopped playing, too. It was meant to be a bit of a gentle dig at his boss, who hadn't let the composer or the musicians have a holiday in ages. He labelled it his *Farewell Symphony* – farewell in the sense of the orchestra buggering off, not in the sense that it was the final time he was going to play Wembley. Mmm. Interesting stuff, eh? I don't know, these musicians. Have you in stitches, wouldn't they? It's his 45th symphony. 45! Can you believe that? And before he's finished he will have more than doubled that count. Of course, he is, by then, forty-one years of age. Wolfgang Amadeus Theophilus P. Wildebeest Mozart☺♬, his partner in crime in the Classical-R-Us© chain, was only coming up to seventeen at this point.

Still, youth never held Mozart back, and in 1773 he came up with the simply exquisite three-movement slice of heaven, *Exsultate, Jubilate.* It's for soprano and orchestra – well, that's not strictly true: it was originally for castrato and orchestra. Mozart had, not long ago, made the acquaintance of one Venanzio Rauzzini, a noted *chanteur sans bals* who had taken a starring role in one of his early operas, *Lucio Silla.* Mozart was clearly impressed and set to work on a new piece using Latin text. It includes one of the most gorgeous bits of composer showing off since Hildegard of Bingen learnt to play mouth organ while riding a bike. It's the last movement. Mozart decides that he can set the *entire* last movement to just the one single word – Alleluia. Clever clogs, he is. In fact, this gives us a perfect chance to take stock and survey how far we've come musically.

Because if you think about this one-word setting in the last movement, and you think of someone like, say, Johann Sebastian Bach when he wanted to do some showing off, then you realize just how poles apart they are. If Bach had done some showing off on this scale – and he frequently did: setting his name as the theme of a piece of music; working out double and quadruple fugues which then went back on themselves♬♬ – well, it would have come out as a largely *academic* exercise. Superbly executed, correct down to the 78th decimal point and yet somehow... not particularly... emotional, as it were. I know I'm on dodgy ground here, for some, because Bachophiles♬♬♬ love their favourite composer with a passion – no pun intended. And I, too, love the man to bits. But with Mozart, working only some twenty-odd years

♬☺*This is only partly a joke. Mozart's full name – the one that would have appeared on his birth certificate – was Johannes Chrysostomus Wolfgangus Theophilus Mozart (the 'Amadeus' was a later substitution, a Latin finessing of the Greek word Theophilus). So I wasn't simply making a gratuitous Lenny Henry reference.*

♬♬ *Which, I believe is called a 'crab' formation.*

♬♬♬ *Bachophiles are not to be confused with the wrappings for cooking turkeys, which go by a similar name.*

after the death of the great man, you get a joyous, uplifting movement that sounds like… well, that sounds like freedom, in a way. It sounds as if Mozart is just improvising on paper – 'Ooh, I could go here, now. I know what, I'll go there after that', a bit like you imagine the mind of a jazz player to work – whereas, only twenty or so years earlier, you could almost smell the working out. Am I making sense? I hope I am. And if I am, then it just proves there's a first time for everything.

So, it's official, then. Into the warm, cheek-shaped indentations left on the twin thrones of music by Bach and Handel move the young and younger new frames of Haydn and Mozart. Baroque is now long dead and *classical* music is the new classical music.

TAME TIME TEAM TOME

The *Time Team*. Don't know about you, but I'm a big fan. Massive. Phil, Carenza, Tony, and Mike of the Strange Pullover, all enthusing to the point of moistness about a two-inch shard of clay: or a different colour line in the trench, which, the computer-generated picture can reveal, is actually the remains of a building the size of Lincoln Cathedral. Honestly. I love it. Absolutely love it. In fact it was here, on this programme, that I first heard about an incredible device that has been developed, in conjunction with ICI, which can extract the previous sounds secreted within walls. It sounds amazing, I know, but the device, if put to proper use, would allow us to recreate all manner of previously lost events, aurally. Concert performances, great speeches, criminal conversations, the applications are endless.☺ Right now, though, I want to put it to use to let you hear the sounds retrieved from a piece of parchment, thought to date back to **1785**. It appears to have picked up the sounds of two people, evidently gossiping. It's patchy, and it all comes out as one general stream of consciousness, but still, let me show you a transcript of what it says:

'Anyway 1785 well yes would you believe it America then eh we repealed all those taxes for them didn't we glass paper dye admittedly we kept tea well you've got to keep a hold on tea haven't you well they just don't know how to make a good cuppa out there I KNOW they had some sort of tea party yes tea party yes in Boston yes well I KNOW I wasn't invited either no and yet I do an awful lot for them Independence I'll give them independence all that no taxation without representation I mean who thought of that eh? who thought of that it hardly rolls off the tongue does it doesn't scan well or rhyme or anything ooh did you hear about that Louis the fifteenth DEAD as true as I'm sitting here with this haircut Right as rain one minute giving it grand with the old nobles next minute DEAD no word of a lie Clive's gone as well yes well I said he'd never survive after that India thing ooh it was a mess wasn't it I told him I said Clive of India I said that was my pet name for him I said Clive of India I said you're better off out of it I said Leave it to 'em I said Besides you burn too easily you do Oh aye he was never one to go brown wasn't our Clive Ooh that reminds me did you see in the papers that Cook fella has discovered somewhere new again I KNOW that's what I said I said It's only more mouths to feed He should just turn right round again leave them to their beach volleyball and just go and Undiscover it again I said

'Anyway wasn't it sad about Mr Pitt wasn't it ooh he was a lovely man lovely he was I met him when he was campaigning Sat on my chaise-longue he did Ooh he was so polite he was insisted I called him Elder for short Goldsmith he's gone too ooh I loved that play of his you came with me didn't you She stoops for conkers ooh I did enjoy it Never did see the conkers mind modern production probably eh have you seen this the Daily Universal Register it's new yeah not bad actually it's got adverts and everything look Mr Broadwood's new improved pianoforte now with pedals dynamics guaranteed or your money back I don't know it's got sports pages too look that's about that new race that Lord Derby started it's really getting popular I KNOW I KNOW I still prefer the St Leger even if you do have to go to

Doncaster ISN'T IT JUST page three has got a great pair of balloons look it says Joseph and Jacques Montgolfier are not all hot air these Gallic goons are flying high after completing the first successful balloon trip at Annonay who knows maybe they'll make it as far as Cook's new island next time then it would really be a case of up up and Hawaii ooh that's awful this paper will never survive...'

And that, sadly, is as much as they've been able to extract, but, I think you'll agree, it does provide a fascinating and perhaps more accurate insight into the real goings-on of 1785. What isn't recorded there, though, is anything about Mozart in 1785, so let me fill you in.

MOZART OF NOISE

Mozart had a weird life. He was born into an already musical family with his dad, Leopold, the Kapellmeister for the Archbishop of Salzburg. Leopold was clearly one of the sharpest quills in the drawer, and he quickly realized that his son had an awful lot of potential. Mozart's sister, Anna – who he called Nannerl – was pretty useful on the piano, but, fairly early on, Leopold recognized that Wolfgang was an all-rounder. He taught him everything he knew, schooling him in harmony, counterpoint and all the finer points of composition. At some point, he must have decided that the world should see his son, too, because most of Wolfgang's early years on the road were spent not so much touring as 'being toured'. The Mozart Family roadshow hit most of Europe, with dates in Paris and London. In fact, if you are ever in London and you happen to be standing in the queue for Ronnie Scott's Jazz Club, take a look upwards and opposite – there's a plaque on the wall commemorating the building where Mozart stayed.

When he was nineteen, Mozart went on tour in his own right, taking his mum along for company. He took in Munich on the way, and it was during his stay with the family of the music copyist, Weber, that he that fell in love. Big-time. Her name was Aloysia and he fell wig over heels for her. Sadly for him, she didn't reciprocate his feelings at all. In addition, his mother fell ill and died on the trip, and so he left Paris doubly broken-hearted. Before long, back in Salzburg, he parted company with his and his dad's employer, the Archbishop of Salzburg – from his letters, it looks as if he jumped virtually seconds before he was pushed – and upped and moved to Vienna, a place which very soon became the city of Mozart's dreams.

From here on in, he would not only write all his best stuff, but he would also find love again – and in the weirdest place. In fact, this is one thing he shares, spookily enough, with Haydn: they both ended up marrying the sister of the woman they had originally courted. For Haydn, it was the biggest mistake of his life. His wife was a complete beast for whom he felt no love whatsoever. She, in turn, had no love for him and would reputedly use the manuscripts of his beloved compositions to line her pastry tins, or as curlers for her hair.♬

Mozart, on the other hand, landed on his feet. When Aloysia went to the trouble of becoming a nun in order not to marry him☺, Mozart married her sis, Constanze, and they got on like a Strauss on fire. Very happy, they were. And even though money was up and down, he was writing prolifically and coming up with the goods – the symphonies, string quartets, sonatas, serenades – lots of goodies.

SIGNIFICANT BIRTHDAY NEXT YEAR

We join Mozart again when he's twenty-nine. Twenty-nine! Remember, by his standards that's almost bus-pass time. He's really motoring, too. He's doing very well with his operas – the crowd just love them – although the first real *belter*, the first one that will really stay around for ever, has yet to come. He's already done the *Haffner Serenade* – a bit of background music, to be fair, written for one of the weddings of the powerful Haffner family – as well as *The Abduction from the Seraglio*, *Idomineo* and the *C minor Mass*, the latter just a couple of years ago.

♬ *That's always baffled me, that one, 'as curlers for her hair'. I mean, it's true, I'm sure, but how do you use, say, the score of the* Clock Symphony *as hair curlers? Or maybe it wasn't the whole symphony, just the highlights. JUST THE HIGHLIGHTS!!!! Suit yourself.*

The big things now, though, for Mozart are his piano concertos. Piano concertos for him were more or less party pieces, for when he stopped off on his travels to visit dukes and emperors and things. They were pieces which not only made him sound – and I imagine *look* – great, in that they were often technically difficult to play and yet had slow movements to die for. The slow movements, alone, had great, heart-rending tunes which had the genteel folk of the 1780s weeping into their snuffboxes. In one sense, they were the '45s' of their period♬, if you like, and, in another, they could be said to be the sort of 'spinal cord' of the body of music Mozart left behind – twenty-seven piano concertos, each one a chapter in the musical diary of his life. Each one can tell you a little bit more about what was happening to him at the time. A little snapshot of him of that moment.

Take the one from 1785 itself, Piano Concerto No 21. A beautiful PC, with possibly one of the best power ballads of its type. Or should that be slow movements? It was written just weeks after Mozart had put the pen down on his previous *Piano Concerto in D minor* – he really was knocking these out – and it was not long after his marriage to Constanze. The outer movements are light and fluffy and full of the joys of spring, but the inner slowie has become justifiably famous not only in concert halls, but also in adverts and movies. In fact, it's often known as 'the *Elvira Madigan*' concerto, just because someone used it in a Swedish film of the same name in 1967. Poor Mozart, I say. Although I suppose it could have been worse. The *It Came from the Swamp!* concerto is marginally less appealing, especially if it becomes 'your' tune.

GOETHE HEAVEN

One year later and Mozart is still reigning supreme. Globally, **1786** is an interesting time. The flavour of the month seems to be coming from the literary world and goes by the name of Robbie

♬ *Mmm, what a great essay subject: 'Mozart Piano Concerto slow movements – the power ballads of their day. Discuss.' Extra points if you can compare and contrast* Piano Concerto 21 *with 'The Power of Love' by Jennifer Rush.*

Burns and his *Poems Chiefly in a Scottish Dialect.* This is the year that sees seemingly everyone doing the Scottish thing – throwing Scottish parties, having Scottish theme nights, failing to qualify for major sporting events, the lot. Elsewhere, Goethe, the toast of Germany – not to mention future Chas and Dave song – is currently attempting to become the toast of Italy too. He's on tour there for a couple of years, taking in the culture, networking, that sort of thing. Other than that, very little of major future significance to impart for 1786, apart from the fact that someone discovered uranium.

Mozart's year is going from strength to strength. For him, it's the year when all his opera experience really begins to pay off, in terms of the 'annals of time' and 'posterity' and all that nonsense. (Remember how we said opera would have its day again?) He's been writing opera for yonks now, of course, but, all of a sudden, he premieres an opera in which everything just seems to gel. Everything manages to just... come together. Right now. It's partly due to the fact that his 'words' man, a new librettist for him called Da Ponte, is coming up with some great 'books' for the operas in the first place. (Very often, just as in musicals, the libretto to an opera is simply called the book.) As a result, it's in Italian – not Mozart's first, but certainly his first for a while, and appeals to the Viennese audience who, for some reason, like their operas in Italian – and it no doubt does no harm that it's a comedy. Da Ponte had taken the story from a play by Beaumarchais, written just a couple of years ago. It was called then, and indeed it is called now, *The Marriage of Figaro.*

Its first night was the 1st of May, 1786, in Vienna, and it is said that its opening night was twice as long as it should have been because virtually *every* aria had to be encored immediately it was sung! In fact, its popularity led to the introduction of a royal order stating that opera houses were not allowed to do over-long encores – just the odd aria.

AMADEUS AND SO'S MY WIFE

Talking of all things Mozart, I make no apologies about staying focused on him for a little while longer. In fact, despite the fact that we've got almost another 220 years to cover in only the next 208 pages, I'm nevertheless going to throw caution to the wind and dedicate the next nine pages… to only *four years.* Four years, ladies, gentlemen and undecideds, four years. Without the aid of a safety net. But these are no ordinary four years as far as music is concerned. These are the last four years of Mozart's life! To do these four years justice, you would need many more pages that I have here, but I can, at least, draw the magnifying glass a little closer and set these forty-eight months apart. If we were a film, these next pages would be in slow motion. But first, let me just place Mozart's last four years in their context of world events. And, fittingly enough, it wasn't just for Wolfgang that this time was to be world-changing. Elsewhere, as well, it was a cataclysmic time.

In **1787** America is beginning to enjoy independence, with both the dollar and the constitution making their debut. In fact, like buses and bridegrooms on a Moonie wedding night, these things all seemed to come at once. France, in particular, is beginning to feel distinctly edgy, with its *parlement* demanding a summit of the three estates: the nobility, the clergy and the commons. Louis XVI is filibustering madly. Well, I suppose you would, wouldn't you? In war, Turkey throws a six, meaning it's their turn, so they choose to declare war on … Russia, please, Bob. Of course, back in the land of Eng, the turmoil, *sturm und drang* of the entire world pales into insignificance when set against matters closer to home – that is, the MCC has been founded. Cue lots of lovely handshakes, handlebar moustaches and an immediate move to Lord's. Jolly good show, I say, catch that, can you? Well done, Wolfgang.

Ah yes, Wolfgang. Let's catch up with him, shall we? For he's currently in a rather bum-punchingly uncomfortable coach, en route from Vienna to Prague. Going through his head must be all manner of things. It's now October and he only lost his father in May. Now losing your father is always a big loss, but remember, this is the father who, genius aside, more or less made Amadeus what he was, in every respect. And Wolfgang had already lost his third child, Johann Thomas, just the year before. He must have been such a mass of different thoughts and feelings on his way to Prague. He's going, with his wife Constanze, to rehearse and premiere his latest opera, at the Prague National Theatre.

It's important for Mozart. Despite the fact that someone with a brain like his must have known the importance of the work in a, sort of, global sense – that is, in terms of its place in history – despite this, he knew it was important in other ways too, chiefly monetarily.

The Mozarts *are* managing to keep the Wolfgang from the door, but money is at a premium. A good premiere here means that it not only does well in Prague, but that it will also have doors opened for it in a number of other cities, too. Indeed, Mozart received this commission as a direct result of the success of *The Marriage of Figaro*. He was soon to get the top job in Vienna of 'Kammermusicus' – which translates as 'big music cheese' – but, for some reason known best to themselves, the powers-that-be♬ would agree to pay him not even half the salary which the previous incumbent, Gluck of the Mildly Amusing Middle Name, had been paid. So, for just a minute, try and put yourself in Mozart's shoes.

Think of that crowd behind you in the Prague National Theatre. *They* haven't heard the opera that's been in your head for months. *They* haven't sat through the rehearsals over the past two weeks: the shouting, the endless repeats, the tantrums, even. *They* don't know that until the night before, Mozart hadn't written the overture, in fact had to be reminded by friends and then produced one literally overnight.♬♬ *They* don't know that so much time, energy and personal tragedy have been invested in the work they are about to hear.

Don Giovanni.

Or to give it its original title, *Il Dissoluto Punito*, or 'The Punished Rake', although this is never used now. *Don Giovanni* is considered by some to be one of, if not *the*, greatest moment in classical music, and, certainly, the Frymobile would subscribe to that point of view. It's set in Seville, and is one of dozens of operas to use the story of Don Juan, lothario and rogue, who strays between the opera's comic and serious faces, laughing in them both. It's full of great music, not least that speedily written overture, the Catalogue aria, 'La ci darem la mano', and the Champagne aria. Gorgeous stuff.

♬ *Do you think, in Cornwall, when you cease as one of the 'powers-that-be' you become a 'power-that-baint'?*

♬♬ *Some say he started writing at midnight and had finished it by 3 a.m.*

Thankfully, the good people of Prague gave it a resounding thumbs-up. It would eventually transfer to Vienna, too, a much more important audience – where it opens on the same evening as an all-night sitting of the British Parliament to debate William Wilberforce's motion for the abolition of slavery – and it then has a good run of some fifteen performances at the National Court Theatre. Just a month later, though, Mozart loses his fourth child, Theresia. No doubt the whole family are hoping that 1788 will play itself out with no more tragedy. Thankfully for Mozart, it does.

1788. If ever there was a calm-before-the-storm year, this was probably it. Louis XVI is in deep doodoo – or *du du*, as they would say there. The French *parlement* have presented their dull list of grievances to him and, amid streets teeming with crowds rioting over bread, he promises to call a meeting of the three estates by May '89. But will that be soon enough? In England, George III has succumbed to a bout of mental ill-health, but, on the bright side, the MCC have codified the rules of cricket. All in all, it's a funny, uneasy sort of year and for Mozart, it's a question of: can he put his bad patch behind him and come up with some great music? Well, of course he can. Come on, this is Mozart we're talking about here!

And not just one piece. It seems the darker Mozart's days become, the richer and more creative his works become. The *40th Symphony*, *Eine Kleine Nachtmusik*, the '*Jupiter*' *Symphony*. The *40th Symphony* is a million miles away from the way most people know it now. I may be wrong, here, but I would imagine that, statistically, more people know the Mozart's 40th because it is one of the most popular mobile phone ring tones. But the shrill, electronic buzz of a mobile is light years from the gloomy and almost morose masterpiece of 1788. Contrast that with the fun, almost throwaway, feel of *Eine Kleine Nachtmusik*, another bit of background music, designed not really to be heard. It's testament to Mozart's genius, really, that something so light and fluffy is still so jam-packed full of melodic, creative invention. And his last symphony, the 'Jupiter'. Not his nickname, unfortunately, but probably something added forty or so years later by people impressed by its jollity – that's what Jupiter is the bringer of, remember. This is seen by many as the *ultimate* classical symphony – its finest hour. And, somewhat ironically, the last movement sees Mozart playing with all manner of devices to weave between no fewer than six full themes. It's as if he's saying, 'Look what I can do. Bach might have been able to interweave acres of themes, and invert them and "canon" them, well, so can I!'

So that's 1788. In addition to those three works of sheer gorgeousnesslessness, there was also the *Clarinet Quintet in A*, written for his friend, Anton Stadler, the principal clarinet player with the Imperial Court Orchestra of Vienna. Despite the fact that Stadler was a bit of a jack the lad, often landing an already impecunious Mozart in further financial hardship, Amadeus provided him, here, with one of the greatest slow movements ever written for the clarinet. Surely he would never top this, in terms of clarinet writing? Well, don't speak too soon. In the end, this undeniably beautiful piece for clarinet proves to be hardly more than a dry run.

JUST GONE HALF SIX

1791. Where are we? Where is the world? Where is the love? Let's try and answer at least two of those questions. I think it's fair to say that the heady smoke of revolution still hangs in the air like a heady smoke of revolution. It seems to be happening everywhere. America has done it – George Washington is in his second year as president. France has done it – Louis XVI desperately putting off that haircut. Even the Austrian Netherlands has done it – gone and got themselves independence just over a year ago and called themselves… called themselves… hang on a minute, I wrote it down somewhere. Here we are. Belgium. Belgium? Oh, well, fair enough. Takes all sorts. What else? The big book of the year is Boswell's *The Life of Johnson*, sitting alongside last year's blockbuster, *Tam o' Shanter*, by the Scottish Jew, Rabbi Burns. Musically, though, it's still Mozart's world. He really *is* the big thing in music, at the moment. Has been for ages – but it won't last. Gone, now, are the days of trekking around Europe. Gone are those awful days, as described in his diaries:

It's Friday, it must be the Hapsburgs' cheese and wine party.

Tomorrow, the Versailles Ladies' Bridge Club Annual Bring and Buy.

Then, Sunday, it's round to the Duke of Esterhazy's for a lock-in.

God, I'm knackered!

Yes, all long gone. Mozart, now, is the greatest thing to happen to music since someone burnt the blueprints of the banjo. But he's nearing the end. His fifth child, Anna Maria, was born this year, but lived only one hour – just how did they take this level of tragedy, year in, year out? Not just Mozart, either, it was everyone. I don't know how they did it. As far as Mozart is concerned, he could always sink himself further and further into his music.

And he did. It's a bit of a cliché but it appears to be true – at times of real pits of despair, composers of real greatness came up with some of their best material. And never was this more true of Mozart himself than in **1791**, the year he died.

For a start, there's *The Magic Flute*, a remarkable opera, no matter which way you look at it, but even more so when you look at it in the light of his final year. He wasn't well, he wasn't in the best financial state, his children were dying around him, so what does he do? He writes a pantomime. (Oh no he doesn't!) *Die Zauberflöte*, to give it its German name, is a weird, Brian-Rix-farce of an opera, a mix of frivolous comedy, fairy tale and Masonic symbolism – Mozart was a long-term member of his local Masonic lodge and had even persuaded his late father to enrol too. There are some lovely musical moments, though, including the Birdcatcher's aria, the fantastic tenor aria 'O zittre nicht', and the amazing dramatic creation that is the Queen of the Night – a part originally written specifically for Mozart's sister-in-law who could reach a glass-breakingly brilliant top F. Unfortunately it is often attempted by much lesser mortals who are a few ledger lines short of a full stave.

With *The Magic Flute*, Mozart's 'Fantastic Four' was complete. Fantastic Four operas, that is. They are: *The Marriage of Figaro* (Mr Fantastic), a comic opera with one of the best overtures EVER, as well as the beautiful aria 'Dove sono'; *Don Giovanni* (The Human Torch), a mix of fun and sinister tragedy, which ends with the anti-hero consumed by the flames of hell, but not before he's sung the rather saucy 'La ci darem la mano'; *Cosí fan Tutte* (The Invisible Woman), a romantic comedy which, were it composed today, would have to star Hugh Grant; it contains the mind-bendingly gorgeous trio 'Soave sia il vento'; and, of course, *The Magic Flute* (The Thing).

The 'True' Yin to this 'Magic' Yang from 1791 is the sublime miniature choral piece which he finished in June, the *Ave Verum Corpus.* It's only a few minutes long, but every second is divine. These two pieces really were, with no disrespect to Mozart whatsoever, the ridiculous and the sublime of his last year.

If that weren't enough, there's the can't-find-a-word-good-enough *Clarinet Concerto*, which he wrote for his friend Anton, again. Two stunning outer movements that are tricky enough to play nowadays, on a modern clarinet, let alone on the one that was around then, which had just six keys. Nestled in between these two is Mozart's divine musical extrapolation of the phrase 'less is more' – the slow movement from Heaven. One often hears the platitude that 'the simple tunes are the best' but nowhere is this more intelligently proven than in the slow movement of the *Clarinet Concerto.* A tune that just seems to get more compelling each time you hear it.

And so the year is almost out, and with it, the age of Mozart. The world will never see his like again. A twenty-one-year-old Beethoven is yet to produce his first big works. Elsewhere, Haydn is still around. Despite being nearly a quarter of a century older, he will outlive Mozart by a good eighteen years. In fact, not for him the melancholia that infected Mozart's music of 1791 – his major work of the year is the *Surprise Symphony*, a jolly little wheeze designed to keep the Esterhazy audience awake, by sounding a huge chord just when they least expected it. 'With hilarious consequences', as the TV listings might say. Gosh, Haydn, you wag – how we all laughed!

Mozart, though, doesn't seem to be laughing. The well-documented story of the dark stranger who totally spooked him by coming to his door and commissioning a Requiem is true. It did happen, but it wasn't, as many have surmised, the Grim Reaper himself. Odd, that. Instead, it turns out it was Count Von Walsegg's cleaner. Walsegg was a local big cheese who did want to commission a Requiem, for his wife. Mozart duly started on it. Elsewhere, Louis XVI tried and failed to escape the Parisian mob, Goethe gets the top job at the Weimar Court Theatre, and a brand-new paper, the *Observer*, reports that William Wilberforce's bill to abolish slavery has been passed.

All big stuff in 1791, but all of no interest to old Wolfgang.
His last surviving letter was written in October and
seems fairly upbeat. He'd been to see *The Magic*
Flute performed at the Freihaus Theatre in
Vienna, and was chuffed that his arch rival,
the composer Salieri, shouted 'Bravo' at
virtually every aria. The week before,
he's even written about how he had
played a joke on the conductor by
playing the offstage glockenspiel
part wrongly. But, just a month
later, he took to his bed.
And some two weeks
after that, on the
5th of December,
at five minutes
to one in the
morning,
he died.

One minute's silence, please. 1 2 3 4 5 6 7 8 9 10 11 12 13 14 15 16 17 18 19 20 21 22 23 24 25 26 27 28 29 30 31 32 33 34 35 36 37 38 39 40 41 42 43 44 45 46 47 48 49 50 51 52 53 54 55 56 57 58 59 60.♬

♬ *This is one of only two times where this book will observe a minute's silence.*

And, well…

He's gone.

So.

What now?

Well, looking back, first, to the *Clarinet Concerto*. It's possible to hear it as merely the beautiful work it is – a delicious slow movement surrounded by two brisk allegros which really throw the clarinet about a bit. But, if you set this piece in its context, then it's almost as if you hear a different work altogether, particularly the middle movement. What was before a simple, elegant and beautiful tune suddenly becomes melancholic and plaintive, almost a lament, and yet, where once was elegance, there is still a retained sense of dignity.

It's the piece he wrote only a couple of months before he died and it's one, now that I know the circumstances, that I will never hear in the same way again.

When he died, the romantic legend says that he was a pauper. I've always taken this to mean that there was no money for funeral arrangements, no money left to his widow and family, and generally that he was whisked off, at dead of night, to an unmarked grave. Well, certainly, the last part appears to be true – nobody quite knows where Mozart lies. You can narrow it down to a cemetery – St Marx's in Vienna – but as for which plot contains the remains of probably the greatest composer the world has ever seen, nobody knows. But as for the rest of it, well, it appears Constanze was more than able to pay the 4 florins and 36 krone in parish fees, as well as the 4 florins 20 krone in church fees and even the 3 gulden to take the composer's corpse from St Stephen's Cathedral to the cemetery. Admittedly, this was what was termed at the time 'a third-class' funeral, but to say he was penniless is more than slightly misleading. In fact, there's no better confirmation of this fact than the list of the contents of his wardrobe on his death. This reads less like the last rags of a pauper and more like a TV presenter describing the guests going into one of Elton John's parties:

> 1 frock coat of cloth, with Manchester waistcoat
> 1 blue, ditto

1 red, ditto
1, ditto, of nankeen
1 brown satin, ditto, together with breeches, embroidered with silk
1 black cloth whole suit
1 mouse colour great coat
1 ditto of lighter material
1 blue frock coat with fur
1 ditto with fur trimming
4 various waistcoats, 9 various breeches, 2 plain hats, 3 pairs of boots, 3 pairs of shoes
9 silk stockings
9 shirts
4 white neckerchiefs, 1 nightcap, 18 handkerchiefs
8 underdrawers, 2 nightgowns, 5 further pairs of stockings

Mmm. Pauper, indeed. I think generations of us have been more than happy to believe a stylized romantic version of events, rather than the actual true picture.

Anyway, no matter. It's all over now. We've witnessed Mozart's last symphony, his last opera, and, of course, his last breath. The great one has gone. Amadeus – literally 'loved by the gods'. The world will never see his like again. So what now? Where are we? Who's still around? And what's happening out there in that rather gory collection of wars they call a world? Well, let's see if we can't find out.

THE RATHER GORY COLLECTION OF WARS THEY CALLED A WORLD: 1796

I'm going to move on some five years from Mozart's death to **1796**, but before I do, let me just try and fill in the gap.

To live in these times is to know the meaning of the word 'revolution' if, admittedly, not always its spelling. Revolution is everywhere – Marc Bolan would have loved it. Republics, too. Republics are the new black. Everybody's wants one. Just as, according to the great philosopher, Sir James Savile, the early 1970s was the age of the train, so this is the age of the Republic. The French Republic, Roman Republic, Lemanic Republic, the... the... the... Helvetian Republic, the Cisalpine Republic... all of them... genuine, 100 per cent kosher republics.

M. Rouget de Lisle's big hit of 1792, 'La Marseillaise', is still popular, although the Commune of Paris has been and gone, and with it some of the leading lights of the particularly French brand of Revolution – the heads of Danton, Desmoulins, Robespierre – all of them, alongside Louis XVI and Marie Antoinette, getting to know what it feels like to be a chicken-in-the-basket supper.

And wars – where are we with them? Well, France has been and gone to war with Prussia and Austria... er, oh and Sardinia. Well, why not, eh? If it moves, declare war on it, that's what I say. In turn, the Holy Roman Empire has declared war on France, and Spain has just this minute declared war on Great Britain, and not before time, too, clearly, Spain! Lagging behind a bit on the old... 'war declaring' front, Spain. See me afterwards. France are, then, current holders of the Jules Rimet Trophy for Services to War, having just this year – 1796 remember – won wars against Italy, Austria, Worthing☺ and Milan. Actually, not sure of my notes, there, on Worthing.

In the more or less non-violent world, things are coming on in leaps and bounds. We've had the new book by the Marquis de Sade, rather racily entitled *The Philosophy of the Bedroom*. I can't think what that's about. Also, the first gas lights have gone on in England, Joshua Reynolds's light has gone out, and someone travelling just near New Zealand has inadvertently discovered the... wait a minute, what are they called...

... the Kermadec Islands.

Mmm.

Yes, I think that was the reaction then, too. Strangely enough, no one goes to war over them. Moving on, Jenner has developed the first smallpox vaccine and someone has sent the first ever telegraph – from Paris to Lille, in fact. The wedding of the year has got to have been that of Napoleon Bonaparte to Josephine de Beauharnais – she of 'not tonight' fame.

But musically, where are we? Who's the ageing Status Quo type, who's the youthful S Club Seven-ers? Well, the smart money is on a twenty-six-year-old Beethoven to come up with something fantastic following last year's impressive Opus 1, *Three Piano Trios*. Would he be a U2 or a Sigue Sigue Sputnik? Also still there, keeping on keeping on, as it were, is his teacher, Haydn. Old Franz Josef may be starring in ads for stair lifts, but he can still knock out a tune with the best of them.

When we left him, Haydn was as happy as a sandboy, coining it in at the Esterhazy Palace, composing his head off and having his meals cooked. But, ohhhh, how his situation has changed in the last twenty years! How? Well, not at all, in fact, apart from maybe he is earning even more money now. He is still in the employ of the Esterhazy Bunch but, by now, his original boss has died. In the true 'jammy devil' style that seemed to stay with Haydn all his life, when the entire orchestra and choir were disbanded and sacked – because his new boss was not particularly into it – he himself was kept on, with an increased salary. As a result, with a salary and no job, he decided to travel. An enterprising type called Salomon booked him to tour London, where he was fêted as a bit of a living legend, making a small fortune in the process.

If it helps, just think of how Tom Jones's career had that wonderful turnaround, not too long ago, when he suddenly found himself all trendy again, with his name coming on some rather 'hip' records, very often after the word 'featuring' – Catatonia *featuring* Tom Jones, White Stripes *featuring* Tom Jones, Peters and Lee☺ *featuring* Tom Jones. Well, so it was with Haydn. London had been fantastic – the audiences couldn't get enough of him: encores galore, special 'London symphonies' written, knickers being thrown from the audience – actually, no, that *was* Tom Jones. Anyhow, Haydn returned to his palace digs with a small fortune in his pocket only to discover there had been a change of management at Eisenstadt. Gone was Paul Anton, who preferred paintings to music – and in had come the new Prince Nicholas II. He revived the old Haydn court orchestra – maybe not quite to the level it had been under Nicholas I, but still, enough to cash in on the new Haydn vogue. And in this orchestra was a sexy new trumpeter, name of Anton Weidlinger, who was not only a fantastic, virtuoso player, but also a bit of a Caractacus Potts.

Weidlinger had invented himself a thing called the 'keyed trumpet' – far too complicated to go into here, suffice to say it allowed you to play faster than the trumpet had ever played before. So Haydn, in the year of Our Lord 1796, duly wrote him a piece, full of the flashy new things that only Weidlinger's trumpet could do.

Unfortunately for Weidlinger, his 'keyed trumpet' became the Betamax of the trumpet world, beaten by the valve system. But Haydn's *Trumpet Concerto in E flat* has weathered every storm and is still considered a good test of even a modern-day trumpeter, particularly the last movement, which goes to show that Weidlinger himself must have been a pretty brilliant bugler to manage it. There are so many versions of this piece around today – on old trumpets, on new trumpets, on 'natural' trumpets,♬ slow versions, quick versions, underwater versions☺, recordings using Haydn's solos, recordings using performers' own specially-written solos – I think it's fair to say there's a recording out there for everyone. Personally, I love the modern, take-no-prisoners sound of Wynton Marsalis. Every time I hear him play it, it makes me realize that this is music that simply *couldn't* have been written any earlier. Well, no, that's not true – it could have been, it's just that no one would have been able to play it, so there wouldn't really have been much point.

VIRTUOSO REALITY

In fact all this talk of virtuosi brings me round to a new theme – virtuosi. Mm, maybe I could have rephrased that. They haven't really been around much until now, to be fair, or at least not in the same way. True, there'd been concertos for ages now, but never with this big emphasis on pushing the performance to the limit, this desire to show 'anything you can do'. And why? Well, mainly because they just couldn't have done it before. I mean, look at Sony Playstation 2 compared with... say, Asteroids. Or Pacman.

♬ *Which are basically ones without the buttons on the top – if you wanted to change the note you were playing, you had to do it with your lips.*

What do you mean 'What's that got to do with it?' It's got everything to do with it. Technology was moving on, and making lots more things possible. Things that composers would never have tried before were soon going to become the norm. And with this new breed of 'virtuoso' instruments came... well, a new breed of virtuoso players. Remember, we ARE still in the classical period but only just – we're dangling by a semi-quaver. In fact, to be fair, the first of these new virtuoso players was already here, and, boy, was he about to make himself known.

1798: the year of Wordsworth and Coleridge; the year the French stormed Rome and declared the 'Roman Republic'; the year that Britain had to declare a new 10 per cent income tax to pay for war; the year that Casanova died, aged seventy-three and nine inches.

1798: the year a sixty-seven-year-old Haydn set to work on another of his 'Indian summer' pieces, *The Creation*.

1798: the eleventh birthday of a virtuoso, Nicolò Paganini.

Paganini had been taught mandolin and violin by his father and, at the age of eleven, he was ready to make his first public appearance. His finest hour, though, is yet to come, so for now, let me show you this ad I discovered while leafing through the files in the Bruce Forsyth Library of Classical Music in Vienna:

Are you tired of the old ways?
Tired of the same old symphonies?

The same old sad little solos and polite little 'prestos'?
You are? Well, why not become an EARLY ROMANTIC!

For just £39.99, plus 10 florins penny postage and packing, you TOO can be both EARLY and ROMANTIC.

Membership of the EARLY ROMANTICS entitles you to write three hugely indulgent virtuoso concertos a year, be grumpy in public, bad with money, as well as the right to wear your hair in a ridiculous quiff, possibly above some broken round spectacles. And remember, if you're not satisfied with being an EARLY ROMANTIC, you... can't have your money back, but you can tear all your music up and throw a luvvie fit...

Remember, all music subject to status. Early Romantic is regulated by Lautro, Imro, Rubato, Libretto and Staccato.

Lovely, isn't it? It's one of the very earliest adverts for the Early Romantics, part of a collection of parchment ads on loan to the Forsyth after having originally been found stuffed behind the sofa in the dean's office at the University of Bonn.

It's **1800**. The year generally thought to have been the start of the Early Romantic period, despite the fact that the classical period is generally reckoned to have gone on to 1820. Well, old dog... new tricks and all that. You see, romantic music... it's just a label, that's all. Some people wrote music that sounded distinctly classical, while some people wrote music that sounded pretty much romantic – and both in the same year.

There was one person who sort of straddled the two periods, though. He wrote in the dying days of the classical and more or less singlehandedly kick-started the romantic. This had happened before – CPE Bach was the end of the baroque and start of the classical. But while CPE is now no more than 'musicologically significant' – that's muso speak for 'pants', by the way – the man who was both the end of the classical and the foundation stone of the romantics would end up being a bit more of a household name. And that's because his 'household name', as it were, was... Beethoven.

Well, thank goodness. He's here at last.

1800: the year of Beethoven's first symphony. Napoleon is now First Consul, Italy is conquered and the age of Beethoven has arrived. His very first attempt at the symphony came at the age of thirty. By composers' standards, that's a heck of a long time to wait – Mozart released his when he was only eight, remember. In fact, Mozart only had another five years left in him when *he* was thirty. Beethoven was an altogether different animal, though – you can say that again – but then he would be. He's being born into a very different world. Alessandro Volta has just, more or less, made the first battery, out of zinc and copper plates. The Royal College of Surgeons has been founded – and you know what that means? Not only is the world getting so much more scientific, but also, well... the golf courses are now going to be full every afternoon.

Enough of this. I'm just 'logging in' with Beethoven for now. We'll be back to check on him soon. For now it's time to check on the comeback kid, the man who wrote more symphonies than, well, than he needed to really – the one and only, you thought he was dead, Franz Josef 'Don't Call Me Boring' Haydn.

Haydn has been coming to the end of his time as Kapellmeister at Esterhazy. Just a couple of years ago, he'd knocked off the Austrian National Anthem for the Emperor's birthday. He'd called it 'Gott erhalt Franz den Kaiser'. Of course, it took on a slightly different tone when its words were later changed to 'Deutschland, Deutschland, über alles'. Haydn was fully expected to retire. He wasn't particularly well, and, at nearly seventy, was thought by many to have probably produced his best work, by now.

Haydn, on the other hand, was having none of it. Just as the sun was setting on the Esterhazy dream, our Franz came up with one of his most youthful-sounding works, which would go on to become one of his most popular choral pieces, *The Seasons.* A year later, he would retire, on full pension, revered as one of the grand masters of classical music.

BEETHOVEN READY

1803. Let me update you quickly. 1803 – Napoleon's doing well. Well, he would be, wouldn't he. Let's leave it at that. The sculptor, Canova, has chipped away at a small but perfectly formed statue of the... small but perfectly formed Grand Fromage himself. Incidentally, France and Britain are at war again... *Ici nous allons, encore*, as they say in Leeds. Moving on, racing starts at Goodwood for the first time and Turner, having been well received with his *Millbank Moon Light*, comes up with *Calais Pier*. Somehow, if he went and got out his easels and painted the same places today, the titles *Millbank Spin Doctors on Mobiles* and *Calais Asylum Seekers Riot* would seem a little unromantic. Call me reactionary.

But back to the angry young man Ludwig van Beethoven. He was born in Bonn in December of 1770. He had a miserable boyhood, beaten into an unreasonable regime of practice by a violent and alcoholic father. The music side of it paid off, though, and he was spotted by Marie-Antoinette's brother, the Elector of Cologne, Maximillian Franz, and made deputy court organist. When his dad lost his job through his drinking, the young Beethoven was forced to go out to earn money by playing viola in a lowly theatre. How degrading. Not the lowly theatre, the viola playing!♬ In 1792, he headed off to Vienna to study with Haydn and ended up never going back to Bonn. He launched himself as a concert pianist three years later, playing his own piano concerto (the first, almost certainly) and his reputation as both pianist and composer begins to spread. As you can imagine, though, fate was never going to allow Beethoven a storybook 'happy ever after' ending. Only a year later, he began to get the first signs of a deafness that would eventually become total.

In 1803, Beethoven was thirty-three, and gradually realising that he was succumbing to deafness. In a letter of 1802, discovered many years after his death, he made it clear that he knew what was happening to him. It's maybe in a sort of race against time that he came up with a massive burst of creativity.

Over the next six years, he would write his *Kreutzer*, *Waldstein* and *Appassionata Sonatas*, as well as the ever popular '*Moonlight*' – not his title, I might add, but one his publishers stuck on. He also produced the oratorio *Christ on the Mount of Olives* and the *Third Piano Concerto*. But in 1803, he also came up with something that has been described as 'the greatest single step made by a composer in the history of the symphony and of music in general'. Big talk, little breeches, as Baloo would say.

But fair, though, because the *Third Symphony* is just not like anything that had preceded it. If you hear a Haydn symphony in concert, it's ... orderly, it's... in place. If you hear a Mozart symphony even, it's still order. Genius, often, without doubt, but still order. Then you get something like Beethoven's *Eroica* – the 'heroic' symphony. It's... well, it's just not on the same playing field. Beethoven was really raising the symphony game with this one. It's EPIC, it's AMAZING.

♬ *For some reason, viola players in the classical world are akin to drummers in the jazz world, i.e. the butt of jokes. Personally, of course, I don't subscribe to such jokes. Such jokes as: What's the difference between a viola and a trampoline? Answer: You take your shoes off to jump up and down on a trampoline. Or: What do you call a guy who hangs round with musicians? Answer: A drummer. Terrible jokes.*

It's the *Star Trek* of symphonies – it boldly goes where no man had gone before. The 'hero' of the title was the man of the moment, too, Napoleon, who was a bit of an idol for Ludwig. Sad to say, it wasn't to last. When, just one year later, Napoleon crowned himself Emperor in Paris, Beethoven ran to his bottom drawer, took the *Eroica* manuscript from underneath his hairbrush, and scratched out the name 'Bonaparte', dedicating it, instead, to 'the *memory* of a great man'.

Strong stuff!

Also composing some great stuff around this time was Beethoven's friend – and, I think, a possible contender in the Mildly Amusing Middle Name stakes – Johann Nepomuk Hummel. In his day, Hummel was considered certainly the equal of Beethoven as a piano player, and some even said as a composer too. Now, though, he's remembered for a mere handful of works and, in particular, his *Trumpet Concerto.* It's a bit of a partner to Haydn's in the trumpet repertoire, with an equally impressive third movement, comparable in difficulty to its predecessor – often considered a blood relation of Haydn. And with good reason, because Hummel's, too, was written for Weidlinger, the guy who invented the new trumpet. The one from Haydn's band. You see, when Haydn got a bit too frail, not able to handle the full job at Eisenstadt, the very cute powers-that-be gave him his pension of 2,300 florins plus all his medical bills, and allowed him to stay on as 'general music bigwig – allowed to potter around, read the papers, no questions asked'. And who took over from him as Kapellmeister? Correct. JN Hummel. Well, isn't it a small world?

In the 'Where are they now?' stakes, it seems to be merely a matter of fate that, despite being extremely popular and indeed influential during his lifetime, the moment he died, his music simply fell out of fashion. Of course, I have a personal theory, which I am willing to share. You see, Gluck... largely out of fashion, isn't he? Hmm? And Dittersdorf? Also, more or less totally forgotten. And now Hummel. Revered by Mendelssohn, Schumann and Liszt in his day, but now the dodo of classical music. And why? Well, my theory... mildly amusing middle names.

Karl Ditters von Dittersdorf
Christoph Willibald von Gluck

Johann Nepomuk Hummel

Need I say more? QED, as the French call the famous cruise ship.

If Haydn were to stroll into the Esterhazy Palace to read the papers in **1806** – and he *was* still there – then there'd have been plenty to catch up on. The Battle of Trafalgar has been and gone, last year, with Nelson doing the most famous snog in history – or not. Napoleon is now, wait for it:

i) First Consul
ii) Emperor
iii) King of Milan
iv) President of the Italian Republic
v) Milk Monitor☺, and
vi) Captain of the Netball team☺

More or less everything, in fact. Pitt the Younger is now going by the somewhat less jolly nickname of Pitt the Dead. What else? Well, *Prussia has declared war on France* – yeah yeah yeah, talk to the Handel, the Façade ain't listening. Moving on, Turner has turned up another goodie, *The Shipwreck*. Think of the impact that a picture like that must have had in that day and age. It wouldn't be just a great picture, it would be a huge shiver down the spine – remember, the sea is a big, relevant image for people. Nelson's victory and death were still big news, press gangs are still all the rage, plus the fact that the sea was less tamed then than it is now, and you've got a bit of shocking image in Turner's *Shipwreck*.

And musically? What about that? Does the music of the time match images like Turner's *Shipwreck*?

Well, if you're talking Beethoven, then the answer's a big, steaming lump of 'yes'.. He's already produced his first draft of his one and only opera, *Fidelio*, with its themes of brotherhood, comradeship and freedom. And 'one and only' – that's important. You see, he doesn't waste paper, our Beethoven, oh no. Haydn wrote 104 symphonies, Mozart forty-one, but Beethoven? Only nine. But they were, no disrespect to the other two, truly greater works – a magnificent nine – and, in that respect, the numbers speak volumes. Much less frivolous than

Haydn's, more demanding, more revolutionary than Mozart's, and, generally, on another level completely. And, then, in 1806, he comes up with his *one and only* violin concerto. It's less 'in your face' than some of his other stuff, with a delirious second movement that is truly ages away from Haydn and Mozart. It's said that, at its first performance, the original fiddler, a man called Clement, was left to sight-read the whole thing, having had no rehearsal, but somehow managed to pull it off. And thank goodness he did: had he completely buggered it up and, in so doing, consigned the work to an eternity of obscurity, then I, for one, would never have forgiven our friend Clement. I don't think I could bear to be without the Beethoven *Violin Concerto*. But, anyway, he didn't. He got through it, everyone applauded, probably politely, he left the concert hall, shut the door and, before you knew it – VOOOMH – it was **1808**.

VAN THE MAN

I'm going to take this opportunity to spend some time going into a little more detail on the next nine years. Just as I did at the last truly intriguing time in music history – the final four years of Mozart – so, now, I'm going to spend a while in the company of Van the Man.

So. 1808. Two years since the *Violin Concerto*, and Beethoven is on a roll. In the last two years, he's come up with *Fidelio*, the 'Razumovsky' string quartets, and *Symphony No 4*. Around him, the world is, as ever, changing. Napoleon, having taken Barcelona and Madrid, abolishes the Spanish Inquisition. Bet they weren't expecting that! Then, for good measure, he abolishes the Italian one, too.♫ In other disciplines, Kaspar David Friedrich exhibits his painting *The Cross of the Mountains*, Walter Scott publishes *Marmion*, and Goethe comes up with a bit of a blockbuster. I think it's fair to say this one will run and run, in oh so many versions: *Faust*, part 1.

Beethoven himself is still as unlucky in life as he is in love. His 'immortal beloved' is from this period too. 'She' is a mystery woman, never to be categorically identified. Some say it was Giuletta Guicciardi, an Italian countess, who is said to have returned his affections before her father forbade the marriage. It was to her that he dedicated the *'Moonlight' Sonata*. Some say it was her cousin, Therese

---

♫ *What Italian one? Why didn't I know about this? Was it a brand extension, franchise operation, what?*

Malfatti, the inspiration for the *Appassionata*. Some even say it was Booboo, the soft toy for whom he wrote the 'Flurble Symphony for Kazoos'☺, although these people like to have someone to sit with them and have been largely discredited. And, finally, some say it's a general letter to 'all women'. Personally, I think this is daft. I mean, if it's an open letter to all women, why not have small A5 flyers printed and left in places where women would see them, like make-up counters or handbag shops? See? It only takes a few moments of common sense to discredit a perfectly foolish theory.

Having said all that, picture Gary Oldman as Beethoven, if you can, from the film *Immortal Beloved*. Strange-looking, bad-tempered, plagued by increasing deafness... and yet capable of stopping a concert audience dead in their tracks. Think how amazing and how *violent*, almost, the *Symphony No 5* must have been when Beethoven let it loose on an unsuspecting public. Up until now, the most amazing thing in the world of symphonies has been Mozart or Haydn. They're both fab, don't get me wrong, but still, nothing in their entire symphonic oeuvre could possibly have prepared anyone for

DE DE DE DERRR
DE DE DE DERRR

You see. Even written out like that, it looks somehow amazing, doesn't it? If you hear a great version of it now, it's still amazing. It's one of those pieces that can make you think that you've never heard it before. And not just the opening movement. Think of the last movement, in all its glory. It's MASSIVE. Huge and glorious, it takes no prisoners, it's immense. History, too, dealt it a helping hand when it became heavily associated with the Allied call-sign for Victory in the Second World War. The reason? The opening motif, which I think you'll agree is splendidly portrayed above, was similar to the Morse Code signal for V – three dots and a dash, or dot dot dot DASH, or, as it were, de de de derrr, see?

One year on, and **1809** is proving to be a very interesting year.

France and Austria are still engaged in a huge game of army wrestling. When a man called Arthur Wellesley gets involved on Britain's behalf, and defeats the French at Oporto and Talavera, he's given the title 'The Duke of Wellington' for his troubles. Oh, and his brother's made Foreign Secretary. Very cosy. Napoleon, though, has had his sights set on the Papal States and pretty soon he has them. Annexed before you can say, 'Not tonight, Josephine!' Which reminds me – the whole stress and hassle of keeping up anything like a decent Napoleonic war has taken its toll on the Emperor, stroke Consul, stroke President, stroke my inner thigh. Indeed, 1809 also sees his divorce from Josephine, so it's a more a case of '... and not any other night, Josephine, either'.

In England, Constable provided the ultimate in escapism with his picture of the delightful *Malvern Hill.* In fact, on a more everyday level, the 2000 Guineas is established at Newmarket Races, and finishing touches are put to Bristol Harbour. On a less everyday level, ST von Sommering invents the water voltameter telegraph. Now, what the *hell* is that?

Whatever it is, it clearly matters not two pins to one Ludwig van Beethoven. In terms of his deafness, he is now seriously suffering. He's not *totally* deaf yet, but, well, if you were to try roughly to convert what he was hearing then to what you're seeing now, well then it was probably something... **like this**. Mm. Not very nice at all, really. And, of course, it's making him more and more irritable and fond of his own company. Being Beethoven, it's a very idiosyncratic state of self absorption. For example, he likes to play the Austrian National Lottery in the hope of winning a fortune. In fact, he was so desperate to come up with shed loads of cash that he used to study the numbers, and gen himself up on the form. Also, by all accounts, he was a little careless about manuscripts, frequently 'borrowing' them for odd jobs. It's said some of his most famous works bear the circular imprint of the times when he used them to cover his soup bowl to keep it hot, or, worse still, to cover up his chamber pot.♬

♬ *His chamber music, one would suppose.*

But despite all, despite the deafness, the lack of money, the various personal hardships brought on by deafness, despite all this he had not yet reached a bad patch musically speaking, and the great works just kept on coming. 1809, the '*Emperor*' *Concerto* – the name didn't come from Beethoven, though. He was very disenchanted with Napolean by this point – definitely wouldn't be sending him a Christmas card this year. **1810**. The *Egmont Overture*. Wow. Each one of them I would be proud to call my life's work. Today, they remain absolute giants of their respective fields. It's unlikely a concert season goes by somewhere in the world without the 'Emperor' in there, somewhere. And although most of the rest of Egmont is not performed much, these days – it was a play by Goethe, for which Beethoven supplied the incidental music – the overture itself is still a stalwart of the repertoire. And, let's not forget, a great pick-me-up drink for coping with hangovers.

1812, now. Yes, 1812 1812. *THE* 1812. 1812 of 'De de de de de de de den dut derrrr' fame. Of course, that – De de de de de de de den dut derr, that is – is not *from* 1812, it's just *about* 1812. Obviously. Good. I'm glad I'm making myself perfectly clear.

Anyway, as I'm trying to say in my own little way, it's 1812 and Napoleon has finally got too big even for his boots and done the whole *invade Russia* thing. I don't know, so 'week one'! Sad time, to be honest. He then had to follow this up with the whole *retreat from Moscow* thing. He finally got back to Paris with a surviving army of 20,000. That's out of the 550,000 he started the campaign with! Quite. Let's see, what else? Well, the big writers of 1812 included Lord Byron and the Brothers Grimm. To be fair, Jane Austen is also one of the big writers of 1812, it's just that nobody knows she is, as she puts out all her stuff anonymously. Last year, it was Anon's *Sense and Sensibility* – big hit – and she's already working on Anon's *Pride and Prejudice* for next year. In other stuff, Lord Elgin has just brought some trifling little marble bits and bobs back to England, Goya has painted the Duke of Wellington and, up north, only last year, a group named after Ned Ludd had destroyed a series of industrial machines that spelt the end of their jobs. Odd times.

As for Herr Beethoven, well, it's finally here. His bad time, that is, as far as music is concerned. He's about to go into a five-year down period. Maybe the deafness was finally getting to him? Maybe he just lost the muse? I don't know. He just finished the amazing *Seventh Symphony* and the somewhat lighter *Eighth Symphony*, and, well, more or less shut up shop. Apart from yet another rewrite of *Fidelio*, he would produce very little, and what he did wasn't masses to write home about.

So, if Beethoven is having some well-earned down time, who *is* around and writing what it would be worth our while covering? Well, there is, of course, the chef. The man who put honey back into symphony – OK, OK, needs work – and who added an extra pinch into the Thieving Magpie. Yes it's Gioachino 'Does this need more pepper?' Rossini. And not only is it going to be Rossini who saves the decade, it's going to be, would you believe it, our old friend opera. And not just any old opera: but only your 100 per cent genuine kosher *comic* opera, no less. As true as I'm holding this carrot.

1816 is the year. And what can you say about 1816 that hasn't already been said? Quite. But let me try, anyway. It's one year on from both Waterloo and the Battle of New Orleans, interesting if only because they both were not only big-hitting battles, but also big-hitting songs. Indeed, the Battle of New Orleans kept Lonnie Donegan very happy in retirement for many years. What else? Canova has sculpted his 'Three Graces', Jane 'You ain't seen me' Austen has written *Mansfield Park* and *Emma*, and Samuel Coleridge-Taylor has finally completed *Kubla Khan*, which he'd started back in 1797. That was back in the classical period. Huh! How primitive. At home in Britain, things are not looking great. Money is tight, some would say non-existent, and the generally gloomy economic outlook is causing a huge migration of people to Canada and the US.

Beethoven, incidentally – well, he's still scribbling a little, screwing up the manuscript paper... scribbling a little, then screwing up the manuscript paper. In fact, he's doing this over and over again. It's not going well, the poor little sausage. So let's see what Rossini can do to fill the gap.

Rossini, of course, was far happier. He was, by now, already becoming known as 'the swan of Pesaro', for reasons perhaps best known to himself. OK, so he was from the Italian coastal town of Pesaro, in Italy? Fair enough, but the 'swan' bit – well, your guess is as good as mine. Maybe it's because it's said that when he went swimming in the Pesaro lido, although he appeared graceful above the water, beneath the surface his chubby little legs were paddling like billy-o.☺ Whatever. By 1816, he was just twenty-four to Beethoven's forty-six, and had already been 'bubbling under' for a few years now. His first operas were utterly unremarkable, but nevertheless led to more commissions. Suddenly, though, things started to happen. The opera *Tancredi* was a huge hit – the aria 'Di tanti palpiti' was massive at the time. It got a nickname 'The Rice Aria' because Rossini was said to have written it in four minutes flat, while his rice was cooking. Then came *The Italian Girl in Algiers* when he was twenty-one and, in an instant, he was famous throughout all Italy. His next opera was very, very eagerly awaited. Could the young man with the ear for some of the most hummable tunes of the day do it again?

Well, the signs looked good when he plumped for a Beaumarchais play as his source. Good start. But then, well, then things went seriously downhill. He had thirteen days to write it. Fair enough. He could do that. And he did – had it finished just the day before the first night. *The Barber of Seville.*

Problem was it was *massively* under-rehearsed. So, on the night, at the Teatro Valle in Rome, singers missed their cues, tripped over on the set, a cat even wandered on stage at one point. Then, nightmare scenario – the audience started booing and shouting the name 'PAI-SI-ELL-O, PAI-SI-ELL-O'. Now this *was* bad news. Giovanni Paisiello was a big Italian composer at the time and he had already set the same play that now found itself being booed in the version by Rossini. Not the best start ever for an opera.

But then, guess what?

No, go on, guess!

Oh, bad luck. No, actually, that's not it. What happened was, come the second night, they loved it. Yes. LOVED IT. Honest. Don't know why, but they did. They just turned it all around, and couldn't stop applauding it. And it's been one of the most popular Italian operas ever since. As well as the overture, which is rightly famous, it also contains the beautiful 'Una voce poco fa', which translates as 'One vodka too far', and the tenor test 'Largo al factotum', or 'Big Al makes breakfast'.☺ When it comes to the latter, I can't hear it without being transported back to my youth. Not to an opera house, not to my father standing pipe in hand by the gramophone, and not to the influence of my knowledgeable music teacher in school. No, it takes *me* back to that rare time, staying up late on a school night, when the Fiat ad would come on the telly, complete with Rossini soundtrack – you know, the one with the factory full of robots doing all the work. Never forget it. Never.

And let me compare *The Barber of Seville*, if I can, to the last great milestone in opera, namely Gluck's *Orfeo and Euridice*. What would you notice if you went to hear the two performed side by side? Well, obviously, it would be a bloody awful mess, with one set of singers and players singing and playing over the other set, thus leading to discords, false related harmonies and a general cacophonous din. But, otherwise, well, we're light years on. Gluck had started to use all those musical effects – you know, musical descriptions, sound effects, if you like – but it was quite tame stuff. Then Mozart had come along with his 'Fantastic Four' – *The Marriage of Figaro*, *Cosí fan Tutte*, *Don Giovanni* and *The Magic Flute*. Now this was the highpoint of 'classical' opera – the full monty. It really didn't get more classical opera than this. So, along comes Rossini and his penchant for steak.♫

Now, remember, he's writing only twenty years or so after Mozart, but already Rossini wants to mirror 'life' more than ever. He could write an opera about anything. His famous quote, 'Give me a laundry list and I could set it to music!' is absolutely true. He doesn't want the polite, form-bound world of the classical period – he wants to wow people in the opera house. And he did. He did with things like his trademark 'Rossini Rocket'. These are the bits in his music where he repeats small phrases over and over again, getting louder and very

♫ *Rossini was a big cook, and left us, among other things, a recipe named after himself, called Tournedos Rossini. If anyone's interested, it goes like this. Ingredients: butter, olive oil, beef tournedos, foie gras, white bread, demi-glace sauce, truffles and Madeira wine. Mix the butter and oil in a hot pan. Seal the tournedos. Fry the foie gras in another pan. Braise the truffles in butter with Madeira wine. Add a brown demi-glace sauce (to taste) and simmer. Toast the bread, then place the tournedos on top, then the foie gras, then the truffles at the summit. Cover in the demi-glace sauce and serve.* Et voilà!

often faster, until they seem to explode – a sort of race to the end. There's one in the overture to *The Barber of Seville*, and probably the most famous one is in the overture to *William Tell* – the end of the 'Lone Ranger' bit. They're *pure* showmanship, and very – open inverted commas – early romantic – close inverted commas. So. If you were to have to write the essay 'Rossini's *Barber of Seville* versus Gluck's *Orfeo and Euridice* – how are they related? Discuss' and it said 'in not more than 4,000 words', only someone had scrubbed off the three noughts so it read 'in not more than 4 words' (OK, OK, big set of ifs but go with me on this). Well, if you did ever find yourself in that predicament, I'm sure you wouldn't be marked down if you wrote the following: 'They're completely different animals!'

But what of the last year in our little nonet, let's call it **1817**? What gives?

Well, to try and answer your questions, let me start in the Americas. James Monroe has just been made the fifth president of the young USA, and, a little further south, Simon Bolívar has set up a groovy new place called Venezuela, and is busy having everyone back to his. Back home, Jane Austen has died, although this in no way seems to diminish her power to release books – both *Northanger Abbey* and *Persuasion* are published, posthumously, a year later. Waterloo Bridge has opened – a bridge that affords the best views of any in London, if you ask me, or even if you don't, and that's even if they have gone and dumped a giant ferris wheel smack bang in the middle of it. In Edinburgh, the newest addition to the rapidly burgeoning portfolio of daily papers is launched, namely *The Scotsman*, with the slogan, 'Och Aye, the news!'♬

Music wise, though, in 1817, who's in, who's out? Who's alive, who's dead? Who's the Michael Stipes, who's the Michael Ball? Well, as you may have guessed, we are now definitely romantic which is why this paragraph is written in a flowery script. Early romantic, it's true, but romantic nevertheless. You only have to listen to last year's biggie, 'The Barber of Seville', to realize that. It simply sounds early romantic. Or, if it's easier, it doesn't sound classical. It was Beethoven who broke the

♬ *Stephen Fry would like to publicly dissociate himself from this line.*

mould, the classical mould, and from then on people needed another word, and the word was 'romantic'. Another leading light of the romantic world was the man we first caught a glimpse of some seventeen pages ago now, as an eleven-year-old boy, fiddling his way round Europe. He's the man in league with the Devil, one Nicolò Paganini.

Thank you. Paganini is touring heavily, at the moment, much like he ever did, although all of it still within his native Italy. He would be well into his forties before he stepped into unfamiliar foreign territories. Much like Mozart had done before him, Paganini takes his own music with him – music that he has specially written himself, to show himself off. Showmanship is the big thing with Paganini, as it will be for many composers of the romantic period.

Actually, at this point, I need to say something stark staringly obvious again – what the marketing types would call a 'no brainer', I believe, and it's this. At any one, given time, there will be three groups of people who are able to make a difference in *any* art form – the past, present and future types. What I mean, there, is the people whose work is stuck in the past, the people who are very content to work in the fashion of their day, and the people who are always in the future – breaking new ground.

Like now – 1817. The people who favour the past are still writing what has gone before; the people who favour the present are embracing, fully, the music that is *now*; and, of course, the people who favour the future – important, restless souls who can only write music that pushes the boundaries – are busy fidgeting and being unable to sit still. If you think about it, at any time, there will always be these three types of people in action, and not just in music, but in anything – art, literature, Wankel rotary engine development, the lot. Eventually, though, one of the groups will get the upper hand, and the influence of the other two diminishes... and so the form will change. And so with music. Music's 'futurists' got the upper hand and so music moved on, as it were. At present, we're seeing off the last tiny vestiges of classical, and romantic is definitely in. Paganini and Rossini are spearheading the 'Romantic for President' campaign and, as it stands, they're doing well in the Primaries, and telling music like it is.

In this year, 1817, Paganini came up with his reality-defyingly difficult *Violin Concerto No 1* and Rossini brought forth *La Gazza Ladra*. The violin concerto is typical of the sort of stuff Paganini would have taken on the road to ensure a return booking – it's all 'double-stopping'♫ and 'harmonics'♫♫ and generally gives the appearance of the fiddler arching all over the place to find the notes. As for *La Gazza Ladra*, some say its finest hour came when a High Court judge in the late 1980s mistook it for Paul 'Gazza' Gascoigne, the then England footballer, causing a resurgence of feeling that High Court judges were out of touch. Only slightly spooky, too, that Gazza – the footballer – did actually play for a football team whose nickname was 'The Magpies' and 'La Gazza Ladra' means 'The Thieving Magpie'. Something to bring up when there's a lull in conversation. Or maybe a powercut.

AFTER THE PREVIOUS NINE YEARS

Great title don't you think, 'after the previous nine years'? I did toy with 'Beyond...' for a few moments but then plumped for the plainer 'After...' in the end. Paves the way, should I ever need it, for a prequel, 'Before the previous...' etc, etc. Can't see as I will ever need it, but still.

The reason I go on about the title is that, to be fair, this isn't really any particular period in history. Yes, it's still 'early romantic', and it's not quite fully fledged 'romantic', but this doesn't earn it its own name: 'the pre-ultra romantic' period, or maybe the 'post pre-romantic period'. Yes, actually, that's better. But, still, it hasn't got a name. And I certainly would never stoop so low as to deliberately *try* to coin a new phrase for some sad nine-year lull, just so that I get quoted in pompous music books. Oh no. Not me.

The post pre-romantic period, as you might call this time, is quite an interesting little time. Quick update: **1819** was the year that

♫ *The bits where they play more than one note at once on the violin.*

♫♫ *The bits where they apply different pressure on a string so as to sound a different note from that gained by applying normal pressure.*

Singapore was leased to the British East India Company, and a bijou but surprisingly spacious settlement was established. Elsewhere, last year, the Allies, in the shape of Austria, Britain, Prussia and Russia, withdrew from France. In another continent, some poor chap is forced to walk the breadth of America with one of those white-line painting machines, as the new border with Canada is established – the 49th parallel. In fact, talking of the US, 1819 sees them going into real estate. A little place called Florida has just come on to the market, put up for sale by Spain, and America is the first to view. There is a small entry in President James Monroe's diaries which is thought to relate to the viewing.

> 1819. Met those nice people, the Spaniards and went round to view F.
>
> It's delightful. Mrs Monroe and I fell in love with it the minute we crossed the border. All its own features – 2,276 miles of tidal shoreline, 663 miles of beaches – lovely for summer. Also has cold running water – St John's river, etc, which is good because Mrs Monroe like to sleep near a bathroom. Also, 7,700 lakes. Nice fishing. In terms of outbuildings, it's got 4,500 islands. Spaniards said it's had only one previous owner, if you don't count St Augustine. Has only 67 counties – we were looking for 70. And it is overlooked – by Georgia and Alabama. In the end, bought it. Fishing swung it!

This year is also the vogue year for the poet John Keats. He's all the rage, having already published *Endymion*, a year ago, and the *Poems* the year before that. In 1819, he's writing not only 'The Eve of St Agnes' and 'Hyperion' but also the odes – 'Ode to a Nightingale', 'Ode on a Grecian Urn' and the gorgeous 'Ode to Autumn'. Staying in England, Turner is still painting madly – this year it's *Childe Harold's Pilgrimage*, and why not? – and also Mary Shelley is still fairly hot on the coffee tables with *Frankenstein*. In France, the powers-that-être have declared 'Freedom of the Press', which, I believe, is rather like 'freedom of the city' only you get the right to drive your sheep across the editor's desk. Science is coming on in leaps and bounds, although, having said that, James Watt has just died. On the bright side, though, the Dane, Hans C Oersted, has just discovered electromagnetism, and a brand-new lock – the detector lock – has just been developed by the sumptuously named Jeremiah Chubb. Don't you just love it when that happens? Next thing you know, they'll try and tell you that someone called Mackintosh invented the mackintosh.

But anyway, on the music front it's a good year for Schubert. Yes, he's around now. In fact he's already twenty-two by now.

Franz Schubert was born in Vienna in 1797. His dad was a teacher, his mother a cook. You get the feeling that he would have 'fallen into teaching' as so many people do, were it not for one thing – his innate musical talent. It simply outed itself! No sooner was he in long trousers than he could rattle off tunes on the piano, organ and violin. Oh, and the viola, but let's not hold that against him. He was enrolled at the Imperial Court Chapel Choir, where one of his teachers was the composer Salieri, who's alleged to have told him that he was a genius who could do everything! It was here, too, that he started to compose – his first song is from when he was sixteen – but, when he left the choir, he set out on his dad's chosen career for him, that of teacher. By all accounts, he was a terrible teacher, totally unable to keep discipline and lacking in conviction. But his heart just wasn't in it. He composed at night, in between marking slates, and eventually packed it in when he was just nineteen.

Luckily for him, he got in with a useful clique that included poets and singers. Handy, really, because he would use the poets' words for his songs and then call upon the singers to sing them. And the writing is flowing too – the muse is good and all that – it's just that he's not doing too well on the public recognition front. Yes, he's written the songs and other pieces till they're coming out of his ears, but virtually none of them are getting performed. Even fewer are getting published. Nothing so far, in fact. He is a tad down about it, but it doesn't stop him keeping on keeping on, and this year he produces a trout. Quite a feat, I think you'll agree. His trout, though, is a piano quintet, written in five movements, the last but one being a set of variations on one of his own songs, 'Die Forelle' – 'The Trout' – which he'd written a couple of years earlier. It's a very pleasant piece, whose significance is more than a little outweighed by its popularity, but, nevertheless, it's fun enough. It's said he wrote it while he was on holiday and, certainly, this would explain its general lightness in comparison to the tragic nature of a lot of his stuff.

Just by way of an aside – well, two asides, really – it's not a particularly well-known fact that Schubert's nickname among his friends was 'Schwammerl' which translates, more or less, as 'the little mushroom'. This is because Schubert was both none too tall and none too thin, and his short, squat frame, complete with his little round face, earned him his own affectionate little moniker. What is more widely known is that Schubert was a great one for routine, particularly when it came to composing. It's said he would compose every morning, come rain or come shine. After lunch, he'd meet friends for walks or a coffee, and then most evenings were reserved for music-making, or 'Schubertiads', as they came to be known. A Schubertiad was basically our Franz saying 'Hey, everyone, back to mine!' and then an evening of jolly good fun round the piano, with all the musician friends he could muster. Add to this all Schubert's friends from the bohemian arty circles of Vienna, and I imagine you got some rather interesting evenings. Rumour has it that, on one occasion, somebody even blew a raspberry. Heady times, I'm sure.

SCHUBERT'S 8TH SYMPHO

Schubert's routine was something he kept almost all his life, particularly with regard to his composing times. Religious, he was, about when he composed as, indeed, he was about *how* he composed. In this respect, too, he had one big rule – he would never start a new composition before he had finished the last one. It was an unbreakable rule of his. Even when he was producing gallons and gallons of music – and Schubert really did knock it out – he would still religiously finish one piece before starting the next. Take the year 1815. In that year alone, he composed a massive 140 songs, sometimes writing up to eight a day! But even then, with so many songs to be written, he would still… finish one before starting another.

Do you get my point? I'm not labouring it, am I? You see, it's because what *I* want to know is this. How did he manage to leave his *Symphony No 8* unfinished? Eh? Answer me that! It was written in 1822, when he still had six years left to live. OK, not an age, or anything, but certainly, at Schubert's rate, plenty of time to finish a symphony. So what about his rule? Why was it left UNFINISHED? I mean! If Schubert was the Magnus Magnusson of classical music, how come he left us only two movements of *Symphony No 8*, instead of four? I think we need to look at this more, but first, let's get our bearings.

1822: Brazil gets its independence, and, consequently, football gets its greatest exponents. Queen Caroline is now sitting on the great throne in the sky, probably as far away as possible from Napoleon, who has also recently gone up there somewhere. Both Spain and Piedmont have had revolutions – well, you have to, don't you? – and, next year, central America, too, has a bit of a general spring clean. Mexico goes it alone, while Guatemala, San Salvador, Nicaragua, Honduras and Costa Rica all join hands to form the Confederation of Central America. In the Confederation of Central Luvviedom – or the Arts, as it's more commonly known – Percy Shelley has made his final overtures to Mary. Or maybe, more accurately, $H_2$0vertures. Canova, he of the Three Graces, has gone too, as has, on a more scientific note, Sir William Herschel. From deaths to births – and the *Sunday Times* is a new arrival in 1822. Stretching it a little, there's a marriage, too, as Stephenson's engineering feat joins Stockton to Darlington.

That's the broad world, then, but what is going on in the mind of Franz Schubert, the absolute stickler – some might say, pain – about not picking up a blank page for one work until he's finished the last. Well, as you can imagine, there have been more than a few theories as to why it stayed at just two movements, and, subsequently, the most famous 'unfinished' in history. Some say he lost inspiration. Some say he did, indeed, finish it but that a friend lost it. And some say no: on this occasion, he simply broke his own rule and moved on to something else. Mmmm, I'm not sure. I don't think I fully buy any of those, to be honest. I just think it's much simpler than all that. I think there is no real mystery. I think Schubert is quite simply the first REAL romantic. True-blue, dyed-in-the-wool, floppy-fringed, bespectacled ROMANTIQUE. And I think he just got to two movements and thought: 'Wow, that's fantastic. You know what? Sod it. It doesn't get any better than that. Who says I have to write four movements? I'm a romantic and proud. There are no rules, now! All bets are off. IF I WANT A TWO-MOVEMENT SYMPHONY... I'LL HAVE ONE!'

Just one year later, in **1823**, Beethoven unveiled his latest offering – a massive, five-movement Mass. Rather like Delius a hundred-odd years later, Beethoven's *Missa Solemnis* is rather less of a hymn to God and more of a personal celebration of all things natural and creative. Where a traditional Mass celebrated God, Beethoven's *Missa Solemnis* celebrates man. It had proved a real labour of love for him over the five years or so it took to write – so much so that the event for which it was written was long gone. On this occasion, at least, Beethoven was not going to find himself, as Schubert had, with an unfinished work on his hands.

A BOTTLE OF YOUR FINEST 1825

1825, and it's not merely by chance that I've chosen to focus on this small but perfectly formed year. If we were talking about a wine, you would have to find a turn of phrase a little more superlative than the old Sinatra line 'it was a very good year'. 1825 was vintage. Classic, as they say round these parts – more than that, really. Let me gradually focus in, if I may. In France, it's a case of 'what goes around, comes around' as a new law compensates the aristocracy for losses incurred during the Revolution. John Nash – yes, *the* John Nash – comes up with a cute little thing at the end of The Mall, called Buckingham Palace. Pushkin follows up his *Eugene Onegin* which he'd started a couple of years ago, with a cool *Boris Godunov*, laying the groundwork for some of the nationalist operas in years to come. The diaries of Samuel Pepys are finally published, some 122 years after they were written. Now that's what I call playing hard to get. All of this, though, pales into insignificance really, when you realize that 1825 is the year that Beethoven came to England.

The previous year, he'd received a commission from the Royal Philharmonic Society. It was for a symphony, which fitted in with Beethoven's plans perfectly. He'd been making the odd sketch for a symphonic work from as early as 1815, and the commission prompted him to look at the last movement again. He revisited a text that had been in his sights for the last thirty years or so. It was by Johann Schiller and called 'An die Freude', but is most often translated into English as the 'Ode to Joy'. Odd to think now that, when it comes to one of the most famous symphonies ever written, one of its defining features, the choral movement, was only added at a very late stage. But for the RPS gig, the work would be perfect – Beethoven would provide them with a symphony. By now totally deaf yet, somehow, able to hear music better than almost anyone on the planet at the time, he set to work hacking away at Schiller's words. In the end, he used only about a third of them, and those he did use he totally rearranged to suit his own symphony. Nevertheless, the result was the symphony's finest hour – something which, today, is enjoyed by millions of concert-goers the world over – in a way the composer himself never could. It's said that at the first performance, with Beethoven himself conducting, the piece came to a close after a somewhat ragged performance, in which the orchestra and the chorus had even got out of sync with each other. Nevertheless, get to the end they did and Beethoven put down his baton, somewhat physically drained from trying to keep his brand-new work together. At this point, he didn't really know how it had gone. He was, remember, totally deaf now. He apparently looked deflated and a little disappointed. It was left to a young alto soloist from the chorus – Caroline, her name was – to come across to make him aware of how it had been received. She walked across and physically turned him round 180 degrees. It was only at this point that Beethoven realized quite what a hit his new symphony had been. The entire audience was on its feet, clapping like there was no tomorrow. Many in the crowd at this point realized that Beethoven had been unaware of the applause, and this made them clap and cheer even louder. To Ludwig, the applause seemed to go on for years. Now he knew his symphony had arrived. If you add to this the fact that William Webb Ellis was busy running with the ball down at Rugby School and 1825 adds up to one hell of a year.

THAT WAS THEN, THIS IS THEN TOO

'Then' is now – **1826**. So who are the mad, bad and dangerous to know people of 1826? One is James Fenimore Cooper. He's just written a book all about early Native American cobblers, and he's called it *The Last of the Mohicans* – you can still see the original last on display at the Museum of Footwear at 27, Rue D'Immelda Marcos, Marseille.☺ Elsewhere André Ampère published his paper 'Electrodynamics' which was, well, basically about dynamics and, basically, how electric they are. Yes, good. Think that's covered it. It was also the same year that Thomas Jefferson died and Russia declared war on Persia. Ooh, Persia! We are getting imaginative.

Au sujet de la musique, on the one in, one out rule, we'd just gained Johann 'The Waltz King' Strauss, and just lost Antonio 'Look, I'm telling you, I never touched him' Salieri. Actually, while we're on the subject of Salieri, can I call a time out?

Salieri Time Out.

It's just that, well, I feel more than a little sorry for Salieri. Let me see if I can build a case for the defence of this man who is now forever vilified as the 'the-man-who-we-know-probably-didn't-poison-Mozart-but-nevertheless-let's-say-he-did.' I mean, why let the facts get in the way of a good story? Salieri was from Legnago, which is now just a short hoik down the 434 from Verona, but was no doubt then a delightful little village on the banks of the Adige river – a perfect place to nurture musical talent. Salieri was orphaned at fifteen, and then more or less adopted by the well-to-do Mocenigo family. He moved to Vienna, where things seemed to fall into place for him and he became court composer at the age of only twenty-four. He was well regarded as an opera composer – it was one of his that opened the new

La Scala opera house, in Milan, in 1776 – and he eventually became Kapellmeister at the Viennese court. OK, so he may have not got on with Mozart, but then Mozart could be a little... what's the word... puerile? One look at his letters tells you that – more bottom references than Rik Mayall and Ade Edmondson put together. And Salieri almost certainly didn't poison him. Yes, he had a few digs at him, but then he was probably one of the few people around at the time in a position to realize quite what a genius Mozart was, and that must have been somewhat daunting. So, I guess what I'm saying is...well, look, lay off Salieri, OK? Good. Now. Time in, again.

This was also the year that a rather ill young man by the name of Carl Maria von Weber had travelled to London, to oversee the premiere of his new opera, *Oberon*. Weber was the head of the German Opera Theatre, in Dresden, and had never been a healthy individual at the best of times. In fact, although he didn't know it, he would never make it back home. *Oberon* was a big hit with the Covent Garden audiences but Weber himself died just a couple of months later, his successor at Dresden being a name that had yet to make its rather large mark. Richard Wagner! Watch this space.♫

There were important things afoot in 1826. Back over in Germany, fun times were almost certainly being had by the sixteen-year-old Felix Mendelssohn – as befits his name, really.♫♫

Mendelssohn came from a prosperous family. His granddad, Moses Mendelssohn, was a philosopher, the Plato of his day, and very much revered and his Dad, Kaschpoint Mendelssohn, had his very own bank and, as a boy, Felix and his cousin ATM Mendelssohn, would shun games of doctors and nurses in favour of tellers and bankclerks☺. The young composer did, however, have to put up with a great many insults, simply for being Jewish. So much so, in fact, that when his Dad realized that his son was destined for big things, he converted to Protestantism, adding the extra name 'Bartholdy' in a cunning and subtle rebranding exercise that would have made Snickers proud.

♫ *Well, obviously, not THIS space, because this is just the mention of his name. I suppose I should say 'watch the space about forty pages further on', really, but no one ever says that, do they?*

♫♫ *Latin dictionary definition: 'felix (1) (adj.) happy, (2) (n.) cat'.*

Felix was the classic 'boy genius' composer – playing piano in public at nine, enrolled in the Berlin Singakademie at ten and home for lunch at twelve. He wasn't yet in his teens before he'd rattled off two operas, several symphonies and the odd string quartet, as well as being able to build, dissemble and then reassemble a fairly complicated Meccano dinosaur. Along with his first pimple, at the age of sixteen, came a work of such vision that it was said not even Mozart had written with such maturity at the same age. The work? It was the overture to Shakespeare's play *A Midsummer Night's Dream*.

It really was a remarkable work for a sixteen-year-old – gorgeous orchestral writing, very light-handed and with a maturity beyond its composer's years. Having penned the overture, Mendelssohn stopped. The overture remained unplayed and largely unknown for some sixteen or seventeen years. By then, he was a celebrated and respected composer, the Kapellmeister to the King of Prussia, and boss of the top music academy in Leipzig. It was at this time that the King of Prussia, an ardent fan and supporter, pressed him to look again at the overture he'd written as a youth, and maybe add some more parts, which could act as both a suite and incidental music to the play. Felix duly stumped them up, and stuck them on the end. The extra pieces included a cute little scherzo, and the now famous/infamous 'Wedding March', which, alongside Wagner's 'Bridal March' still to come, has formed the entrance and exit to virtually every wedding ceremony since. Until, that is, the late 1960s onwards, when many folk started to get a little bit more adventurous with their choice of in and out music. Hence, today, a bride can sweep majestically down the aisle, white-knuckling her impoverished father, while the beautiful strains of Bryan Adams's 'Everything I Do, I Do It For You' echoes around the nave, in an ill-advised arrangement for Bontempi organ. Still, that's neither here nor there. Humour me a moment, will you, if I tell you it's 1829.

It's **1829**, and here's how things stand. Since Mendelssohn coughed up the overture to *A Midsummer's Night's Dream*, the world has changed. Not surprising, really. We've lost William Blake and Goya and, indeed, Sir Humphry Davy's lamp has finally been snuffed out. On the world stage, the combined powers of Russia, France and Great Britain have banded together to give Turkey a sort of diplomatic 'clip round the ear', as it were. In fact, and this is true, they literally sent Turkey a note. Honest! True as I'm wearing this shalwar kameez, it's true. They sent Turkey a note. Turkey goes to war with Greece and so three of the world's greatest superpowers at the time get together and SEND IT A NOTE!

I say, Turkey, lay off, old chap. There's a good fellow.

Something like that. Needless to say, it ends up lining the Sultan of Turkey's wastebin and he carries on regardless. Russia, meanwhile, has won its little spat with Persia, taking Erivan – or Armenia – as the spoils. In Britain, the Duke of Wellington becomes Prime Minister – the boy done well – and London gets a brand-new police force. There've been some jolly good reads in the last three years, too. Dumas wrote *Les trois mousquetaires*, Tennyson wrote his sequel, *Timbuctu* – the further adventures of Tim – and the *Spectator* starts publication. And, leaving the literary world behind us, London's *Evening Standard* appears for the first time.

In fact, it's a great time for 'firsts', as you might imagine – first *everythings*. The first sulphur matches from John Walker; the first Oxbridge Boat Race, at Henley; the first Webster's Dictionary; and the first real train – George Stephenson had won £500 with his new train, the *Rocket*, at the Rainhill Trials. Elsewhere, another George, this time George Ohm, formulates 'Ohm's Law', which, er, which states that, er, well, it's all about resistance. It's left-handed, I think. Or is that Fleming? Anyway, it's all about resistance. Yes. Er, which I think, it says, is futile. Roughly. Good.

HIHO, ROSSINI... AWAY!

Over to Paris now, and the French capital seems to be rapidly becoming the centre of the musical universe – that is, if there is a centre of the musical universe. To be fair, the epicentre is probably still Vienna, but France, particularly Paris, and Italy are essential territories to crack, as it were. London? Well, London is somewhere to earn money if you are famous in the classical music world, but it's not anywhere near as important as the rest. Just five years ago, Rossini moved here. He'd already sampled the delights of Vienna and London, but now found Paris *un peu* more to his liking. He stayed for some six years then left, before returning, late on, for his twilight, 'Indian summer' pieces. The first Paris period, though, saw Rossini at the absolute peak of his powers. Under his belt already – *La Cenerentola* (*Cinderella*), *La Gazza Ladra* (*The Thieving Magpie*), *Il Barbiere di Siviglia* (*The Barber of Seville*) and *Semiramide* (*Half a Pint of Mild*☺), as well as a goodly number of pies. Emboldened by his worldwide fame, he decided to reel off a couple of operas that would really suit the current French tastes – ones written particularly to please the Paris audience of the late 1820s. The first came out as *Le Comte Ory* (*The Tory Bastard*)☺ which went down well enough and was very politely welcomed. His second attempt, though, was to put it in the shade – in fact, it would almost become his signature tune.

Now obscenely wealthy and feeling that he was writing the best stuff he'd ever written, he finished his second Paris opera – *William Tell*, his grand masterpiece. Even the overture was, almost, the culmination of everything he'd been trying to do with all the other overtures, up to that point. It all just came right. Everything came together in this overture. So much so that it is now played separately from its opera probably more than any other. And, of course, it was at one time – still is for some, me included – inextricably linked to the Lone Ranger, the masked man who had a strange 'Morecambe and Wise' type relationship with his sidekick, Tonto (although, I've got to be honest, I never saw the episode where they are in bed, with Tonto working on his latest play). And this is OK – the link to the Lone Ranger, I mean. At least, I think so. It used to be said that the sign of an intellectual was someone who could hear the *William Tell Overture* and not think of the Masked Man. Well, personally, I don't mind people linking it. To me it just says classical music is getting out there, people are hearing it, whereas, were you to get all precious about it, then many of them wouldn't be hearing it. And how is that better? Exactly. These days you might say the same about the Hamlet cigar ad. Some people only know Bach's *Orchestral Suite No 3* because of the Hamlet ad. But is that a bad thing? If the alternative – and it almost certainly would be the alternative – is that they don't know the *Orchestral Suite No 3* at all, then give me the former, any day. Good. There we are, then. Now, somebody help me down off this soapbox, please.

The opera *William Tell* is, sadly, less known in its entirety than its near-perfect overture. (But then again, it would be, wouldn't it. You're not really going to find someone using an entire opera as the theme to a Toilet Duck ad, are you?) Maybe this has something to do with the story, though, which, if you're a fruitarian, is highly disturbing, telling as it does the tragic story of Granny Smith, who is cruelly slain, her body cut in half by the evil Tell.

The other big thing about the opera *William Tell* is that it marks the point at which Rossini simply shut up shop. Stopped composing. Finito. Kaput. The End. Everybody go home. Yes, he simply stopped writing. Apart from a couple of little corkers, right at the last minute of his life, some thirty-four years later, that was it. From then on, he concentrated on becoming the nineteenth-century version of Nigella Lawson, only with a somewhat less attractive figure.

CH-CH-CH-CHANGES

To paraphrase the great Robbie of Williams, let me edutain you. Uggh. Sorry. Sorry I ever said that. Edutainment – supposedly a cross between education and entertainment – was a bit of a buzzword, recently, but, thankfully, has fallen on hard times, as my English teacher used to say. Despite the ughism, though, let me just catch up with myself for a moment. It's hard, you see, whizzing through an entire 6000 years in just 304 pages – that means I have to average about twenty years per page. You try that, some time. In fact, I've just spent seven whole lines saying that I'm about to tell you something. Seven lines! In seven lines I should have advanced a full four years. Onward, I think.

What's happening? Who's composing, who's decomposing, to borrow a line from Monty Python? Who's leading the pack, who's following like sheep? Plus, of course, the perennial question, Who's sorry now? Well, much like any other time in history, change is the key word.

Everything always has, everything always will, change. But in the early nineteenth century, the sheer rate of change was bordering on the mind-blowing. Railways, for example. They now start to pop up all over the place. In just under twenty years, the amount of rail being laid in the UK goes from a couple of hundred miles' worth to more than 2,000. A change is gonna come, as Viscount Sam of Cooke aptly stated. Change, in the words of Lord Tears of Fears.

Ch-ch-ch-changes, to quote Earl David of Bowie. If you were to stick a pin anywhere in the map of **1831**, and stick your head above the parapet, what would greet you would have been a mass of change. After the obligatory revolution in Paris last year, this year has seen a huge slave rebellion led by Nat Turner in Virginia. Lots of the change is 'social', as people are beginning to refer to it, with new groups forming the world over: Joseph Smith's Latterday Saints, for example, or Mormons, get under way in Fayett, New York State, and almost immediately commence foreign missions as far afield as Europe. It was also around this time that a twenty-three-year-old Charles Darwin got the job of naturalist on board the HMS *Beagle*, setting sail for South America, New Zealand and Australia. It would be a very different mission from that of Joseph Smith and his followers, and it would be one that simply wouldn't stop *repercussing*. There were also experiments galore: Faraday, with light and electromagnetics, for example. It's a big time for change, you see. Hope it was wearing clean underwear.

But what about music? Is all this *res novae* reflected in the world of black dots and baton waving?

THE LONG AND THE SHORT OF IT – ONLY NOT IN THAT ORDER

So is it? Is it reflected in the world of music? Well, if you want the short answer, yes.

Of course, if you want the long answer, then:

Yeeeeeeeeeeeeeeeeeesssssssssssssssssssssssssssssssssssssssssssssssss.

In fact, tell you what: let me go into a little more detail, in just a moment. But first, I want to keep you posted on two old friends.

Mendelssohn is the first, and the strange netherworld that is opera the second.

Mendelssohn first. If you can imagine that Roger Hargreaves had written the history of classical music, then, for example, Handel would be Mr Greedy. Schoenberg might be Mr Topsy-Turvy, and maybe Wagner could be Mr Bossy. Whatever. Some of them are open to discussion. One that isn't in question, though, is Mendelssohn. Mendelssohn, without a shadow of a doubt, is Mr Happy. His music is rarely, if ever, too taxing. It's almost always beautiful, or, if not beautiful, chipper, or if not chipper, then relaxed. The world according to Felix – and remember, his name even means 'happy'. Never really wanted for money, was quite happily married, was recognized as a great composer while he was still alive – something that doesn't always happen – and generally was the sort of person who took his library books back and 'rallied round'.

Anyway, the reason I want to catch up with Mendelssohn relates to the fragment of paper that was recently uncovered during an exhibition entitled 'More than just a Big Circle and a Line Down – Composers and their Minims' at the University of Baaden Blackschiep. It appears to be a scrap of the minutes of a meeting, attended by FM-B, during the latter half of 1832.

Chairman spoke: 'This week we have a new member of Bachaholics Anonymous, and his name is Felix.'

General murmurs.

Chairman spoke again: 'Hello, Felix. Is there anything you'd like to tell us?'

More general murmuring and chairman calls for quiet. Chairman spoke: 'Felix?'

Murmurs die down. FM-B speaks.

'Hello. My name is... is Felix, and, well, I love the music of Bach. I am a Bachaholic. THERE!'

Murmurs from crowd.

Chairman spoke: 'Well done, Felix. That's the first step!'

Yes, Felix Mendelssohn-Bartholdy is about to do what no one has been able to do for almost a hundred years, and that is to single-handedly start a Bach revival.

Despite the fact that we take Bach very much for granted these days, as one of the staple parts of the classical music diet, it was not always thus. Bach's output had been more or less forgotten after he'd died in 1750, and it was going to take someone with a fortunate mix of passion and clout to make people sit up and take notice of it again. Such a man was FM-B. He was, remember, a 'great composer' in his own lifetime. He was, also, the boss of a music academy, the Berlin Singakademie. Under his guidance, the academy had put on, just two years ago, the first performance in recent memory of Bach's *St Matthew Passion*. Combined with a significant championing of the great man's music, this was enough to relight the Bach fire, a fire that has not gone out to this day.

Around the same time he embarked on his love affair with Johann Sebastian, he also embarked on a second love affair to run alongside it, namely a love of Britain. By 1831, he'd made the first of a long line of trips to the land of the knotted hankie, and was being hailed as a bit of a celeb.

He took in Scotland, and came over all Celtic, not only with a *Scottish Symphony* but also with a piece of 'programme music' too, as it was known – that is, music with an unspoken story or picture attached, which the composer is trying to depict in the music. It was an overture called *The Hebrides*, or *Fingal's Hohle* (*Fingal's Cave*), and was prompted by an actual excursion to the cave itself in 1829.

Mendelssohn was evidently totally overwhelmed by Scotland, and the small Hebridean island of Staffa in particular. It's said that he wrote down the opening bars of his now famous overture the day before his trip to Staffa, and that it was some time before he eventually gave the overture he had written the name 'Fingal's Cave'. Indeed, despite the romantic notion that you 'can hear the waves lapping in the cave', it probably wasn't quite as hunky-dory as that. There's even a case for arguing that Mendelssohn would have liked to get Staffa out of his mind. Indeed, his travelling companion in Scotland, one Carl Klingemann – reported that Mendelssohn 'is on better terms with the sea as a composer than he is as an individual or a stomach.' Mendelssohn himself wrote, from the comfort of dry land some days later, 'How much has happened since my last letter and this! The most fearful sickness, Staffa, scenery, travels and people...' So, you see. Next time you're waiting for lights to die down in a concert featuring the Hebrides overture, and the smartarse next to you offers to point out the musical depiction of 'the waves lapping gently and ever so beautifully into the cave', just tell them: 'Actually, you're mistaken. I'm pretty sure that's meant to portray Mendelssohn with his head down the loo, doing a Technicolor yawn.' I'm sure they'll thank you for it. Whatever the reality of the situation, Mendelssohn managed to produce a work that simply reeks of Scotland – it's music with a kilt on, music that says 'CELTIC', music that says 'I'll never win the World Cup.'

OPERA III – THE RETURN OF THE LIVING DEAD

OK, you may think, judging from that title, that I've got a bit of a downer on opera, but nothing could be further from the truth. True, the people who attend opera on a regular basis are, on the whole, a strange, often slightly paranoid breed, who tend to be either over-animated or shy to the point of torture. Some say they are, like organists, a breed apart, but I prefer to give them a chance. After all, some of my best friends are regular opera-goers, and, let's face it, well under 50 per cent of them have ever been a cause for concern. Admittedly, most of them smile a little too much and look over their shoulder a lot, but that should not be borne against them. Besides, I, myself, like nothing better occasionally than to sit back and let *Don Giovanni* wash over me. So I don't want you to think I'm anti-opera. Far from it.

Anyway, it's 1831 and more or less three people are upholding the interests of opera. Rossini is one, as we saw earlier; Donizetti, as we'll see soon; and Bellini, as we'll see now.

Bellini was the classic opera composer. In fact, you could say he was the classic composer, period. He wrote only a handful of masterpieces, then died young and left a beautiful corpse. In the gospel according to Roger Hargreaves, again, he would be, what, Mr Tragedy? Or Mr Consumption, perhaps. In fact, gosh, what a jolly little book that would have made – just right for the first book for your god-daughter: 'Mr Consumption went to the door. "Oh look," he cried, weakly, "it's Little Miss Tuberculosis, come to cough!"' Best leave that one there, I think. Anyway, Bellini it was who put more *feeling* than you could shake a stick at back into opera. Whereas Rossini and Donizetti would rattle off a couple of operas over lunch, Bellini would take around a year to produce just one, wrenching the notes from his very soul. Or whatever. He also decided to move away from big, vocal displays for their own sake, and went instead for sheer intensity. So gone were the 'stand and deliver' arias, which showed off just what a singer could do, simply because they could do it. In their place were bywords like passion and feeling, and all that malarkey. It frequently left his audiences in tears.

Take his offering from 1831, for example; 'a work of genius', according to Richard 'Just you wait' Wagner, 'a great score that speaks to the heart'. It was called *Norma*, set in Roman France (Gaul), and, today, the title role is still considered one of the most important roles for a soprano, not least because it's exceedingly hard to sing. But it's also because it contains one of the, if not the, most beautiful soprano arias EVER – 'Casta Diva' – divine in every way and best, in my view, in the version recorded by Maria Callas. Sorry, not exactly a revolutionary view, but, nevertheless, a heartfelt one. In terms of plot, it lives up to the prerequisite rules of opera that all plots must be (a) hard to work out without reading the programme notes, and (b) complete bollocks. *Norma* is both. If I remember rightly, there's druids, Roman soldiers, a pet rabbit, and extras in togas. Actually, better check the rabbit.

FRENCH POLISH?

1832: a very good year for Paris. Musically speaking, at least. As I said earlier – hope you were paying attention: might not even have been a bad idea to have written it down!! – anyway, as I said earlier, the musical centre of the universe seemed to be shifting towards it, or at least, as you might say, 'in black and white terms'. That is to say, Paris had suddenly become the place to be not only for opera, but also if you happened to be one of the new breed of 'pianist–composers'. And, boy, were there lots of them around! So many, no doubt, that only a handful were bound to survive. And of this handful, the greatest was no doubt Chopin. In 1832, he found himself in Paris, at around the same time as the completely potty Hector Berlioz. But before we get on to the French and the Polish, a brief update.

MDCCCXXXII. Ah, those were the days. The days that the term 'Socialism' was first used – in England and France, oddly enough – and also the year a twenty-three-year-old William Gladstone started on a distinguished political career as both MP for Newark and handy clasp-type bag. The population of Britain stood at an amazing 13.9 million while the population of the US, wait for this, was an astonishing 12.8 million. Incredible. By the time the year was out, Johann Wolfgang von Goethe would be dead and gone, Sir Walter Scott would be dead and buried, and economist and social reformer Jeremy Bentham would be dead and stuffed. Constable gave the world his view of *Waterloo Bridge from Whitehall Stair* and the Alcotts, Bronson and Abigail gave the world their little woman, Louisa May.

Back in France, two very different composers are sharing the same heady Parisian air: Berlioz and Chopin – two very different sides of the Romantic coin. Quick toss and heads, it's Chopin.

Frédéric Chopin was very much the 'sensitive' romantic one, one for whom the word romantic meant *pure* and *subtly intense*, *reserved* even. He was born to French and Polish parents and had studied at the Warsaw Conservatory before leaving his native Poland complete with an urn of genuine Polish earth which he kept with him to remind himself of home. (Indeed, he would end up having his urn buried alongside him when he died.) He was now fitting in perfectly with the polite '*levez votre petit doigt*' Parisian salon society. They adopted him as one of their own, albeit after a somewhat shaky debut. He was introduced into the salon of Baron de Rothschild by a count, Count Radziwill, and, from then on, could do no wrong, his every note deemed to be of national importance.

As the chalk to his cheese, the *craie* to his *fromage*, as it were, there was Mad Hector.

Louis-Hector Berlioz, to give him his full name, was born in the countryside near Grenoble, which lies around a hundred kilometres south-east of Lyons, on the edge of the French Alps. His father was a doctor, who would have liked nothing more than if Hector himself had signed up to the Hippocratic oath. As a result, Berlioz was shipped off to med school in Paris, but allowed to take music lessons on the side. Of course, after three years, he gave it all up and enrolled himself at the Paris Conservatoire, where he pursued music to its then limit, with all the ferocity of a dog let off the leash.

Now, Great Hec is often referred to as an Arch-Romantic. Interesting, this. All this means is that he was romantic… and bonkers. Not for him the laid-back, effete, 'sketches' of Chopin. Berlioz worked in huge, colourful brushstrokes, the size of Bournemouth. MASSIVE statements that positively screamed 'LOOK AT ME, I'M ROMANTIC AND PROUD!'

Now, I know what you're thinking – I'm overdoing the *bonkers* bit! Well, maybe, but let me just go over the events that led to the second performance, in this year, 1832, of his *Symphonie Fantastique*. As early as 1827, Berlioz had fallen madly in love with the Irish actress, Harriet Smithson, having seen her as Ophelia in *Hamlet*. He then went after her, with all the obsession of a stalker. Followed her morning, noon and night. When his advances failed, what did he do? Become a monk? Throw himself into the Seine, while chained to his grand piano? No. He went off and wooed someone else. The someone else was a woman called Camille, and, sadly for her, she was just a pawn in Mad Hector's rather idiosyncratic game of love. He'd decided to do the jealousy thing – going after someone else, in front of the *nez* of his beloved, in the hope that it would make her see sense. Also, he'd just won the Prix de Rome, which was the big Paris composers' competition, and part of the prize was a stay in Rome. So, he upped and went to Rome, too. Maybe this was all part of the classic, French 'treat them *mesquin*, keep them *très fin*', as they say in Leeds.

His plan started to go a little awry, though, when, while in Rome, he heard that Camille had taken a lover. Damn. This buggered things up completely. How would Harriet Smithson ever be jealous if she had nothing to be jealous of? So what did he do? Well he did what any 'mad as a spoon' romantic French composer of the 1830s would do. I mean, it's obvious, isn't it? He immediately headed back to Paris, *disguised as a lady's maid*. OF COURSE! (This is, I assure you, totally true. No ☺ symbol here, you notice?) Well, who can honestly say that they haven't done that in their time? I know I have. Anyway, Hector le Fou only got as far as Genoa, when he somehow lost his disguise – which is a great shame, because I for one would have loved to know the outcome. Sounds like perfect material for a bedroom farce. In the end, he went back to Rome, deflated.

When he finally did return to Paris, he discovered that Smithson was in town. Oh, no – here we go again. He had to act fast. What would be the thing that would convince her that he was the best thing since sliced baguette? Fill her room with flowers? Send her a leather-bound book of the most romantic love poetry she'd ever read? No. HB – the man who was clearly one lead short of a pencil – decided he knew what would win her over. He would arrange a performance of his ridiculously large *Symphonie Fantastique* – the five-movement hulk of a symphony, containing four brass bands and a Dream of a Witches' Sabbath. That was bound to be the best love token she'd ever had.

But get this. It worked! She was won over! He got her! Well, I've got to say, Berlioz – and indeed Harriet – and I will clearly never see eye to eye on the subject of romance. To be fair, the *Symphonie Fantastique* is a tremendous work, and, also to give him his due, it does contain a 'Harriet Smithson' tune, which keeps cropping up all the way through. So she must have been quite touched. He subtitled the whole thing 'An Episode in the Life of an Artist', and the artist of the subtitle has apparently poisoned himself with opium, leading to him having all manner of strange hallucinations, which are depicted in the music – so not a million miles from what Velvet Underground were doing in the '60s. Throw in Timothy Leary, and you're about there.

At the time, as most forward-thinking works are prone to do, the *Symphonie Fantastique* provoked quite a few 'disgusted of Tunbridge Wells' reactions. Schumann hated it – with a passion – but probably the best quote about it came from the light-hearted lunch-lover,

Rossini, who said 'What a good thing it isn't music' – not only one of the best quotes about the *SF*, but, I think, one of the best quotes about any music. And there are these two composers: the frank Frenchness of Berlioz, the forward-pushing romantic, with the emphasis on the antic; and the Polish polish of Chopin, with his delicate, tweaking romanticism, with the emphasis on the 'twea' – the two major romantic forces in Paris at the time.

RPM ♬

Let me step back, for a moment, and try and gain some sort of overview, if I can, of the first half of the nineteenth century. It's basically all about one word: revolution. How many revolutions per month you have all depends on which part of the world you live in. The background is still that of France and the US – huge, world-changing revolutions, which made their effects felt everywhere, not least in the field of music. Hand in hand with this is, of course, nationalism. Everybody wanted to be *themselves*. They wanted to be *of their own country*, as it were. I can understand that. It's all just about 'a heightened sense of worth, individual freedom and personal expression'. Now, hold on to that phrase, if you would; hold on to that thought – 'a heightened sense of worth, individual freedom and personal expression'. Because if you lift that phrase and graft it on to the world of music, well, what you have, more or less, is a viable definition of the word Romanticism. In fact, you didn't need to separate the worlds of music and political revolution: ever since Beethoven had been some two parts revolutionary to three parts artist, revolutionary life and art had been inextricably linked. You not only *didn't need* to separate them, you COULDN'T.

Various people seemed to be on the move: **1836** – the Boers started the Great Trek; ten years later the Mormons would set out for the Great Salt Lake. And, oddly enough, with the exploration of the new, came an increased passion for the old – it may sound odd, but it's

♬ *Revolutions per minute.*

true: the homeland becomes all the more cherished when it is left behind. So nationalism would increase apace – and it would be matched in music. Not just Chopin, with his urn of Polish earth, but deeper, in the very heart of music. Glinka wrote the first *truly* Russian opera in 1836 – *A Life for the Tsar*, with its story of *real* Russian peasants, not nobility, and complete with *real* Russian folk songs, embedded into the score.

BLACK AND WHITE RAGE

Elsewhere, one of the chief phenomena that would advance the Romantic manifesto, as it were, was the further rise of the pianist-composers. Chopin himself, as well as Schumann, Mendelssohn, Liszt, were the real big movers and shakers of this part of the romantic era, and not surprisingly, really, considering that Beethoven's nine-fold legacy left many composers in absolute fear of taking on the symphony, for want of appearing inadequate. Berlioz, of course, was too loopy to care, but the rest were more than a little daunted.

As he couldn't play an instrument to any great level, Berlioz, then, became the standard bearer for the romantic orchestra. So, if Chopin was, say, Billy Joel (gentle, thoughtful stuff for piano), and Liszt was Elton John (rather camp, over the top stuff for piano), then Berlioz is like James Last – a mad, orchestra man, with big hair. It is true, of course, that other people composed for the orchestra around this time, but, because he took it on in such a different way, Berlioz brought it to another level, before anyone else. His orchestral works were both highly individual and EPIC – the perfect recipe for moving any art form into its next phase.

Finally, into all this, add the ever-present ingredient of *better technical resources.* Instruments became so markedly different too. New trumpets, with keys, were now becoming more and more common, whereas previously the trumpet played would have several different 'crooks' – a crook was a piece of the trumpet tubing that could be removed. If you put a crook of a different length back in, you were effectively changing the length of the trumpet tubing, and, thus, the notes it could play. This was all eventually replaced by keys. Similar things happened with the clarinet, with more keys added to increase its versatility. The orchestra could make almost a completely different sound from the one available to, say, Mozart, only thirty-odd years ago. Thirty-odd years ago – amazing, isn't it? It seems like another world. Pianos, too, were just beyond comparison. The advent of the iron-stringed piano made dynamics so much more pronounceable – so, not only did the Romantic pianist–composers want to go somewhere different, they also had the means to get there. What more could you want?

WELL, BERGAMO

Zooming back in, now, and the time has come for another opera composer to get his fifteen minuets of fame. Post 1829, he was becoming as popular in Paris – remember, the current centre of the music world – as he was in his native Bergamo. He was the final three-ninths of the opera triumvirate that was: Rossini, Bellini and... **Donizet** [pause for full Italian effect] **ti**.

Donizet ti was a man who'd been given a huge shot in the arm, as far as composing operas went, in 1829, the year Rossini stopped composing. The shot in the arm was, well, that Rossini stopped composing, frankly. Up to this point, Donizet ti had produced more or less one opera every twenty-five minutes. OK, I say 'more or less', but, to be fair, it was in fact less. OK. It just seemed like he was producing an opera every twenty-five minutes. And, also to be fair – because I do like to be fair – more or less ALL of them were not so good. Of course, the audiences enjoyed them enough, and so he kept churning them out. Well, why not, I suppose. Who would be prepared to say they would have done any differently? But then, all of a sudden, Rossini made his sudden and unexpected move – suddenly and unexpectedly retreating from music. And, lo and behold, the effect on Donizet ti was astonishing. He started to write his best ever stuff. In fact, all his operas which could fairly stake a claim to be labelled 'masterpieces' came from the time after Rossini had decided to shtay shtum: *Anna Bolena*, *Maria Stuarda*, *Don Pasquale*, *Lucia di Ilkley Moor*,♬ and, my own personal favourite, the darling *L'elisir d'amore – The Elixir of Love*.

The Elixir of Love, from 1832, is a comic opera that conceals a divine tragic kernel in its best-known aria, 'Una furtiva lagrima'. MMMMMMMMMMWHAH! A gorgeous aria, on many people's list of Top Five Tracks to Propose To, alongside 'Long-Haired Lover from Liverpool' by Little Jimmy Osmond. Donizet ti is said to have composed the entire opera in only two weeks – which, if it's true, makes it all the more astonishing. Try it some time. The Royal Opera House used to have an 'oldie but goldie' production of it, which was quite charming in a quaint, country bumpkin sort of way. The only thing which I ever found hard to take about it was the fact that I always seemed to see it with Pavarotti in the role of Nemorino – the guy who gets to sing 'Una furtiva lagrima'. This is meant to be the young, virile lover, but sometimes the sight of Big Luc in a country smock, trying to gambol and skip, strained my limited suspension of disbelief. And in opera, that's saying something.

A full five years and, it would seem, a whole million miles separate *L'Elisir d'amore* by Donizet ti from the next MASSIVE work by Bonkers Berlioz, the *Grande Messe des Morts*. In between, he'd had a strange run-in with Paganini, which I want to tell you all about.

BERLIOZ'S STRANGE RUN-IN WITH PAGANINI (WHICH I WANT TO TELL YOU ALL ABOUT)

Paganini was, by now, a bit of a megastar.

If you remember, apart from a passing reference, when we last really came across Paganini, he was only eleven and both he and his acne had just made their first public appearance. Well, the fiddling had gone well for Mr P. He'd spent virtually all his teens practising and

♬ *Correction –* Lucia di Lammermoor. Lucia di Ilkley Moor *was one of a triptych of operas, only ever sketched out, following a brief stay in Yorkshire, and was, along with its sister operas,* Il Barbiere di Otley *and* The Italian Girl in 'alifax, *never actually finished.*☺

performing and, financially, it had paid off. He did blow a great deal of it on gambling, but, ever since he'd landed the job of violinist to Princess Elise – Napoleon's sister – in Lucca, his pizzicato prowess had led to fame and fortune.

In fact, in our age of manufactured pop and even manufactured classical, it's hard to put into perspective quite how much of a star Paganini was. He had, as I mentioned, toured just Italy for most of his life, only venturing abroad when he was well into his forties. When he did, though, he became the toast of every venue – London, Vienna, Berlin – you name it. And, of course, Paris too. Wherever he went, he was hailed as a truly miraculous player. The now famous legend that he had sold his soul to the devil in return for his playing skills – which really *were* beyond any performer that had gone before – was something which he himself did nothing to disprove. For Paganini, he had nothing to lose from the story – people simply flocked more and more to his concerts to hear the 'devil' playing in person. One critic even swore he had seen a small devil, perched on the fiddler's shoulder during a concert, helping him reach notes beyond the grasp of mere mortals. Some even came to simply try and touch the man himself, to see if he was genuinely human. Whatever the reason they came, Paganini lapped it up and continually raised his ticket fees – occasionally quite simply doubling them.

Over the years, then, Paganini made an absolute fortune from his performing and he spent the last few years of his life wondering quite what to do with it. He'd kicked up a bit of a stink already, trying to open up a gambling house, the 'Casino Paganini', in Paris. He clearly had money to burn. Which is why, when he acquired a beautiful – and, let's not forget it, expensive – viola, he ended up on the doorstep of one Hector Berlioz with a request for a new work. He commissioned the composer – who was, after all, the shock jock of 1830s music, the Damien Hirst of romantics – to provide him with a viola concerto. What Paganini had in mind was something that would allow him to do with the viola what he already did with the violin. Quite why he didn't just write one himself, as he had done till now, is anybody's guess. Maybe he had lost his muse, a little. Whatever. He asked Screaming Lord Berlioz to write the dots for him.

What Berlioz had in mind, however, came out as the 1834 work *Harold en Italie*, which he subtitled *Symphony in G for Viola and Orchestra*. In this piece, the viola was more of a parallel commentator, an ethereal, often melancholic will-o-the-wisp, giving off all manner of molten impressions. It was not quite the 'JEEPERS, this is so BLOODY hard to play it makes me look FANTASTIC for pulling it off' showstopper that Paganini had hoped for. As a result, he threw a luvvie fit, and he refused to play it. In the end, the premiere fell to someone else, a performance which Berlioz himself conducted. Amazingly, Mr P attended the concert. He ended up being so overcome by the work he had rejected, he went on stage at the end, walked over to Berlioz, and knelt down in homage in front of him.

The very next day, Paganini had a message delivered to the French composer's door. It read: 'Beethoven is dead and Berlioz alone can revive him!' Inside the letter was a cheque – for 20,000 francs! WAS PAGANINI LOADED OR WHAT?

Ironically, the strange run-in with Paganini, which I've now told you about, was to prove invaluable to barmy Berlioz. The 20,000 francs made for a much easier time of it while he was writing not only his *Romeo and Juliet*, but also his headbanging, Ozzy Osbourne of a work, the *Grande Messe des Morts.*

ANOTHER FINE MESSE

The Italians call it *Messa per I Defunti*. The Germans *Totenmesse*. But the best version, by far, comes from the silver-tongued French. The Requiem form is almost as much a part of music as it is a part of life and death, and it's obvious, in a way, that someone like Berlioz might, at some point, want to get his hands dirty having a go at it. Of course, Berlioz wouldn't just write a 'Messe des Morts' – how could he? He had to write a *Grande Messe des Morts.*

It is hard to think what kind of mayhem the first audience for the Berlioz Requiem thought they were witness to. Time is not so much a great healer, in this case, but more of a disguiser, a 'brusher under the carpet'. As mad, bad and dangerous to hear as the Requiem is to *us*, now – and that's from a point of view of not just *all* the romantics, under our belt, so to speak, but also, the late romantics, the modernists, the avant-garde, the post-modern ironicists, the *oncle-thom-cöbblicists*, everyone: we've heard it all before – time has misted the perception of just quite how shocking such a work might have been to the Class of **1837**.

It was inspired by the deaths of French soldiers, killed in the French Algerian campaign, and Berlioz really did want to make it monumental – a huge, towering cenotaph of music in tribute to those who had lost their lives. It may have been a work that people might not have liked, but it was certainly a work which they couldn't ignore. It calls for over two hundred voices. Bearing in mind that even a standard symphony chorus – the ones you see at the back of the Albert Hall, huddled round the organ – would only normally ask for around seventy to eighty, you can get some idea of the scale of this work. Indeed, Berlioz himself favoured using around seven to eight hundred singers. Do you want to go back and re-read that line? Yes, I did say Berlioz himself favoured using around seven to eight hundred singers! The orchestra is also massively enlarged – the standard drum section, for example. You can picture in your head the person playing the timpani drums, can't you? Usually he's got three, maybe four, drums in front of him, yes? Often there's only two, even. Well, 'the Composer in White Coats', as he was known, wrote an amazing sixteen kettledrums into his score – sixteen! There were also four separate brass bands, playing at all four corners of the concert hall.

To be fair to Berlioz, it really must have been a tremendous spectacle, and, if he wanted to have the soldiers of the Algerian campaign remembered, then he certainly achieved that not only with the scale, but also the fact, almost in spite of the towering scale, it is still regularly mounted today. He, himself, was very proud of it, too. 'If I were threatened with the destruction of all my works but one,' he once said, 'I would beg for mercy for the *Messe des Morts*.' A beautiful sentiment, spoilt only marginally by the fact that he also chose 'The Birdie Dance', six other records, and a cuckoo clock as his luxury item. His fellow romantic in the opposing camp, Chopin, had a different view on the Requiem, describing it as 'composition by spilling ink on a page'.

Sobering to think that 'modern music' and the shock of the new, as it were, has always been with us. It might be Birtwistle or Berio today, perhaps, but back in 1837 it was Berlioz.

Stand by your beds, now – I'm going to skip four years. But first let me briefly 'mind the gap'.

SPECIALIST SUBJECT 1837–1841: 'YOUR TIME STARTS NOW...'

In order to rid myself of the unbearable guilt of skipping four years, I have put together a series of questions and answers which might prove useful if you were ever to go on *Mastermind*, with 1837–1841 as your specialist subject. Admittedly, it's only a faint possibility, I grant you, but, well, it might be better than 'the novels of Sir Arthur Conan Doyle'. And it sure beats auto-flagellation as a way of coping with guilt. Well, for some. So, if you could bring to mind one of those films where they show the passage of time with the flapping pages of a calendar and superbly crafted montages of music and images, denoting the important events, then that would be useful. Have it in your subconscious as you read the next section. Here goes.

Q. Was Constable alive in 1837?

A. No, and neither was Pushkin now that you mention it, but at least we had got Morse's 'Electric Telegraph', which looked like it was here to stay, and, with any luck, if given 150 years and a prevailing wind, would one day be refined into that joy of joys, the delight that is... mobile phones on trains. Good. Hope so.

Q. Who is on the throne in 1838?

A. 1838 is the year that Queen Vic was crowned. It's also the year the Boers defeated the Zulus at Blood River, with more than a little help from Michael Caine. 'You're only supposed to blow the bloody Boers off!'

Q. What else is 'big' in 1838?

A. Well, ships are 'big', so to speak. Quite literally, too; huge great ocean-going steamers are the 'in' way to travel, and they're getting bigger. AND faster. Not long after the 103-ton *Sirius* docks in New

York, the mighty 1,440-ton *Great Western* clocks in with a time of fifteen days, Bristol to Big Apple. Impressive.

Q. Who was 'in the picture' in 1838?

A. You must be referring to Daguerre, who may or may not have been around to shoot the *Great Western* crossing the finishing line. He was probably too busy presenting his new system, the 'Daguerre-Niépce' photos, to the French 'Académie des Sciences'. Say 'Rocquefort'!

Q. Name one of the bestselling novelists of 1839.

A. OK, you could have Charles Dickens. 1839 saw the release of *Oliver Twist* and *Nicholas Nickleby*. There was also Poe's *The Fall of the House of Usher*, as well as it being the year that Auguste Comte officially christened the emerging social science of 'Sociology', thus single-handedly making it OK for future generations of students to spend three years drinking in the union bar, so long as they popped in to see their tutor on his birthday.

Q. What was the size of Britain's Navy in 1838?

A. Hah, bet you think that's a tough one, don't you? Not a bit of it. Britain had 90 ships, while Russia had 50, France 49 and the fledgling US a very respectable 15.

Q. Who was fighting whom?

A. Good point. The First Opium War had broken out between Britain and China, in fact. Elsewhere, the Dutch and the Belgians tripped to London to sign a treaty – London: very nice, good venue for a treaty, tea- and coffee-making facilities in the rooms, etc – and promised not to be beastly to each other any more. Also, the Boers founded the independent republic of Natal.

Q. Which composer was born in 1839?

A. Mussorgsky. In other worlds, there were also Paul Cézanne and George Cadbury – not two people you normally hear spoken of in the same breath. Being both an art lover and a chocolate lover, I do feel we have to bear them both in mind, though. The man who gave us Cadbury's chocolate. MWAH!♬

♬ *Although, of course, with my name, I do have some allegiances to the makers of Chocolate Cream.*

Q. Who married in 1840?

A. Well, that's rather vague, isn't it? I imagine thousands of people married in 1840 – Enid and Keith Sprogg, for example, of 6, The Sewers, East Grinstead. The nuptials to which I must assume you refer, though, were those of Queen Victoria to a rather dull foreign royal, the Prince of Saxe-Coburg-Gotha. Or, Albert the Square, as he was known to Londoners.

Q. Which great wit and man of fashion died in 1840?

A. Again, rather a vague question, but I presume you are referring to Beau Brummell, although, if you ask me, he didn't exactly go out on a high. Beau Brummell, man of genius wit. But what were his last words? What nugget of ingenious observation did he come up with on his deathbed? I'll tell you. 'I do try,' he said. I do try. Marvellous. Add to that the fact that, when they got his death certificate, they discovered his real name was in fact Bryan, and, well, I think he's ripe for the revisionists.

Q. Who would love to have run out of ham?

A. Now you're just being silly. Napoleon, I guess, is your man. He tried another unsuccessful conspiracy and found himself in the fortress of Ham.

Q. Who's in and who's out in 1840?

A. Your vaguest yet. Let me try and round up. Fenimore Cooper's new one, *The Pathfinder*, is out. Work starts on building the Houses of Parliament, transportation to New South Wales for convicts is stopped. The German romantic painter Caspar David Friedrich dies, but Monet, Renoir and Rodin are born – what a year! – as are Thomas Hardy, Emile Zola and Peter 'Is this my glass?' Tchaikovsky. While we're at it, two new places of interest get on the map. Kew Gardens has its first queue, and Nelson's Column has its first... er... column.

Q. How many people lived in 1841?

A . Wow, now that's a tough one. Not sure I know. Let me tell you what I *do* know. The population of Britain stands at 18.5 million, only narrowly beating America's admittedly fledgling 17 million. Other news: in Britain, Lord Melbourne has resigned and Sir Robert Peel is the new PM – a Whig for a Tory, as Paul Daniels's dresser was once heard to say.

Q. What kept Queen Victoria up at night in 1841?

A. Well, if you're suggesting it was the baby, then I would say you're wrong. I imagine the last person who was going to stay awake at night was Victoria herself. Yes, in 1841, QV gave birth to a bouncing baby boy, Edward. It's said he had his dad's eyes, and his mother's beard.

Q. Name a famous Belgian.

A. Ooh, I love these – thanks for the cue. 1841, and Adolphe Sax makes *his* bid to be included in the game of Ten Famous Belgians when he invents the saxophone.

Q. Name a famous novelist of 1841.

A. Another easy one. Charles Dickens will do again, because he's still knocking 'em dead with, this year, *The Old Curiosity Shop*. While we're talking of old curiosities, let me just add that it was also this year in which Sir Joseph 'Don't call me boring or I'll sue' Whitworth proposed… wait for this… proposed THAT SCREW THREADS SHOULD ALL BE THE SAME! Mmm. The words 'get', 'out' and 'more' need very little rearranging, to be honest. Bring on the music, that's what I say. And what a good year to be around, too, because Rossini is about to break his vow of silence.

A SERIOUS MATER

Good. I'm glad we caught up, because it's very important to know not just *when* things arrived, but also in what context. Could it have been any of those things we've just mentioned that prompted Rossini to come out of musical hiding and spring his first work in years on to an unsuspecting and unready public? Who knows. He'd been working on the piece since 1831 which, in itself, may give the odd clue to what's been keeping him. Remember, this is the man who wrote *The Barber of Seville* in, some say, only thirteen days. For him, spending twelve years is nothing short of phenomenal, and would maybe hint at there being possibly a crisis of inspiration rather than just that he'd decided to sit back and simply enjoy his money and his cooking. You could give him the benefit of the doubt even here, though, especially considering that the two works he did produce following his self-imposed silence were both religious – this year's *Stabat Mater* and then, some twenty-two years after that, the *Petite Messe Solonnelle.* Could it be that he was devoting himself to a greater, somehow more valid, way of working that forced him to write and write and write, until a piece was perfect in the eyes of God? The fly in this argument's ointment is possibly *The Sins of Old Age*, a series of small and light pieces which Rossini dashed off in his later years, and which are no more than pleasant and amusing little favours.

The *Stabat Mater*, though, is something different. It sets the words of the thirteenth-century Franciscan, Jacopone da Todi, describing Mary, the mother of Jesus, grieving at the foot of the cross. It was added to the Roman Catholic liturgy, officially, in 1727 and had been set by an illustrious line of composers over the years, before Rossini had a go: Josquin des Pres, Palestrina, the Scarlattis, Pergolesi, Haydn and Schubert. Maybe this long line of settings, too, added extra pressure on Rossini's need to leave a lasting impression on the *Stabat Mater*?

Its sad subject matter would continue to inspire beautiful music, long after Rossini too: Verdi, Dvořák, Szymanowski and Poulenc – many were attracted to this delicate little verse. By the time he wrote his version, Rossini was back living in Italy – not in his native Pesaro, but in Bologna. He travelled back to supervise the first performance of the *Stabat Mater* at the Salle Herz in Paris and, thankfully for him, it was immediately recognized as a late work of beauty and genius. Some have referred to it as a late opera, but this just seems to make light out of what is one of Rossini's chief virtues – his ability to show the human voice in its best light, even if that usually meant, as it would do for an opera composer, a dramatic light. And so Rossini brought out the drama in the lines of the *Stabat Mater*. I'd say the idea of a mother standing by the cross of her only son is drama enough to justify it. Nip along to hear it in concert, and judge for yourself. In the meantime, let me tell you who else is still around.

NEBUCHADNEZZAR OPUS

1842, then. Who's up, who's down, who's flying around, and who *are* those magnificent men in their flying machines? Well, I'll answer a full 50 per cent of those questions right now.

Chopin's still around, for one. Tragically, despite being only thirty-two, he's got just another seven years left to live. But 1842 finds him in Paris, probably at his creative peak. Even though he really didn't have the ideal constitution for it and was in somewhat dubious health – in fact, in the flighty world of the ultra-romantic Pole, someone had once remarked that the 'only constant thing about him is his cough'. Just last year, 1841, despite all his debilitating nerves and personal turmoil, he'd gone down a storm in Paris, and a follow-up concert in February 1842 was just as good. When I say 'personal turmoil', I mean chiefly the fact that this was the time Chopin was at the height of his affair with the novelist Amandine Aurore Lucie Dupin, Baronne Dedevant, better known as George Sand. At first, he'd resisted her charms – indeed, he'd not immediately recognized any charms at all. 'I did not like her face,' he said. 'There is something off-putting about her.' Maybe it was the fact that she smoked and wore men's clothes in public. Maybe it was her well-known coterie of lovers. Whatever the initial setback, they were now lovers, living separately in Paris but summering together in Nohant, some 300 kilometres south of Paris, in the heart of Indre et Loire.

Although the concert of 1842 was to produce some of Chopin's best ever reviews – 'sheer poetry superbly translated into sound' – it proved to be the penultimate public concert of his life, the last being at the Guildhall in London, just a month before he died. In fact, from here on in for Chopin, the going appears to be pretty much downhill. A split with Dedevant Sand, failing health and somewhat convenient if soulless marriage. But let's look on the bright side, eh?

Actually, what is the bright side? Is there one? Of course there is, but, as so often with composers, it comes in the form of the 'pay now, receive later' standard artist format. In 1842, he was the undisputed bantamweight champion of the romantic piano. Everything's black and white to him, he's the sort of nineteenth-century 'Fat Reg from Pinner' – and, let's face it, he's still writing virtually *nothing* that doesn't have a piano in it. More 'bright side' comes if you look at the facts, too, because, in a career of only thirty years or so, he utterly transforms what the piano can and can't do, both on a technical level – sometimes – and on an emotional one. Add to this the fact that his influence would be felt for at least a good fifty years after he died, and you're talking a premier league player, here.

Berlioz, of course, is still around, big-time. The man who put the mad into 'madrigal' is still very much a contender in Morecambe's Mr Romantic 1842 competition, I think it's fair to say. And if Chopin is the bantamweight of the early romantic movement, then Louis-Hector is certainly one of the heavyweights, pushing orchestral rules to their limits, refusing to be fenced in by old forms and – and this is quite a key thing for Berlioz – managing to get his imagination into his music. In fact, I need to stop here and go into how important this is.

STOP

Good. Now how can I say this better because, throughout history, this becomes more and important. What I mean is, of all the early romantics, Berlioz was one of the best at being able to say, 'Right. I'm imagining a... pair of lovers,' and VOOM! there they are, quite literally AUDIBLE in the music. There's a particular bit from the 'March to the Scaffold' from the *Symphonie Fantastique*, in which he's writing music that depicts a guillotining taking place, and so acute is his symbolic orchestration that you actually hear the decapitated head bobbling into the basket. Gruesomely macabre and very Berlioz, but yet SUPERB romantic craftsmanship. As music progresses through the periods, composers had sought more or less – usually more – realism in their music. Remember Gluck putting thunder into his opera on page 83? Well, it's just a very sophisticated form of that. As time passes, the deepening levels of this musical picture-painting will rock to and fro.

It's a similar concept to when artists paint pictures; if you put it at its crudest, they can either paint EXACTLY what they see, or they can paint something totally abstract. You have a set like the Impressionist painting a sort of half-way house, and then lots of points on the curve, too: Seurat, with his pointillist version, Braque with his cubist outlook – all manner of different takes on 'painting what it is I see'. And so it would be with composers. Some would want you to be brought face to face with an event in their heads, others would want to give you merely a general impression of what it was like and indeed some would just continue to want you to hear simply the music that was in their heads. And it will hopefully *always* be like this.

START

Good. 1842 wasn't all plain sailing, though. Sadly for arts lovers everywhere, a Czech national dance, known as the polka, has come into fashion with the elite circles of high society. Poor darlings, making right pillocks of themselves, skipping around like hermits on their day out. Around the same time as polkas, a paper is published called 'On the Coloured Lights of the Binary Stars'.

So what? I hear you say. Well, let me tell you that it was written and published by one CJ Doppler.

Still so what? I hear you cry. So let me tell you, then, that it was the same paper, and the same Doppler, that isolated the effect known as... the Doppler Effect. What then, hmm?

Right. OK. I see. So what, still. OK, let's move on – nothing to see here.

And so to the 'Nebuchadnezzar Opus', as it were. Not merely or even necessarily the 'magnum' opus, so to speak, but one that was to prove a turning point for a young composer from Busetto, in the Parma district of Italy.

Giuseppe Fortunino Francesco Verdi, to give him his full if slightly worrying name, was born in the small Italian village of Le Roncole, near Busetto. He led a fairly ordinary Italian village life, too, give or take the odd early incident. In Verdi's case, it was that, while serving at the altar at church – as an acolyte, to be precise – the priest had noticed that he was paying too much attention to the sound of the organ, and not enough to his sacramental duties. As a result, he did what any priest worth his salt would have done – he kicked him sharply up the arse, sending him tumbling down the altar steps and leaving him almost comatose at the bottom.♬ Oddly enough, Verdi never really sought a musical opening in the Church – so maybe that Catholic priest did Italian opera the biggest favour possible.

At the age of twenty-three, Verdi might have had even more reason to give up on the whole music thing, too. By then, he'd been to the big city, Milan, to seek his musical fortune, only to be unceremoniously dumped on before he even got into music college: the powers-that-be denied him a place at the conservatoire. 'Lack of piano technique', said one; 'over age', said another: 'insufficiently gifted', said a third. So he slunk back to his native Busetto and got a local job, as Director of the Philharmonic Society. And that's how it could have stayed. A big albeit undeveloped fish in a very small pond. But it didn't.

Back in Busetto, Verdi married. Her name was Margherita, and despite the fact that she was plain – only cheese and tomato – they had two children. Tragically, though, his kids died in infancy, and, just two years later, he lost his wife too. Verdi did what many musicians before him had done – he threw himself into his music.

He grafted hard on the city's music by day, and then on his own by night. He was working on an opera. He had high hopes for it and spent every unallotted moment tweaking a note here or reorchestrating a phrase there. So convinced was he that it was a winner, his magnum opus, that he moved back to Milan, and took his now completed opera with him. It was 1840, and, amazingly enough, for the man rejected by the conservatoire, the most famous opera house in the world, La Scala, Milan, agreed to stage his opera. Verdi was right. The world would sit up and take notice of his opera.

Well, OK, he was partly right. The world would sit up and take notice, only not of this opera. Let me try the title on you, and you tell me when was the last time you saw it in any opera house's forthcoming season brochure:

Oberto, Conto di San Bonifacio

Quite. Says it all, eh? Despite the fact that it maybe didn't achieve its

♬ *OK, any priests reading, I'm using irony here, OK? Or is it litotes? I can never work that baby out.*

place in history, it did, nevertheless, achieve its place in the La Scala season of 1840/41, and to modest success, too. As a result he was commissioned to write another. THIS ONE! THIS ONE would be the magnum opus. This would be one to go down in history. And so he came up with:

Un Giorno di Regno

OK. Wrong again. In fact double wrong, with cheese. Wrong Royale, as it were, because not only would this not go down well in history, it would not go down well in the La Scala season of 1841. Verdi was nearly broken. Look at him – he'd lost his wife and children, he'd given up his safe job in his hometown, he'd had a minor hit with his first opera, and now he'd had a turkey with his second. It was not the start he had hoped for. In fact he was on the point of giving it all up. Indeed, he visited his opera producer, a chap called Merelli, with the express purpose of telling him that he was packing it in. Merelli, however, had other ideas.

He'd been approached by a librettist, Solera, with a 'book', as they say in opera circles, for an opera of the story of Nebuchadnezzar, set in the Jerusalem and Babylon of 568 BC. Ignoring Verdi's protestations, he forced the manuscript into his hands, ushered him out, and locked his door. Verdi spent a few minutes pleading with his colleague from outside, but to no avail. Exasperated, he retired to the nearest coffee house for an espresso.

Over coffee, the libretto fell open. It was at the page where Verdi could read the words 'Va, pensiero, sull'ali dorate' – 'Fly, thought, on wings of gold.' His mind immediately began to wander over the musical possibilities of the words, and he started to think. After a few minutes he put on his coat, flung some coins on the table and rushed home. By the time he got there, virtually the whole of one chorus was written in his head. All he had to do was 'copy it out' of his brain, so to speak. The chorus was 'The Chorus of the Hebrew Slaves': the opera was *Nabucco*. It was to turn Verdi's career, and the path of Italian opera, completely around. Within the year, Italian opera was, once again, King, and Giuseppe Verdi was its most famous composer.

Officially, it's called *Nabucodonosor*. Thank goodness he shortened it to *Nabucco*. But then operas are like that. They're a bit like show dogs – they have a normal name and a ridiculous kennel name. Many operas of which we think we know the title are, in fact, officially called something else. *Cosí fan Tutte*, for example, when displayed in show, goes by the name of *Cosí fan Tutte ossia La Scuola degli Amanti*. Catchy, huh? Beethoven's *Fidelio* won best in breed as *Fidelio, oder eheliche Liebe*. Obviously! Fairly rolls off the average Italian tongue, as rumours used to go about Vivaldi.

Another reason for the success of *Nabucco* might also have been the state of Italy at the time. The Italian nationalists were less than twenty years away from a unified Italy, and the symbolism of *Nabucco*, with its enslaved heroes, was not lost on Verdi's countrymen. 'Va, pensiero' was taken up as a national signature tune in the fight against the Austrian oppressors.

NATION SHALL SING A PIECE UNTO NATION

Alongside Verdi and *Nabucco* in Italy was Glinka and *Russlan and Ludmilla* in Russia. Both of them jam-packed full of great pieces to sing, both of them from 1842, and both of them the early expressions of the seeds of nationalism in their own countries.

Glinka was, as we all are no doubt, an amazing blend of different influences, chance acquaintances and minor quirks of history. Born in Smolensk in 1804, he'd been brought up largely on one of those stunning Russian country estates that you can now only dream of – his uncle even had his own house orchestra. After some lessons in St Petersburg with John Field – yes, John Field the composer: Field had gone there on tour with his then boss, the pianist–composer Clementi, and when Clementi left, Field stayed on. Bit complicated but stay with me – Glinka then, quite consciously, decided that he needed to be able to write 'a great Russian opera'. But before he could do that, he quite simply need to be able to write 'a great opera'. Seems fair. So what did he do? He quite simply took himself off to the home of opera – Italy – and decided to learn from the masters. He got to know Bellini and Donizetti but, more importantly, got to hear operas. Many, many operas. This done, he went to study with a Great Dane. Sorry, my mistake. That should read with the great Dehn: Siegfried Wilhelm Dehn, a very much respected musicologist and theorist. When Dehn thought he was ready, he sent him off with the line 'Go home, and write Russian music', and Glinka duly obliged.

For his first opera, he picked for his subject the invasion of Russia by the Poles in 1613. So a nice light opera, then. This is still very 'Italian' in style, it has to be said, and yet demonstrates lots of the new, up and coming 'nationalism'. For his second opera, though, he adapted a poem by Pushkin, *Russlan and Ludmilla*, and it was this opera that was to be the turning point. It's now looked upon as setting the standard for the new, truly Russian opera style. It also, ironically, was the start of a mini-craze for 'orientalism', incorporating, as it does, authentic oriental themes, and what's known as 'whole tone scales': this is simply a technical, muso way of saying 'sounds a little eerie, with a bit of suspense, and more than a hint of sinister'. (Hope that helps.) Sadly, these days, the showstopping overture to *Russlan and Ludmilla* tends to do precisely that – stop the show. At least, many more people now only ever hear the overture and nothing of the opera. Ah well. As they say in Germany, '*Sie sind zwei menschen, die anlich aussehen, und am gleichen tag geboren sind!*' How true, how true.

All in all, what with Glinka and his first Russian opera, Verdi with his resistance-friendly tunes and even Chopin with his Polish stuff, it's fair to say that the first seeds of musical nationalism have been sown. Now talking of Germany, lock up your daughters, hang on to your hats and do whatever else it is that you do in clichés before something cataclysmic happens.

Whatever you do, do it.

Because...

...Wagner has arrived.

THE WHOLE WAGNER THING, PHENOMENON, BIT. OR WHATEVER

Quite. Quite. I agree. What a fantastic subject – the whole Wagner thing, phenomenon, bit. Or whatever. Absolutely. Couldn't have put it better myself. Nail-on-head-hitting mission accomplished, I think. Because to call Wagner a romantic is not really accurate. You can't just say Wagner was a romantic – I mean, he was. But he was much more than that – he was... well, he was just... Wagner. A one-off. There had been nothing like him before, and there would never be anything like him again. Thank goodness, some might say. But not I. Oh no. I will come right out of the Bayreuth closet and gladly shout, Peter Finch-like, from the windows,

'I'm a Wagnerian, and, as a result, I'm clearly as mad as hell, and I'm not going to take it any more!'

Well, something like that, anyway. What I mean, really, is that I think we need to look into this whole Wagner thing a little bit deeper. So put your horned helmet on – we're going in.

THIS WHOLE WAGNER THING, ONLY A LITTLE BIT DEEPER

Wilhelm Richard Wagner was born in Leipzig in 1813, the product of an affair his mother had with an actor called Ludwig – how ridiculously apt – whom she later married. He had two sisters who were both singers, and was often to be found bunking off his piano practice in favour of trying to sight-read opera scores. If you add in a talent for poetry and a predilection for Beethoven, it's not hard to see how the whole Wagner world took hold.

After an early flop with an orchestral overture, he turned to opera, writing his own words from the start. He became a chorus master when he was twenty, which meant he summered in Lauchstadt, near Leipzig, and wintered in Magdeburg, some 250 kilometres west of Berlin. It was here that he met his wife, Minna, an actress, and they were married in 1836. **Wagner**'s third opera, *Das Liebesverbot – The Love Ban* – was written for his Magdeburg company, but it ended up more or less bankrupting it. Just two years later, the couple sailed to Paris. Yes, I did say sailed to Paris. Don't ask me why, but they did and it was to prove a memorable journey in more ways than one. The boat took a full eight months to get to Paris – I'm still not quite sure how you sail to Paris – and the stormy voyage would provide **Wagner** with not only a deeper knowledge of his insides but also inspiration for his future opera, *The Flying Dutchman* – based on an old sailors' legend. More of that in a moment. **Wagner** was one of those people who thought the world owed him a living. And that's not just me being glib and reactionary, he honestly did. Listen:

> *'I am not like other people... The world owes me what I need. I can't live on a miserable organist's pittance like your master, Bach!'*

See? I imagine it was little moments like that that did a lot to endear him to the people of Dresden.

And that more or less brings us incompletely and utterly up to date with Richard the Lionbreath. It's **1843** and he's just hit the big thirty. A quick look around will maybe get you right back up to date. There's been a revolt in Spain – General Espartero has been ousted. Nothing new there, you might say, except that, in this case, he's been ousted in favour of a thirteen-year-old, which must have been a bit galling to say the least. Imagine it now: 'Ah, hello, Queen Elizabeth? Yes, glad I caught you. I hope it's OK with you, just wanted to check: we've decided to rationalize your post as part of a modernization process. And in your place, we're having Charlotte Church. She's sitting for the stamps as we speak. Would you mind if we borrowed a tiara?' Mmm. Not sure it would go down a storm, really.

Anyway, in Spain, the thirteen-year-old is called Isabella, although, before long, she is officially declared 'of age' and people start to call her

Queen Isabella II. There's been a revolt in New Zealand, too – the Maoris are none too happy about singing 'God Save the Queen'. Seems fair, really – awful dirge. Elsewhere, Washington to Baltimore have just got Morse – presumably Series I. Also, the first nightclub has opened up in Paris, although it is rather perversely entitled 'The English Ball'. What else can I tell you? Well, in a place called Tromso, Norway, they've really started to get into the brand-new pastime called skiing. In the world of science, JP Joule has determined how much work is needed to produce one unit of heat – the 'mechanical equivalent of heat', as it's known – while next door, in literature, Tennyson has just published *Morte d'Arthur*. In fact, taking the 'neighbours' lark a bit further, next door but one, in philosophy, the feminist and radical John Stuart Mill has come up with his latest book, simply entitled *Logic*. But, three doors along, in the music department...

GOING DUTCH, MAN!

Well, in the music department, our hero, Wilhelm Richard Wagner, to give him his full name, is now thirty, as I mentioned. By the time they were thirty, most composers had done lots of their best stuff. In fact, if you take a goodly percentage of them, they'd more or less done it all. I mean, Mozart hadn't long left to live in which to do much more work, anyway, and a large number had already popped their clogs.

Wagner, of course, was Mr Exception that proves the rule. Mr Perverse, if you like. A late developer, as it were – you know the sort, who get that first, whisper-thin, slightly pathetic moustache just before they leave school. Well, I think that's Wagner. True, he'd produced *some* things by now – operas such as *Die Hochzeit*, *Die Feen* and the aforementioned *Das Liebesverbot*, but, well. Just reread that sentence again. Better still, let me help. Here:

> True, he'd produced some things by now – operas such as *Die Hochzeit*, *Die Feen* and the aforementioned *Das Liebesverbot*, but, well.

Exactly. Ever heard of any of them: *Hochzeit*, *Feen* and *Liebesverbot*? Unless they made up the midfield for Borussia Mönchengladbach in the '70s, then I imagine the answer is probably no. Which tells you a lot about what calibre of work he'd produced up till now. To be fair, he *has* yet to realize his potential. But, equally, to be fair, not everyone around him is agreed that he even *has* potential. After all, he'd been expelled from Leipzig's Thomasschule, and then spent most of the short time before he left university – *early*, I might add – gambling, drinking and womanising. (What you might call, these days, a model student, but, in those days, a disgrace.) Also, his formal musical training amounted to no more than six months with the Cantor at Leipzig Cathedral. When he finally *got* a job, the one at the Magdeburg Opera House, when he was twenty-two, his first ever production – his own opera, of course – had succeeded in bankrupting the place, and he'd been forced to flee the town, along with his wife Minna, and head for Riga, in what was then Russian Poland. So, a genius-in-waiting or an unpleasant megalomaniac with 'small-man' syndrome? (He was only 5 foot 5 inches, by the way.) Well, as the Geordie voice on Channel 4 might say, 'You decide!' Whatever the case, one thing was for certain. All of a sudden, quicker than you could say 'I love me, who do you love?', Wagner's luck was about to change.

His new opera, *Rienzi*, was staged in Dresden, and it was a huge success. Messrs *Hochzeit*, *Feen* and *Liebesverbot* were well and truly last year's men. *Rienzi* was a hit and, as they say in Internet world, a hit is a hit is a hit. Interestingly enough, the music of *Rienzi* is still very much *early* Wagner, even at thirty. It's not his mature style, and you might even say it was pretty much in the style of the current vogue composer, Meyerbeer. Of course, if you did say that, it might be best to say it out of earshot of Tricky Dicky. As far as he's concerned, he's got a hit on his hands and it's all his own work – what I did in the summer holidays by W. R. Wagner, aged thirty and three-quarters.

So, when Wagner was asked to follow it up, rather than come up with more of the same, he decided that it was time to unleash something completely different on the unsuspecting Dresdonians. After all, they'd loved *Rienzi*, they would love his next one. All he had to do was to get down on paper the amazing sound-world that was in his head, and – VOOM – he'd have another hit on his hands. He cast his mind back, just a few years, to 1839, when he'd had that particularly unpleasant, and rather gut-wrenching, sea voyage. Er, to Paris. Three times, his ship had almost gone to the bottom of the ocean in much the same way as the contents of his stomach. The other abiding memory of the trip, though, was a tale he had heard, the story of the wandering Jew of the ocean, who had boasted that he could sail round the Cape of Good Hope in all conditions, and had been sentenced to sail the seas for all eternity. Bit harsh, if you ask me, but still. The conditions of his sentence allowed for him to put into port just once every seven years – presumably to stock up on sickbags – and his plight would be over only if he could find a love that would be true to him till death. What a totally ridiculous story, thought Wagner, and therefore absolutely *perfect* for an opera. Before long, he had the libretto written. Oddly enough, he offered it to the Paris Opera, hoping for a commission to finish it off, music and all. Instead, they gave him 500 francs for the story, and bade him good day. In his financial position, he wasn't going to turn it down, so he took the money and ran back to Dresden. There, he was able to use his earnings to give him time to finish the music. And he did.

His brand-new opera – still a bit beholden to Meyerbeer but nevertheless with many of the remarkable soundworlds that would make his later work the stuff of legend – was complete. It was finished. It was concluded. It *was*... accomplished. It *was*...

...a flop.

A big, flaccid, floundering flop.

It was also called *The Flying Dutchman* or, in his native German, *Der Fliegende Holländer*. And they hated it. Couldn't wait to get out of the opera house. Positively ran to hills to avoid it. Obviously, the world was not yet ready for the maturing Wagner.

To be fair to the audience – and, indeed, to all first-night audiences at major music events in history – can you imagine being in their shoes? Put yourself there. It's 1843, you're in Dresden. You've just heard Richard Wagner's first semi-mature work. Previously, the most shocking thing anyone would have ever heard up to that point was probably, what? Well, maybe the *Symphonie Fantastique* by Berlioz, or even *Les Huguenots* by Meyerbeer? And, to be fair, only a lucky few hundred have heard those, too, so far – you can't exactly download the MP3 of Meyerbeer's *Robert le Diable* off the Internet. So what do you do after the first night of something like *Der Fliegende Holländer*? What DO you DO?

You're probably speechless. I mean, who could have dreamt up such a series of sounds? Lots of it didn't quite make sense to you. And the people around you appear to be speechless, too, so it can't be just you. So what do you do? It's ended. And you're speechless. The curtain has come down. In less than a moment, it will come back up again. What DO you do? Do you stay silent? Do you dare… clap that first clap? Well, you don't really even like doing that when it's an opera you absolutely love, so you definitely won't do that. You don't know what to do. Do you? No!

So?

So, you boo like crazy, more out of discomfort than anything else, and because you're pretty sure no one around you liked it either. Then you reach into your pocket for that lump of rotting artichoke that you just happened to bring for your interval snack. Ah well. Too bad, Wagner, you think as you lob. Ooh, great, got him right in the small of the back, too. Good shot. Made the bugger fall flat on his arse. Fantastic.

Still, Wagner's day will come. In fact, in about, let's see, just two pages' time, give or take a concerto. Which gives me the perfect excuse to skip a couple of years and come up in **1845**. Let me fill in the news gaps.

IT'S 1845: HERE IS THE NEWS

Good evening, this is the last two years' news in brief, and I'm John Suchet reading it. The Anglo-Sikh war has now begun, which is a big nuisance to the civil servants back home in Blighty, who were already having a spot of trouble with the rather tedious and aforementioned Maori rising.♬ Interesting things are afoot in the US,

♬ *Sounds a little odd, really: 'Hello, my name is Stephen. I'm an Aquarius, really, but I do have Maori rising.'*

too. Texas and Florida have come into the family of states, and – possibly more importantly – the rules of baseball have been codified by the quaintly named Knickerbocker Baseball Club. Presumably, somewhere in there are the rules that (a) no game shall take less than three weeks, (b) you must all eat junk food, and (c) you must learn to love the electric organ. As far as more *handlebar-moustache* sporting events are concerned, so to speak, the Oxford and Cambridge University Boat Race has transferred allegiances: not from BBC to ITV but from Henley to Putney as a venue. It's possible that one or more members of the teams might have been taken with the new book of this year, *The Condition of the Working Classes*, which Friedrich Engels published in Leipzig. In fact, it had been only last year that Engels had met Karl Marx in Paris. History has it that they found they agreed on virtually everything except who would pay for the cappuccinos. Other recent books on the shelves included *Vingt Ans Après*, the sequel to *Les Trois Mousquetaires* by Dumas, as well as a little something called *Carmen* by Prosper Mérimée. The master of French neo-classicism, Ingres, has just exhibited his *Portrait of the Countess Haussonville* and JT Huvé had finished *La Madeleine* in Paris.

That was the world in 1845. Now the weather, and light wars are expected around Lahore next year, with the odd blustery annexation out towards New Mexico. The rest of the world will be sunny with showery intervals.

THE NAME'S WAGNER... RICHARD WAGNER!

As one of my favourite people, Oscar Wilde, once said, 'I like his music better than anybody's.' Absolutely. I wholeheartedly concur. OK, if I'm to be honest and decent and true, then what he actually said, in *The Picture of Dorian Gray*, was, to be precise:

> *'I like his music better than anybody's. It is so loud that one can talk the whole time without people hearing what one says. That is a great advantage.'*

OK, well, yes. He was being facetious. But, regardless, Wagner really is one of my favourite geniuses. Before we refocus on him, though, what's happening with his fellow luvvies, the composers of the day? Who's still around? Well, Chopin, Berlioz and Liszt are still the big noises. Mendelssohn is still alive, though, as are Verdi, Schumann, Gounod, Offenbach, Suppe... lots of them really. The Classical Music First 11 is fielding an odd, some would say illegal, 4/2/20-odd formation, and the big four, attacking up front, are Frederick, Hector, Franz and new boy Richard. Of that attacking front four, it is, to be fair, Wagner who is going to become top goalscorer, in terms of history, and eventually command the biggest following, or claim the biggest influence.

In a way, Wagner basically carried out a root and branch overhaul of music. Gone were the rules. Gone was the form book, the structure. Wagner, and indeed many of the romantics, but Wagner most of all – to be fair – said simply, 'Why should we?' and then did his own thing. As a child, he had loved Beethoven, and used to spend hours and hours copying out the scores and making arrangements of his music. He also loved the operas of Mozart – the first true German opera composer, he called him – and, if you add to this as healthy respect for the composer of the day, Meyerbeer, well, you can see how it all came about, in a sense. Throw in the fact that, as we know, he was only 5 feet 5 inches tall, and everything becomes crystal clear. The equation would read:

$$\frac{\mathbf{pB \times kB + lM(o)}}{\mathbf{-h}} = \mathbf{WO}$$

That's **'Passion for Beethoven x knowledge of Beethoven + love of Mozart opera, all over lack of height = Wagner operas'**. Obviously. Now open your text books at page 182 and work quietly through chapters 7 and 8, while I go off to the staff common room.

Wagner wanted to make a *new* form – not just music, not just opera, but a real living, breathing, organic new form. In Wagner's new form, the music and the plot would be inextricably linked – one couldn't move independently of the other, both were of equal importance. He called it 'music drama', a harking back to the *dramma per musica* of the Renaissance. They weren't just operas, though, to him – they were different. The music had to grow out of the drama – and the drama could advance only with the help of the music. So, no, you couldn't simply stop, every now and again, and 'stand and deliver' a pretty aria, for the sake of having an 'extractable' song which people could sing in recitals. His music would build and build, taking its cue from the story – and, as we know, he could write his own librettos too. Well, who else would know how to write librettos exactly how he wanted them? Who else would *get it*, as it were? But, if the music was going to be more or less continuous, how would he keep the audiences involved? He did want them to be able to at least keep up, but if the music was all just constantly new and unheard, page after page, how could they? How would they get what was going on, if there was no stopping, and everything flowed from what had come before? And more importantly,

WHERE WOULD THEY COUGH?

LEIT MUSIC

The way he got round it was this. He kept writing what he called 'leitmotiv' – short, snappy(-ish) tunes that denoted either characters or moods or general themes. These would crop up, whenever he needed to get his point across, often over and over again, and sometimes long after they had been first heard. In fact, there is a great quote from the conductor, Sir Thomas Rentagob Beecham, which comes from the time he was taking an opera orchestra through its Wagnerian paces:

> *'We've been rehearsing [this opera] for two hours, now, and we're still playing the same bloody tune!'*

What a wag he was. But also, imagine you are not stopping a piece of music for two, maybe three hours even. After a while, you begin to lose any sense of what key you are in, because Wagner was always flitting around, shifting seamlessly between different keys. It must have been a whole new world for people, hugely unsettling. And that's not to mention the staying power you needed to simply sit through the opera – sorry, music drama – in the first place. In fact, while we're in the mood for great quotes, one of the other best quotes in all music concerns this aspect of Wagner operas. It's got to be one of my all-time favourite Wagner quotes after Woody Allen's 'I can't listen to that much Wagner. I start getting the urge to conquer Poland.' It is:

> *'A Wagner opera is where it starts at 6 o'clock.*
> *After two hours you look at your watch and it says 6.20.'*

True, it's not for everyone, the five-hour-long works, with intervals which, honestly, last as long as some of his rivals' entire operas.

And the reason we pulled in in 1845 was because he was about to let it all hang out for the first time. October the 19th, 1845, was when he unveiled his first all-singing, all-dancing, *true* music drama. It went by the fantastic kennel name of:

Tannhäuser and the Singing Contest on the Wartburg

...or simply *Tannhäuser*, for short. So, you see: despite the fact that he might have been getting everything else right, he was hopeless at titles. I mean, *Tannhäuser and the Singing Contest on the Wartburg*. Reminds me of our old family holidays – we had a Wartburg. Yes. Never had a singing contest on it, though, as far as I can remember. Had an aerial that you had to pull up by hand, and those funny ventilator slats at the back. Made an awful noise, it did. Loved it, though. Sorry. I'm off with the fairies.

As I said, they're not for everyone the humungously long operas of Wagner, and this may account for the popularity of this early masterpiece, *Tannhäuser*, which nowhere near tops the scale when it comes to length, coming in at a mere four days, eighteen hours. It also comes complete with one of the best overtures in opera, a storming and rounded piece of work which manages to warn the listener about most of the tunes that are going to come up in the opera. As a result, it's become one of the most played opera overtures not only of Wagner's personal output, but of all opera.

Now, if you don't mind – or, indeed, if you do – I'm going to move on to the period of 1848/49/50, which means skipping some five or so years – or one whole Wagner opera length, if you like.

ISN'T IT ROMANTIC?

OK, let me take you right to the edge, now. Imagine it's 1849. The next year, 1850, is the year, according to the music books – and you will note I don't include *this* book in that august number – that music became true ROMANTIC and not just EARLY ROMANTIC. Or, as some like to call it, HIGH Romantic, which I presume means Romantic but they still use incense and Latin. 1850 is the year when we are allowed to think of music as *really, fully fledged* Romantic. So, in 1849, we're right on the edge. Officially, we're still *early* Romantic period, but only just. If someone gave us a leg up and we could see over the wall, you'd see the High Romantic garden in all its lush glory. But what was it that tipped everything over the edge, as it were, into fully formed, card-carrying Romanticism? Well, partly it was a case of things just working themselves through – people will always take a movement to its limit, before someone presses the hooter and it's on to the next big thing. But more importantly, if you take romanticism as being a by-product of music + world events – remember Beethoven: half man, half real-life revolutionary – well, then it becomes clear that revolution is the fuel of the romantics. Ever since *Eroica*, you haven't been able to have one without the other. So what was the main thing that tipped the early romantics over the edge, into becoming out-and-out high romantics?

Well, more than anything, it was the events of last year.

RICHARD, THE GREAT, AND VIV THE REVOLUTION

1848 was THE year for revolution, more than any other year had been in recent history. In Paris, Louis Philippe had abdicated and the French National Assembly had elected the recently escaped Louis Napoleon as President of the French Republic. In Vienna, Prince Metternich resigned during the first uprising, then, during a second, Emperor Ferdinand I decides to get out too, while the going is good, and nips to Innsbruck for a spot of skiing. A further, third uprising sees him abdicating fully in favour of his nephew, Franz Joseph. In Rome, Count Rossi, the papal premiere, is assassinated and Pope Pius gets out, sharpish. It's happening all over, too. Paris, Vienna, Berlin, Milan, Parma, Prague, the Isle of Sheppey☺, Rome – all of them undergoing a massive period of ***Revolution***, with a capital R. Er, and in bold. And italics. And underlined. I think I've made my point.

Come **1849**, and Wagner himself is caught up in it all, too. He starts giving hardline, radical speeches, in support of the rebels, and even selling revolutionary pamphlets on the street. Can you imagine that? Bumping into Wagner on the street, trying to sell you a magazine?

> 'RW: Guten tag, Guv'nor. Buy a Groß Issue?
> Pleb: Sorry?
> RW: Go on, buy a Groß Issue, support the keinen Haus mensch...
> ...er, please?
> Pleb: Oh, I, er, I already bought one, Wagner, honest. It's...at home.
> RW (tuts): Er, well, wass about du, squire? Buy a Groß Issue?
> Come on, Groß Issue, who'll take my last eins?

What a strange concept. Anyway, as a result, when the revolt in Wagner's bit of the world, Dresden, eventually comes to nothing, Wagner is forced to flee to Zurich to escape prosecution. In fact, he's forced to stay in Zurich for thirteen years, until the heat dies down. Thirteen years! That must have been some heat. It was left to friends and champions, like Liszt, to keep Wagner heard in his native land. That's 1849's amazing turn of events. What about 1850, hmm?

EVERYTHING YOU EVER WANTED TO KNOW ABOUT CLASSICAL MUSIC BUT WERE AFRAID TO ASK, LIKE: 'WHAT ABOUT 1850, HMM?'

So. **1850**. Right, well, let's see, Chopin has been dead for a year, Mendelssohn for two years, and even Edgar Allen Poe has finally found out whether death puts on a red masque or not. In England, William Wordsworth has shuffled off, too, and is replaced as Poet Laureate by Alfred, Lord Tennyson. California is the newest recruit to the American state roster – not surprising after the Gold Rush of a couple of years back – and, over in China, the Taiping rebellion is causing all sorts of trouble, with Hun Hiu-tsuen proclaiming himself Emperor.

Actually, what a jolly good wheeze – proclaiming yourself Emperor, I mean. Great idea. In fact, I might try it now. Let's see:

'I hereby proclaim myself Emperor of the United Kingdom, and of all its colonies, including all of Norfolk, of course, and not forgetting the Grand Isle of Sheppey.'

Mmm.

Well.

I don't feel any different.

Wonder if it's worked. I might be Emperor now, for all I know. I'll see if I can annex a small country, maybe, or – an even better test – see if I can't get a cabbie to take me south of the river.

JAKE AND ELWOOD. AND RICHARD

Back to 1850. Around the same time that Turgenev produces his play, *A Month in the Country*, Wagner is still enjoying the second of his thirteen years of enforced exile in the mountains. But he hasn't stopped writing. Of course not. This is a man who, to borrow from the Blues Brothers, is on a mission from God. Or, as he himself put it:

> *'I am being used as the instrument for something higher than my own being warrants… I am in the hands of the immortal genius that I serve for the span of my life and that intends me to complete what only I can achieve.'*

Mmm. I've got to say, I think the Blues Brothers' line is a little snappier.

But that's not the point in 1850. The point, in 1850, is that Richard 'Don't call me Lindsay!' Wagner comes up with his best work yet – his first TRUE masterpiece, as some would have it. It is, of course, an opera. Sorry, a 'music drama'. But this opera has no overture. Instead, it has a prelude. It has leitmotivs coming out of its ears. It is more seamless, more perfect than any of his other attempts so far.

It's fan – bloody – tastic!

But who would conduct it? In Germany, I mean. Let's face it, the world premiere of Wagner's new opera wouldn't create quite as much of a stir anywhere else really – it has to be Germany. But who would be brave enough to stage the work of a self-confessed revolutionary, wanted by the authorities for crimes against the state?

Well, step forward good old Franz Liszt. Liszt has been making people sit up and take notice with his music-making in Weimar. In fact, both he and Weimar are, as a result, the talk of the country. His uncompromising commitment to good music has brought it an international reputation – a bit like Sir Simon Rattle and Birmingham in the 1980s. And where better to premiere the work of the revolutionary exile, Wagner? (That's Weimar, I mean, not Birmingham.) And the work that had them all worked up?

Lohengrin. Or to give it its full kennel name:

'Lohengrin, the Holy Grail and the legendary Knights of Hemel Hempsted, go off for a long weekend orienteering in the country' ☺

OK, so I'm lying about the full title. So shoot me. Anyway, best get to 1851. I've such a lot to tell you.

WOMEN ARE LIARS

1851. Quick rain check on the population of various parts of the world as they stand in 1851. Britain is currently on around 20 million, America an amazing 23, France 33, Germany 34, but in first place, with a whopping 430 million, the winner is China. Well done, China. Come on down!

And what news to impart? Well, big news really. Cuba has just declared its independence, France has a new constitution following a coup by Louis Napoleon, and Britain? Well, the first double-decker buses appear. OK, not exactly *huge* news for Britain, but still. Things are a little quiet.

In the US, the brand-new *New York Times* carries an ad for the equally brand-new, first-ever, continuous stitch sewing machine, freshly patented by one Isaac Singer, while, over in Paris, photographic pioneer Louis Daguerre keels over, on his own doorstep, and dies. So – he not only invented the first photographs, he also pioneered the mat finish.

The English art cognoscenti are also mourning the death of one of their finest painters, JMW Turner. The big read this year is Herman Melville's *Moby Dick*, and the brand-new modern building for everyone to complain about is William Cubitt's King's Cross train station. Although platform 9¾ had yet to be added. But in the world of music, Verdi has something up his sleeve. His green sleeve, you might say.

Imagine you're there.

Where?

There. In Venice. At the Teatro La Fenice.

Let's say... you're in the orchestra. Yes, that's it. You're in the orchestra. You've been to three dress rehearsals so far and, every time you get to a certain part of the opera, you hit a blank page. And I mean literally. Where there should be an aria, there's a blank page. Bloody odd. Whenever you get to it, everyone looks up at the conductor, questioningly. The conductor – who is also the composer – says something like, 'Oh... we'll... fill that bit in later.' Bloody odd. It happens again. And again. In fact, every time you get to that particular bit. How dashed, decidedly, brow-beatingly, breathtakingly, bloody odd! Until, that is, the very last dress rehearsal, which is on the day of the opening night. Only then, does Verdi – our conductor/composer – stump up the missing aria.

Why? Well, it turns out Verdi knew he was on to a winner. In fact, so convinced was he that he was on to a winning, hit tune, that he wanted to make sure it stayed under wraps until the opening night, for fear of some unscrupulous composer stealing it. And he was right, too. By that I don't mean someone stole it – I mean he *did* have a hit tune on his hands. It is usually translated as 'Women are fickle', but I do remember one amazing production at ENO, by Dr Jonathan Miller, which had it translated as 'Women are liars', which I thought was certainly giving it some. His opera, *Rigoletto*, opened that night, complete with the hit tune he had kept from even his own orchestra until the same day – 'La donna è mobile'.

And you've got to admit – corking tune. You could see why he'd want to protect it. It's one of those that, once you've heard it, you can't get it out of your head. And the words are so good too.

'Women are liars....tum tum tum teedle tum......dum dum dum, deedle dum....'

EIGHT MINUTES TO SEVEN

One year on from *Rigoletto*, and, my, what a lot has happened. Louis Napoleon is now more or less a king – or at least has given himself the powers of a monarch, in much the same way I gave myself the powers of an Emperor, earlier. Got to be honest, it hasn't changed me. I still eat in the staff canteen, park in the staff car park – everything. Louis N, however, is still calling himself President. Again, much like me – I don't make a big thing of insisting everyone calls me Emperor. Obviously, if they *do*, I do tip more. Along some of the same lines, the Iron Duke has died at the grand old age of eighty-four, living just long enough to witness the very first England Cricket Eleven. Presumably, that means he lived long enough to see the very first England Cricket Eleven Batting Collapse, too. Charles Dickens seems able to write no wrong, so to speak, and the blockbusters keep on coming – this year, it's *Bleak House*, which is competing for shelf space alongside Harriet Beecher Stowe's *Uncle Tom's Cabin*. Artistically speaking, William Holman Hunt's *The Light of the World* and Millais's *Ophelia* are probably the most important works. As regards 'the music' in 1852, the big noise is still Richard Wagner.

In **1852**, Wagner was still in exile in Zurich. Although Liszt had kindly premiered *Lohengrin* in Weimar, Richard was, as he himself used to say, still one of the few Germans not to have seen it. And yet it had made him the most famous composer in his own land. You can see why, putting all this together, he might one day have the desire to build his own opera house, can't you? That would solve the problem of not being able to mount your own work.

RW is, however, by no means wasting his time out there in the land of cows and chocolate. He is hard at work on his grandest project yet – well, to be honest, would you expect me to say anything else? I mean, I can hardly imagine myself writing the line 'He had decided to tone things down a bit, go smaller-scale, maybe only write in his spare time when he wasn't committing to his love of insurance underwriting!' No. Richard was clearly one of life's 'bigger, better, grander' people, and this next idea is not just an opera, but a huge CYCLE of operas. Four, in fact, which would form one huge opera-event, and which were going to tower over all opera before or since, from the very moment they were first heard. Wagner gave his project the title *The Ring of the Nibelung*, and it was conceived in much the same way as the *Star Wars* films were. First of all, he wrote the words – the libretto – to something that he called 'Siegfried's Death'. Siegfried is the hero – so, if it helps, picture him as the nineteenth-century Luke Skywalker. He was then about to set out on the music to go with his words when he thought that, in fact, he really should explain the story that led up to it. So he wrote the words to the 'prequel', as it were, which he called 'The Young Siegfried' – a sort of 'Siegfried, the Phantom Menace', if you like. Then, he wrote the words to another prequel to that – 'The Valkyrie' – and then yet another prequel – 'The Rhine Gold'. Wow – one book and three prequels. So you see: *Star Wars*, then *Star Wars – the Phantom Menace*, then *Star Wars – Attack of the Clones*, etc – it was all more or less done by Wagner some 150 years earlier.

Finally, after all that writing of just the words, he sat down and set about writing the music to it all. And by 1853, he had finished the first two parts: 'Siegfried's Death', which he'd now changed to *Twilight of the Gods*, and the first prequel, 'Young Siegfried', which he was now calling *Siegfried*. Phew. Hope you're understanding all this. If you are, could you by any chance explain it to me, because I haven't a bloody clue.

Of course, he wouldn't finish all the music until 1874, so you get some idea of quite how mammoth an undertaking this all was. In their finished form, they take a full four nights to perform, a full fifteen hours of opera. If you ever happen to walk past an opera house and see people entering in full dickie-bows and DJs at 3.30 in the afternoon, you can probably bet that either (a) they are students, on their way home, lost and pissed from the night before's May Ball, or (b) *The Ring* is on.

The Ring is definitely an acquired taste, but nevertheless it is one which can be as hugely rewarding to the inspiration as it is challenging to the bladder. Lots of it is utterly GORGEOUS music, music you can quite honestly get lost in. That having been said, not everyone agrees. It's known that Rossini wasn't a fan. Neither was Friedrich Nietzsche.

'Is Wagner a human being at all?' he wrote. 'Is he not rather a disease? He contaminates everything he touches – he has made music sick. I postulate this viewpoint: Wagner's art is diseased.' Don't hold back, Fred.

Let me move on now, not even one year, but to just January and March of **1853**. I only mention it because it will help focus on the two dominant styles prevailing in music, and indeed opera, around this time.

JANUARY 19TH AND MARCH 6TH 1853

The dates are, in fact, the first days on which the opera-going publics of Rome and Venice, respectively, were to hear the new works by Verdi – *Trov* and *Trav*. Or *Il Trovatore* and *La Traviata*, to be more precise. And why is this important, apart from the fact that they are both stonking operas, still performed every five minutes, today? Well, it's important because when you put these two operas up against the two operas that we were discussing above – *Götterdämmerung* (*Twilight of the Gods*) and *Siegfried* – then you have the basic gist of the two big schools of romantic music going on at this time: Italian and German.

In the bold corner, there's Wagner, obviously, who, despite his unique, one-off individualism, is straight from the German tradition: his operas are logical extensions – well, logical in Wagner's brain, at least – of the legacy of Beethoven and Weber and the current legacy of Meyerbeer.

In the italic corner, there's Verdi. He's directly continuing the line of Bellini and Donizet ti, and all their 'bel canto' Italianate characteristics.

Wagner wants to advance his art form.
Verdi is, ostensibly, a crowd pleaser.
Wagner wants the heights.
Verdi wants the hits.
Wagner deals with Gods on horseback.
Verdi deals in bums on seats.
T*o*g*e*t*her*, t*hey* a*r*e *ro*m*a*nt*ic* *o*p*e*r*a* i*n* 1*8*5*3*.

But guess who is said to be about to put in an appearance, some twenty-six years after he'd died? If you guessed Beethoven, then award yourself ten points and a pair of glasses.

BRAHMS AND 'THE MAN'

The year I'm talking about, when the late Ludwig is said to have put in an appearance, is **1858**, just some five years after *Trov* and *Trav*. To be fair, the person I'm on about is not Loud Wig, back from the dead. This guy is a whole different kettle of fish, altogether – different hang-ups, different style – later on, certainly – and different notes, generally. The man in question was said, in his youth, to have played piano in pubs and brothels to earn a living, and didn't actually start composing until pretty late on in life. He also kept a bronze bust of Chancellor Bismarck in the room where he did all his writing, as a constant reminder of his belief in a dominant Germany. And who was this rather corpulent composer, rarely seen without a cigar in his mouth, who had a full-on white beard and was said by many to have written 'Beethoven's Tenth'? Step forward Johannes Brahms, spinster of this parish.

But before the connection from Brahms to Van 'The Man' – Herr Beethoven, that is – let me bring us up to date a little.

There is – obviously: goes without saying – war a-plenty. Always is. The Anglo-Chinese is just coming to an end, but the Indian Mutiny has just started and the Taiping Rebellion has been put down (all that fuss over a brooch). Garibaldi has founded the Italian National Association, just last year, in Italy, while, in Britain, Lord Derby is now PM. On a more diurnal level, shall we say, the *Daily Telegraph* has been founded and Florence Nightingale has had her fifteen minutes of fame in the Crimea. Further afield, Livingstone comes across a simply breathtaking set of falls, on his exploration of the Zambezi river. It's in some of the most unspoilt and raw country you could imagine: it's exciting, it's breathtaking, it's deafening in its ferocity and... well, apparently, for Livingstone, it brings to mind a thirty-nine-year-old dame-like, stern-faced monarch with a bit of a Mona Lisa smile. So. He calls it Victoria Falls. Not Amazing Falls, or Ferocious Falls, or 'Jeepers, will you look at that' Falls. No. He calls it Victoria Falls. Doesn't seem right, somehow, does it?

Elsewhere, in the world of books, while Livingstone has been away, the past few years have seen some very fine additions to the local libraries: Flaubert's *Madame Bovary*, a couple of years ago, Baudelaire's scandalous *Les Fleurs du Mal* – 'The Flowers of Evil' – and Trollope's *Barchester Towers.* There are exciting developments in other areas, too: the world of art had just gained *La Source*, a painting by Ingres; the world of naughty substances has just witnessed the first extraction of pure cocaine; and, finally, the world of 'people named after bells' gained its first, and possibly only, member – the then Director of Public Works in London, one Sir Benjamin Hall. It will eventually sit up in St Stephen's Tower, and be known as Big Ben. Very cute way to go down in history, isn't it? As a bell. Not as 'the one who led thousands of people to their deaths' or 'the guy who first contracted that rather nasty skin disease'. But 'the man who gave his name to the bong you hear on *News at Ten* and at New Year'. So remember to drop it in, if you ever find yourself wading through tourists outside the Houses of Parliament and the clock bongs the hour: something like 'Ah, good old Sir Benjamin Hall, striking away in St Stephen's Tower.' Funny to think that this was all going on around the same time as a shy, fourteen-year-old girl, Bernadette Soubirous, claimed to have seen an apparition of the Virgin Mary in the southern French town of Lourdes. Big Ben and Lourdes, you see. Never knew they were connected, did you?

Back to Brahms, though, and well, to put it diplomatically, I think you could say he is another of the what's termed 'late developers' in the world of composing. The proper form for a composer, as you probably know, is to have your best work done in your teens, then it's syphilis at twenty and dead by twenty-seven, thank you very much. Well, it wasn't to be the way for Brahms.

Brahms is, how shall I put it, well... scared, really. He's quite a big fan of Beethoven, you see, and, for a long time, he feels very much in 'The Man's' shadow. In fact, on a bad day, he couldn't quite see the point of trying, almost, after what Beethoven had achieved. As a result, he's staving off writing his first symphony – not a bad idea, to be fair, considering the critics were always going to call it Beethoven's Tenth – and generally, well, filibustering. In 1858, though, he overcomes his nerves in order to produce his first piano concerto, in D minor. And, to be fair, he needn't have worried. It is still, today, seen as one of the chief weapons in the concert pianist's armoury – along with surprise, fear and an almost fanatical devotion to the Pope (sorry, best not get into that) – although, admittedly, at its premiere it did not go down too well. In fact, come to think of it, the *PC No 1* wasn't regarded very highly in his lifetime, at all. And now that I think of it, it only came into the mainstream concert pianist repertoire during the twentieth century. So, to be fair, he did really have something to worry about. So, sorry, Brahms. You were right to fret.

Still.

I like it.

Anyhow, Brahms's *PC No 1* comes out around the same time as the latest surge of creative juices from Mad Hector's house. Sorry, let me rephrase that. Berlioz writes another masterpiece in the same year. Yes, he's still around, still bonkers, and still knocking 'em asleep with his EPic stuff. (That's EPic with a capital EP.)

1858 brings forth the EPic (with a capital EP) OPera (with a capital OP):

Les Troyens

How's that for an Epic typeface? These days, it's Wagner who has gone down in the history books as the man who simply couldn't put his pen down, and, therefore, left the world HUGE long operas that you can only watch in their entirety if you have a thermos, some glucose tablets and a bladder of steel. But Berlioz did it too, you see, and long before Brad Pitt in a skirt. In fact, with *Les Troyens*, it's not just a case of it being ridiculously long – four and a half hours, when you count nipping up to the crush bar for a smoked salmon sarnie and an overpriced mini-bottle of fake champagne: with *Les Troyens*, it's also a case of it being just too big.

Les Troyens translates, as you may have guessed, as *The Trojans*. Sorry, let me do that title justice, first.

Good. Feel better for that.

Anyway, about the size thing. Well, let's dig a little deeper, here. Berlioz based *The Trojans* on *The Aeneid*, by Virgil, no small tome itself, as any schoolboy will tell you.♬ So Berlioz decided to split his opera into two – jolly decent of him – namely *La Prise de Troie* and *Les Troyens à Carthage*. All well and good so far. Problem is, he made them both disproportionately long, a problem that could be got round if it was the only issue. Thing is, he also made the opera one of the most expensive to produce – well, think of Brad Pitt and all those extras! Not to mention nobody makes a good wooden horse, these days.

As a result, Berlioz never saw the whole thing performed in his lifetime, and, even today, you're likely to fare little better. Very few opera companies would have the budget to be able to take on such a huge project as *The Trojans*, and live to tell the tale. Having said that, Opera North did it a few years ago, I think, and they are still very healthy, thank you very much, so it can obviously be done. And, indeed, although I've never actually seen it, I'm told the rewards are great, with much of it being very beautiful – the 'Nuit d'ivresse' duet, for example. For now, then, maybe nip off and buy yourself a good 'highlights' CD and just imagine what it might have been like to be there. At a performance, I mean. Not... inside the wooden horse, nose pressed up against the rear end of some sweaty Greek oik in front of you.

It's a funny thing, size. Size was clearly important to the then current batch of opera composers. Berlioz, Meyerbeer, Wagner: they were all obsessed with size. Looking back, now, it's tempting to see them as a little too obsessed, but that might not be totally fair. Back then, in 1858 for example, you really are DEEP in the thick of High Romantic Opera, and, as we've said before, where you are in the life cycle of any particular 'era' or 'period' largely dictates what type, style and, it's got to be said, size of music you're going to get. Early in any given era, you will get perhaps smaller works in that idiom, first

♬ *You know, I can still hear the sound of my Latin teacher shouting the phrase, 'It's an ablative absolute, boy, isn't that obvious? It's "He, having been about to... HAVING BEEN ABOUT TO..."' Ah, those were the days. Such a shame that a teacher isn't allowed to launch one of those wooden board dusters at your temple, these days. Takes all the danger out of being taught Latin, don't you think?*

ventures into previously unknown areas. Later, the works will get bolder and bigger, with the era now established – and more or less everybody doing it. Then, towards the end, you get the biggies – the 'You want "era X?" I'll give you "era X!"'-type pieces. People will ALWAYS do this. They will always take an era, a style, an art form, whatever, to its absolute end. And that's what these guys were doing now. 'You want high romantic? I'll give you HIGH ROMANTIC... with knobs on!' Berlioz and Meyerbeer had very much blazed the trail in this area, but Wagner was about to leave them all in the shade, somewhat, with his go at it. But, and this is a beautiful irony, the man who wrote operas longer than is medically recommendable is about to WOW the entire world...

...with just one chord.

TRISTAN SHOUT!

1859. There was such a lot going on, musically, and yet it is a year that is largely going to be remembered for more or less one chord. OK, so I'm pushing it a bit, but still, there is something in it. It is the big chord in 1859, yes, but it's also the big chord of the next 250 years. People never forgot it. Maybe they never will. Certainly, music professors are still talking about it in 2004. It is, possibly, the MOST FAMOUS CHORD IN HISTORY – if you don't count 'The Lost' one or the one that held up Adolf Hitler's father's trousers. And, oddly enough, this chord has a name.

It's called 'Tristan'.

Tristan, the chord with a name, is the latest little baby of Ric 'I'm hard' Wagner. We've already had *Ring Cycle* Parts 3 and 4 – *Siegfried* and *Götterdämmerung* – and so, by way of a little light relief, he starts to busy himself on a little love story. Of course, Wagner being Wagner, he comes up with one that will take its place in history. To the illustrious list of lovers that include Orfeo and Euridice, Romeo and Juliet, and Mills and Boon, is added the eternal pairing of... Tristan and Isolde. At the time, Wagner was having one of his many extra-marital affairs, this one with the impressively named Mathilde

Wesendonck. Some say she inspired him to make the character of Isolde, whereas other say it was the other way round – writing Isolde made him yearn for an affair with her. Who knows? What *is* certain is that *Tristan and Isolde* was to go down as one of the most important works of the entire nineteenth century, not least for its harmony.

Harmony, yes. Especially in that chord, 'Tristan', or, to give it its posh full name, 'The Half-Diminished Seventh'. That chord was just part of the whole, well, shifting sort of 'gear changing' stuff that Wagner was doing with the harmony in this opera, *T&I*. He pushes the 'key' thing to its limit, so that you can't really tell, musically speaking, where the original key is at all. Or indeed, where the current key is.

If the word 'key' means nothing to you – as I am frequently told it means nothing to me, usually after I've sung something – well, try this instead. Imagine you can hear home – your own home, imagine it has a sound. Much like it has a smell. Yes? Come on, get it in your heads, what does your home 'sound' like? Right? Is it there? Well, that's it's 'key'. Now, imagine: most composers, up until *T&I*, had stayed 'around the home', as it were, in their pieces of music. Sometimes they wandered off, but never too far, or if they did go too far, they always knew how to get back. And they always *did* get back. Home, that is. And, more importantly, if they did wander off, they could always see home – or hear it – and maybe even left themselves a good old ball of wool as a trail. Well, if all that is the case, then in *Tristan and Isolde*, Wagner has basically walked way out of the garden, miles away from home, and has taken an amazingly complicated route round town – like a cabbie on low money day. You can't see home at all, now. Not at all. In fact, you are unsure if you ever did know where home was in the first place.

Does that help? No, didn't think so. Still. Anyway, that's what Wagner was doing. He was pushing the whole 'key' or 'home' thing to its limits, and calling it 'chromaticism', which is, strictly speaking, the word for it.

And he was doing it in 1859. Now, though, of course, it's soap-box time, and the subject is the rather convoluted: 'Going to See Live Music, Especially Stuff you Might not Normally Consider'. I know I keep mentioning this – and why not? – but *Tristan and Isolde* is a perfect example of something you have to go to hear live to appreciate fully. Someone once said, 'Delius is all the same intoxication, but Wagner has a hundred different ways of making you drunk' – and nowhere is this more apt than in *TampersandI*. Sorry, *T&I*. It is the music of utter speechlessnesslessness. Music that can make you unaware of the time. So that famous quote about Wagner I shared with you earlier – well, ignore that completely. That was clearly said by someone who didn't know shinola from anything. Wagner operas, if done well, are exactly the opposite. They make you hate the interval with its crush bar and its wine glasses resting on one of those gadgets for perching wine glasses on the side of plates so that you can still have one hand left over to do the actions to the word 'Daaaaaaarling!' Wagner operas done well are Lost Worlds where you are lost for words, where you can go to forget other inferior music. In fact, come to think of it, talking of being lost for words, it's said that Wagner hated the saxophone. Absolutely loathed it. He said it sounded like the word '*Reckankreuzungsklangkewerkzeuge*', a lost word itself, which translates as... well, something untranslatable, really – it's a series of German puns, all in one word. *Reckankreuzungsklangkewerkzeuge*. Absolutely. Write it down and bring it out at parties. Will clear a room in seconds.

Now let me build a bridge between Wagner's 1859 and Verdi's 1862.

RECKANKREUZUNGS KLANGKEWERKZEUGE!

Well, as good a title as any for a section that bridges three years. It's 1859 that we need to jump from, the year that a fifty-year-old naturalist really puts the cat among the pigeons when he finally writes up the notes from his trip on the HMS *Beagle* some twenty-three years earlier. Clearly a one-finger typist. He calls his finished opus *On the Origin of Species by Means of Natural Selection*. Very nice. Caused quite a stir, I would imagine. Elsewhere, in **1860**, a soldier and one-time member of Giuseppe Mazzini's Young Italy Society, marched on Palermo and Naples with 1,000 men, dressed in red shirts, and claimed them for Victor Emmanuel II. Not the red shirts, you understand – Palermo and Naples, I mean. He then proclaims Victor Emmanuel 'King of Italy' after the seizure of the Papal States. Garibaldi and 'I mille' – the thousand – as it comes to be known.

Across the pond, Abraham Lincoln is inaugurated as the sixteenth president of the US and, immediately, South Carolina secedes from the union. What a gorgeous phrase, 'secedes from the union', isn't it? A beautiful and almost poetic way of saying 'goes off in a sulk'. I wish I'd tried it when I was young. Imagine it.

> [Scene – somewhere in Norfolk.]
> *'Where's Stephen?'*
> *'Oh, I told him he couldn't have one of my liquorice allsorts, so he said he was seceding from the union.'*
> *'Not again.'*

Well, it might have worked. Who knows? Anyway, 1861 now, and it's not only South Carolina, it's Georgia, Alabama, Mississippi, Florida, Louisiana and Texas – the Confederate States, as they were known – and America has itself a civil war. In the UK, Queen Victoria goes into an age-long period of mourning, and begins to contemplate living the next forty years without her consort and companion. And so to **1862**, then, and Abraham Lincoln makes his 'Emancipation Proclamation', which will, in just a short while, bring about the freedom of slaves. What else? Of course. Prussia gets a new PM, one Otto Eduard Leopold Bismarck.

Artistically speaking, it's been a good few years too: George Eliot's *The Mill on the Floss* and *Silas Marner*, Dickens's *Great Expectations*, Dostoevsky's *House of the Dead*, Victor Hugo's *Les Misérables*, new stuff from Manet and Degas – all of them since 1859. Also worth mentioning is the debut of Sarah Bernhardt – went down a storm in Racine's *Iphigénie*. Also in 1862 a forty-nine-year-old Giuseppe Verdi makes the long trip to St Petersburg, to the Imperial Opera, the august body who had commissioned his latest opera, *La Forza del Destino*: *The Force of Destiny*.

Verdi, like Wagner, was advancing from work to work, although maybe not quite as dramatically as Little Richard. The harmony and orchestration in *The Force of Destiny* are steps up from his last work, *Un Ballo in Maschera – The Masked Ball* – and that was a step up, itself, on the previous *La Traviata/Il Trovatore*. Oddly enough, it's considered by some to be the opera equivalent to *Macbeth*, in that its name is not meant to be mentioned in the theatre or opera house. Don't know why. It just is. Personally, I think it's gorgeous, even if I can't prevent myself thinking of Stella Artois every time I hear it. And, if you're into connections, then it was written the same year that Bizet offered up his classic opera *The Pearl Fishers*, with its hit duet, 'Au fond du temple saint'.

THE CURIOUS CASE OF THE SLEEPING GIANT

zzZZZZZZZZZZZZ

Ah yes. Curious indeed, this one. The Sleeping Giant. Far off, away with the fairies, way off up the wooden hill to dreamland.

To be fair, I should explain. The Sleeping Giant is actually a composer, and, again to be fair – because I like to be fair – ...zzZZZZ he isn't really sleeping. He's just... not found his ...zzZZZZ voice, shall we say. Finding your voice is ...zzZZZZ c o m p o s e r - s p e a k ...zzZZZZ for finally writing in a style with which you are ...zzZZZZ comfortable and which is your own. So the Sleeping ...zzZZZZ Giant is a composer who hasn't found his voice. ...zzZZZZ He's forty already. Forty! And he hasn't published a ...zzZZZZ note. He's been studying composition for some ...zzZZZZ twenty-three years, but hasn't felt confident enough ...zzZZZZ yet to let the great unwashed hear his work. So ...zzZZZZ instead, he has just carried on playing the organ – ...zzZZZZ which was one of his passions – studying, sketching ...zzZZZZ the odd composition, studying, learning music ...zzZZZZ zzzzzzzZZZZ theory, studying, learning harmony… did I mention zzzzzzzZZZZ studying? Anyway, some time soon, the giant is due zzzzzzzZZZZ to wake up, and you'd do well to be around zzzzzzzZZZZ when he does. In the meantime, let me fill you in zzzzzzzZZZZ on the last couple of years.

1863, was zzzzzzzZZZZ quite an important one for the USA. Following the zzzzzzzZZZZ battle for one small town, the Federal forces set zzzzzzzZZZZ about making a cemetery to take the war dead. At zzzzzzzZZZZ the dedication of the cemetery, Lincoln gives a zzzzzzzZZZZ speech. The speech goes down in history, named zzzzzzzZZZZ a f t e r zzzzzzzZZZZ t h e small town where the cemetery was built – zzzzzzzZZZZ Gettysburg. The following year, he is re- zzzzzzzZZZZ zzzzzzzZZZZ elected President. zzzzzzzZZZZ

What else? Well, Florence is, albeit briefly, zzzzzzzZZZZ the capital of Italy in place of (a) Rome, (b) zzzzzzzZZZZ Turin or (c) Milan? The answer's Turin actu- zzzzzzzZZZZ ally, with Rome having to wait another six zzzzzzzZZZZ years before it achieves capital status. zzzzzzzZZZZ Elsewhere, on the world's battlefields, the zzzzzzzZZZZ Geneva Convention is set up to establish the zzzzzzzZZZZ neutrality of medical facilities in war, the zzzzzzzZZZZ words 'In God we Trust' appears for zzzzzzzZZZZ t h e first time zzzzzzzZZZZ on American coins, and, let's see, Louis zzzzzzzZZZZ Pasteur invents 'pasteurization', initially for zzzzzzzZZZZ wine, would you believe. I raise a glass to him as zzzzzzzZZZZ I write. Good old Louis.

zzzzzzzZZZZ

zzzzzzzZZZZ Other than that, nothing much else to report. zzzzzzzZZZZ Charles Dickens churns out another one, *Our* zzzzzzzZZZZ *Mutual Friend*, and Tolstoy starts *War and Peace*. I zzzzzzzZZZZ say 'starts' because it takes him a good five years. Five zzzzzzzZZZZ YEARS! Jeepers, you could write *War and Peace* in zzzzzzzZZZZ that time. Last year was a good year for art, zzzzzzZZZ though. A couple of biggies saw the light of zzzzzzZZZ day – Manet's *Déjeuner sur l'herbe* and Dante zzzzzzZZZ Gabriel Rossetti's *Beata Beatrix*. Lovely. Now zzzzzzZZZ back to the 'Z'

The Sleeping Giant, I zzzzzzZZZ called him, and I think that's fair at forty. He'd zzzzzzZZZ been training and studying for most of those forty zzzzzzZZZ years, but just lacked the confidence to publish. But zzzzzzZZZ t h e n , t h i s zzzzzzZZZ year – **1864** – just as Meyerbeer dies, he wakes up, so zzzzzzZZZ to speak, and finishes his first symphony. Well, actually, zzzzzzZZZ to be more accurate, he finishes his first symphony, then gets another fit of insecurity and decides it's not fit to publish, so renumbers it 'Symphony No. Zero!' Can you believe that? I'm not kidding, honest, he did. Thought it simply wasn't good enough to be called his first symphony. Composers – funny bunch. And he was an organist, too, so that might explain it some more. Anyway, the world disagrees with him, eventually, and, I have to say, so do I. It is now a published and recorded symphony, known as *Die Nulte* – literally, the Nought, the 'Zero'! Astounding. You couldn't make it up. Anyway, let's wake him up, shall we? I want to introduce you. Bruckner... you're on, love. Bruckner, this is the reader: reader, this is Bruckner.

Someone once said, 'Gothic cathedrals of sound!' And they weren't talking about Frank Zappa. Bruckner, they meant. And if you've ever been to a Bruckner concert, you'll know what they mean. Gorgeous, it is. The symphony he called the *Zero* is simple and beautiful. And – and this is amazing – there's even a *Symphony Double Zero*, which is actually a sketch he'd written a year before the *Zero*. Are you following this?

All in all, a beautifully simple person, Bruckner. You can hear the organist in him coming out in his symphonies. He composes entire long passages all in a certain register or soundworld – much like an organist choosing a certain setting of stops on the organ for a while. Do you get my drift? If you are unfamiliar with the organ and its workings – and, I've got to be honest, you'd be wise to be! – then imagine it like this: you know those people who eat their food separately and in order? You know, the ones who eat all their peas first, carrots second, and then they spend some time eating the potatoes, before finally eating the sausage? You know those people? Well, Bruckner was the sort of composer version of that – different registers at different times. In fact, if you listen to *Die Nulte*, you can just about hear the horns being the carrots towards the end. Or not, as the case may be.

NIGHT ON A BALD MOUNTAIN (WITH BOBBY CHARLTON COMB-OVER)

I've never really got beyond the sniggering schoolboy stage when it comes to the title of Mussorgsky's work. As impressive as the piece sounds, I found it very hard to take in the title, *Night on a Bald Mountain*. Even when it was modernized to 'bare' – in much the same way that you watch the news on TV, one day, and find out that everyone is now pronouncing a particular word a different way, and you feel like a citizen in the 'Emperor's New Clothes' if you don't go along with it: I'm talking here about words like Nike (which used to rhyme with 'Mike' but apparently now is 'Nikey') and Boudicca (which was once 'Boa-da-see-er' and nobody seemed to mind) that seem to change overnight and nobody so much as lets on that it they had ever said them differently.♬ Even then, I couldn't seem to get 'bare' witches or, for some reason, bare knights, out of my head. I know, I know, it's probably just me. Still. For now, though, let me join some of the dots and complete the picture from here to the 1867 of Mussorgsky's *Night on A Bare Bottom*. (Sorry, there it is again. Can't help it, see!)

The main, big wow, my-word-did-you-hear-the-news was from America, namely the end of the Civil War. Very sad end, too, for Abraham Lincoln. He took the Confederate surrender at

♬ *In fact, I heard a radio announcer say 'DyLAN Thomas', just recently, and thought, 'Oh, here we go again, are we all going to have to change this, now?'*

♬ ♬ *If you were to guess the meaning of that word, Appomattox, having come across it for the first time, I'm sure you'd plump for a cosmetic operation over a Confederate surrender venue. Just a thought.*

Appomattox♫ on April 9th, only to be assassinated five days later. Sad. It was all over bar the shooting, as it were. The American constitution does get its Thirteenth Amendment, though, the abolition of slavery – and not before time. In England, there are a couple of important debuts: the Salvation Army goes into battle for the first time, and WG Grace goes into bat for the first time, both of them, in their own ways, with a war cry – the Sally Army initially going by the name of the Christian Revival Association. Also in 1865, Edward Whymper scales the majestic chiselled features of the Matterhorn, the first of a select and illustrious line that would eventually include Ronald Lihoreau in the late 1950s. Louis Pasteur, no doubt already the toast of Parisian bacchanalian society from his service to wine, probably becomes the toast of French haute couture, too, when he manages to cure silkworm disease, thereby single-handedly saving French silk. Silk hats off to him.

A year on, **1866**, and Prussia, Italy and Austria are in a right mess. All over the place, to be honest. Too tortuous to explain now, save to say that, after lashings of jiggery-pokery undertaken for reasons best known to themselves, Schleswig-Holstein becomes part of Prussia. I'm sure it won't end there. What else? Well, TJ Barnardo opens his first home for destitute children, in Stepney, and Swedish chemist Alfred Bernhardt Nobel, the man who gave rise to the peace prize, invents dynamite, the thing that gives rise to all manner of war, death and destruction. It's an irony that is never lost on me, no matter how often I hear it repeated – the fortune that came from dynamite goes to fund over a century and a half of the promotion of peace, amongst other things.

A year on, still – **1867** – and Garibaldi marches on Rome, an event that will forever be known in Italy as, wait for it… The March on Rome. Gosh, they were an inventive bunch, weren't they? When he gets to Rome, he is eventually defeated by a combination of French and papal troops. Ah well. No doubt one or other side wasn't quite playing strictly in accordance with the newly introduced 'Queensberry Rules' of 1867. Anyway. Year out, round 2. (Ding.)

And indeed the last few years have been pretty good for all things arty-farty. Somebody called CL Dodgson used the pseudonym Lewis

Carroll to write *Alice's Adventures in Wonderland* and Cardinal Newman, writing under the cunning pseudonym of 'Cardinal Newman', comes up with the poem 'The Dream of Gerontius', which will eventually be food for thought for one Mr Elgar. At present, though, little Edward is only, let's see... eight. Awwww, look at him, little love. Eight years old... awww. Still. Handlebar moustache coming on nicely! What else for the arts? Well, Degas has started to paint ballet scenes – could do well – Millais has done *The Boyhood of Raleigh* (cue bicycle jokes), Dostoevsky has done *Crime and Punishment* and Email Zola, the first writer to get on the net, has written *Thérèse Raquin. Et bien!* On the downside, though, we have lost Rousseau and Ingres. Bof! I think that's about it. Now, though, to paraphrase the great Elvis Aaron Presley, 'One night... with you. Er, and Mussorgsky.' Yeah, I know – needs work. Leave it with me and I'll write out parts for The Jordanaires.

So. Mussorgsky. At last, we're here. Always loved the name Mussorgsky. I think it's because, when you are very young, and have no knowledge of repertoire at all, you associate composers with either the sound of their name or the one, maybe two pieces you know by them. With Mussorgsky, it was a bit of both. I loved the brassy sounds of the 'Great Gate of Kiev', and his name seemed to match it perfectly – a bit brassy, almost as if it were imitating the air as it was blown through as tuba or a horn. MUSSORGSKY! MUSSSSSORRRRRGSKY! No? Never mind, then. There was also his first name, which I could never escape – Modest, usually pronounced 'Moe-dest' (as in Five Guys Named Modest), with the accent on the moe. What a groovy, cute name for a composer, I always thought. Modest. Modest! Modest Mussorgsky. Great name.

He was born into land-owning aristocracy and became an officer in the elite Russian Preobrajensky Regiment. Following the emancipation of the serfs in 1861, his family went bankrupt and he was forced into a succession of civil service jobs that left him in poverty. Added to this, he had a drink problem that left him with an official portrait that looked like 'The Dong with the Luminous Nose', and you could have forgiven him had he wanted nothing to do with the current vogue for 'Russian nationalism' in music. But not a bit of it. He wanted you to be able to hear 'the people' in his music, as well as being able to hear their stories, too. And it was against that backdrop that, in 1867, he produced what was to become one of his most memorable small works. It's meant to be the music to the events of a midsummer night, a night during which the witches' sabbath is held on a bald mountain, near Kiev – STOP SNIGGERING, FRY MINOR, OR I'LL SEND YOU TO SEE MR RUTHERFORD. Now, as I was saying, it's meant to sound like a witches' sabbath, and is probably better known in the version that was reorchestrated by his friend, the composer Rimsky-Korsakov. *Night on a Bare/Bald Mountain* is one of those pieces that storms out of the traps and hooks you in from the start, a whirling tumult that seems to paint a near perfect musical picture. If you happen to think of Maxell tapes rather than witches, then I think that's fine too.

'TYPICAL. YOU WAIT AGES FOR A GORGEOUS CONCERTO, THEN...'

. . . Two come along at once. Isn't it always the way? Anyway, more of that in a moment. On to **1868** first, the year of the last Shogun. Yes, following the abdication of Shogun Kekei and the abolition of the Shogunate, the Shoguns are no more. 'The abolition of the Shogunate', what a fantastic phrase. In fact, there's something about the word 'Shogun' itself which inspires feelings of awe and, I think, fear. Not surprising, then, to find out that the word is simply the Japanese for military dictator, an abbreviation of '*seii tai shogun*', which means 'great barbarian-conquering general.' Wow. Does *that* come with baggage, or what. This is also the year that Disraeli became PM, and also the year that Disraeli became NOT PM again, as he was out a few months later. It's the year of the brand-new in sport, devised and named after the Duke of Beaufort's residence in Gloucestershire, Badminton, and the year of the first TUC conference in Manchester. Wow, do *they* not seem to go together. It's also the year of Darwin's flop follow-up to *The Origin of Species*, namely *The Variation of Animals and Plants under*

Domestication. Ooh, I say, what awful branding, eh? Really needs work, darling. I can just see him bringing in the '80s ponytailed brand consultants to advise him.

> 'Charlie, baby, people don't want all this Animal/Plant scene any more, man! It's so last year. You've got to sex it up a little. The boys in the focus groups have come up with another title that retains the key elements of yours but... well, you know, just... cranks it up a gear, yeah? Try this.
>
> *The Animal UNLEASHED* or *You Can't Keep a Good Plant Down – From the writing team that gave you "Species 1 – the Origin!"*
>
> 'What do you think, C? Wicked, huh? That'll be 50K. Ta. Hey, Neville, get me another latte, yeah...'

This was also the year of Marx and *Das Kapital*, Renoir's *The Skaters* and Degas's *L'Orchestre*, as well as the first twitchings of the soon-to-be-named art movement, 'Impressionism'. All this, and two of the greatest concertos ever written. One was by Grieg, the other by Bruch.

Edvard Grieg came from quite a musical family – his mother was a good pianist. And if the name 'Grieg' seems a little out of place in Norway, it's because it was actually from the composer's Scottish great-grandfather, who had emigrated after the Battle of Culloden, setting up a small enclave of Griegs in Bergen. The young Edvard had always wanted to pursue music, except a brief time when he considered the priesthood, and was eventually sent to study at the Leipzig Conservatory, where his contemporaries included Arthur Sullivan. After Leipzig, he settled in Denmark for a time, in Copenhagen, where he became friends with the grand old man of Scandinavian music, Niels Gade, under whose influence he set up the Euterpe Society to promote Scandinavian music. Just the year before he wrote his only piano concerto, he'd married his cousin, Nina. Their only child, a daughter, died in the year that the concerto was premiered, 1869.

Bruch is a completely different kettle of fish. He was born in

Cologne, and, in his day, was considered to be one of the greatest German composers. Then, his highest achievement was thought to be his choral works, many of which he had composed by the time he was in his mid-twenties. They brought him fame and some fortune, and he travelled across Germany, conducting and teaching as well as composing. The year before he wrote the *Violin Concerto* of 1868, he'd been made Director of the Court Orchestra in Sonderhausen, midway between Dortmund and Leipzig, where he spent three happy years before returning to Berlin. Still to come, at this stage, were the three unhappy years as director of the Royal Liverpool Philharmonic Orchestra, where his abrasive personality went down like a performance of John Cage's Silence (see page 287) at a Hard of Hearing Conference.

Both, however, gave birth to concertos in 1868, and both concertos can still claim to be among the most popular in the field – Grieg's by dint of a stunning first movement and mesmeric slow movement, and Bruch's by way of a delicious slow movement and a breathtaking finale. Both are fine examples of how MASSIVE popularity cannot ruin truly great works. Both as delectable a couple of concertos as you're ever likely to come across in a dark alley on a Friday night. Gorgeous. Now, it's over to our man in Russia, Pyotr Ilyich Tchaikovsky.

BRING ME THE HEAD OF PYOTR ILYICH TCHAIKOVSKY!

The Tchaikovsky Mini-Quiz:

Before we get on to Russia, where **is** Tchaikovsky? I don't mean geographically, I mean in the general scheme of things?

(a) Where does he fit in?

(b) Why did he write what he did?

(c) Who were his mentors?

(d) And did he really think his head was going to fall off?

Well, let me see if I can answer all those. Award yourself ten points each if you gave the answers, (a) sort of in-between, (b) er, why not?

(c) oh, a bunch of people, really (I'll accept 'a number of people, actually') and (d) yes, apparently. Good. Quizette over. Now, let me magnify.

A little overview, first. Wagner... is still HUGE. Gi-NORmous, with a capital NOR. So much so that a lot of composers are under his spell – Bruckner, for example. Many, though, aren't. One of many in the 'aren't' camp is Brahms, a very 'classical' romantic, shall we say? In fact, Brahms did everything that Wagner didn't, when you think about it. Brahms did chamber music, concertos, variations and symphonies, all without the huge, what he considered to be 'over the top', excesses of the real Wagnerian 'high romantics'. Beyond Wagner, though, the big thing is still 'nationalism' in music – that is to say, putting the sounds, smells, ideas and even tunes of your own country into your music. It's no longer just a 'colour', as it once was. It's now everything. Well, it would be – these are revolutionary times, still, and it is almost the done thing, de rigueur, to reflect your country's roots and traditions in your music.

In the Russia of **1869**, composers divided straight down the middle.

There were the Nationalists, led by the five composers whom Russian critic, Vlad Stasov, had dubbed 'The Mighty Handful', namely...

Balakirev, Borodin, Cui, Mussorgsky and Rimsky-Korsakov.

On the other side, there were the 'Europeans', shall we say, who preferred to write in the western tradition. In this group, there was...

er... Tchaikovsky.

As you can see, Tchaikovsky was the only significant member of the latter group. His music was much more a case of what HE, Pyotr Ilyich Tchaikovsky, was all about, not what Russia was all about.

♬ *What a shame we don't have a non-musical job called 'teacher of harmony' – someone who just teaches people to love one another, and spread love. OK, I'll get down off my hippie soapbox.*

By 1869, he had already lost the mother he doted on, and was living in the house of Nicholas Rubinstein, the pianist and composer, brother of Anton Rubinstein, the pianist and composer. (Musical lot, the Rubinsteins.) He was making his living as a teacher of harmony♪ at the Moscow Conservatory. He had also been on the verge of marrying a Belgian soprano, Désirée Artot, which would have been somewhat disastrous for three reasons. Firstly, he was gay. Secondly, Désirée was as famous for her sexual flings as she was for her voice. Thirdly, it's not good for a composer to be married to someone named after a potato. They parted company with no real harm done to the very sensitive Mr Tchaikovsky, although it was immediately following this episode that he produced his overture to *Romeo and Juliet*. Ironically, it was Balakirev who had put the idea of writing an *R&J* overture into his head, and it was to him that Tchaikovsky turned for help and advice as he was completing it. Tchaikovsky called the finished work a 'fantasy overture', which basically means it's not an overture in the strict sense of the word – with all the 'overture rules', etc – but more a flight of fancy in music. An overture where the composer is allowed to go off on one, whenever he wants. It has that gorgeous, lush tune in the middle, which has been used, ever since, when a film director has been in need of portraying something ULTRA romantic.

And that final question. Did Tchaikovsky really think his head was going to fall off? Well, yes, actually, he did. Tchaik was afflicted with several all-consuming neuroses, one of which was that his head was going to fall off if he conducted an orchestra too energetically. It's as true as I'm standing here! And – and this is no word of a lie – he was often to be seen, when he did conduct, with one hand holding the baton, and the other holding on to his chin, for fear it would fall off. Honest!

Well, now. We're about to hit the '70s. But don't worry – your flares are safe in the wardrobe. This is the **1870s**. Before we do, though, let's catch up with Little Richard and Big Joe.

THE SEVENTIES – FLARES AND FALLIBILITY

I imagine the 1870s were little like the 1970s. OK, OK, specialist subject the bleeding obvious, yes, I know. But that's not to say there weren't some similarities. In the 1970s, you had love and peace – in the 1870s, Mahatma Gandhi was born! Eh!? Need I say more? I need to? OK, well, in the 1970s, you had Abba. In the 1870s you had the Pope, just having been declared infallible, courtesy of Vat. I! Eh!? Spooky, huh? You want more? You do. Right, OK. Well, in the 1970s you had saucy postcards, in the 1870s you had the very BIRTH of the postcard. In the 1970s you had a ride of your Raleigh Chopper, in the 1870s you had a Ride of the Valkyries. In the 1970s, YOU HAD THE WORZELS, in the 1870s… OK, the cod similarities end there. Sorry. Can't match the Worzels (as Melvin Bragg once said).

Let me just spool back a bit. 'The Ride of the Valkyries'. Yes, that was 1870 – OK, actually it was premiered in 1869, but it was 'the big thing' in 1870 and beyond. Just as the Suez Canal opened, Wagner gave the world the music of the nine daughters of Wotan; the music of the weird and wonderful horsewomen of the air; the music of napalm, depending on your generation. It was the fourth in his bladder-testing cycle of operas, *The Ring*, or to give it its full kennel name, *The Ring of Lady Benedictine-Trixibelle, the Third.*☺ OK, that's a lie. Its full name is only *The Ring of the Nibelung*, but personally I think mine sounds better. If the *Ring* were an American Football match, then, with The Valkyries, we're in the third quarter. Not long before, he'd wandered off again for some light relief from the *Ring*, much like he did with *Tristan and Isolde*, a little earlier. It was in 1867 that he'd premiered his comedy, *The Mastersingers of Nuremberg*. The word 'comedy' is applied a little loosely, here, as you might be beginning to guess. In fact, the word should be applied *so* loosely that it becomes free to roam off and never contact *The Mastersingers of Nuremberg*, ever again, save for the occasional postcard. Just how UNFUNNY this '*comedy*'♬ is can be gleaned from this sentence: 'Set in sixteenth-century Nuremberg…'

♬ *In inverted commas, italicized, ironically underlined, complete with the accompanying disclaimer 'Notice: this "*comedy*" will not make you laugh. Any experience bearing any resemblance to any other amusing experience, either living or dead, as a result of this "*comedy*" is entirely unintentional.*

♬♬ *All hail the great Ronnie of Hazelhurst. Sorry, just wanted to see his name in the book alongside the great Wagner.*

In fact, stop there. That's captured it, I think. 'Set in sixteenth-century Nuremberg.' It's hardly the cue for a light, knockabout half-hour, accompanied by the strains of a Ronnie Hazelhurst♫ theme tune, starring the guy off *'Allo 'Allo*, is it? No. I'm glad you agree.

To Wagner, comedy meant 'the human comedy', only comedy in so far as the subject matter does not make you want to reach for your revolver. Well, usually. It concerns the (apparently true) story of a Mastersingers contest. The 'meistersinger' tradition is one which goes way back, and was also called 'minnesinger'. This story concerns one of the most famous, Hans Sach, who offered his daughter's hand in marriage to the winner of one such 'meistersinger' competition. There's a great baddie, Beckmesser, and a rather pompous goodie, Walther the Franconian knight. Sounds a hoot, doesn't it? Anyway, I said we'd catch up with Big Joe, too, so get your period Y-fronts on and don the foppish 'What's that over there?' stance of a John Collier catalogue – it's the 1870s proper, and we're going in.

FASCINATING AÏDA

1871, it is, to be precise. The year of the Paris Commune – more or less the first socialist government in history, running from March to May of that year, a lifespan that was to set the standard for all socialist governments of the future, until Tony Blair's. It was the year the French also ceded Alsace Lorraine to Germany, along with an 'indemnity' of FIVE BILLION francs. FIVE BILLION francs. Sorry, my needle got stuck. FIVE BILLION francs, though. Sorry, there I go again, repeating myself. No doubt it was doppels all round for William I, the first being the very first Emperor of the new Germany. It appears to have been an unusually – and no doubt temporarily – peaceful time, too, with the Treaty of Washington settling up all the existing niggles between the USA and Britain. How lovely. Add to that the fact that the FA Cup was started, bank holidays came into being and Stanley met Livingstone at Ujiji and, well, God was in his heaven and all was right with the world. 1871 also had a couple of particularly good book launches to keep the literati happy – Lewis

Carroll followed up with *Through the Looking Glass* (good canapés) and George Eliot with *Middlemarch* (particularly impressive dips). Gosh – pseudonyms everywhere. Amazing. Come to think of it, I've always though of using one myself.

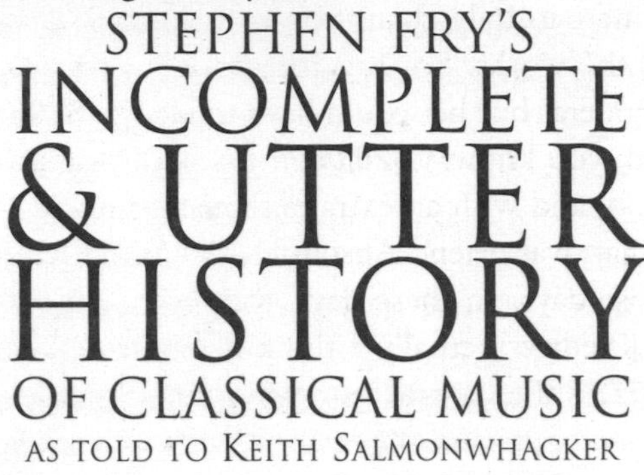

Mmm. I think I'll sleep on that. Anyway, now to the music of 1871, and if it isn't Big Joe. Our man Green. Giuseppe Verdi was by now a very sprightly fifty-eight-year-old, and was loved by the Italians only a smidgeon less than Parmesan cheese. Anyone who could wander round virtually ANY Italian town and expect to see his name graffitied across the walls in virtually every backstreet piazza knows he has made it. To be fair, Verdi's name had become synonymous with the now successful nationalist movement, in part due to Verdi's own nationalist leanings and subsequent use of nationalist plots in his operas, but also, in part, down to a quirk of fate with his name.

The words 'Viva Verdi' were to be seen in backstreet piazzas because of a serendipitous piece of luck. The then incoming King of Italy was one Vittorio Emmanuel. As a result, the letters VERDI were used as an acronym of **V**ictor **E**mmanuel, **Re D'I**talia – or **V**ictor **E**mmanuel, **K**ing **O**f **I**taly – and, in long form, Viva VERDI. In other words, Long Live Victor Emmanuel, King of Italy. It's an oft told but nevertheless beautiful bit of serendipity, one which wouldn't have worked half as well if Verdi had been either (a) not a nationalist or (b) a crap composer.

In 1871, though, Mr V received a very nice letter from the Khedive of Egypt. Khedive... I think it's some sort of root vegetable. Whatever. Anyway, he was writing to ask Verdi for a nice BIG opera to open up his nice BIG opera house, the brand new Cairo Opera. He'd like it nice and BIG, please, preferably hummably tuneful, and could he have it ready Thursday? Well, the way I see it, Verdi probably didn't want the gig. Cairo? I mean, it was miles away, and he was doing perfectly well here in Italy, thank you very much. Name in every back-street piazza, the works. So, Big Joe sends a letter back saying he'll gladly do the opera, but he would have to charge $20,000. **$20,000!** (that's in bold, you know?) ***$20,000!!*** Just so's you know, that was in bold, italics too, and with an extra exclamation mark! Well, just think how much that was then. Absolutely STAGGERING amount of money, in those days. In these days, too, even. Anyway, much to his surprise, the Khedive (actually I think it might be a small canapé or something) agrees the fee and stumps up the twenty grand. So, Verdi duly supplies the opera and the rest is his story, as it were.

Oddly enough, the opera had originally been conceived as a celebration of not just the brand-new 'Italian Opera' House, but by way of a general party for the opening of the Suez Canal, in 1869. It has an amazing lineage, commissioned, as it was, by an Egyptian Khedive (I think it's possibly, literally, a funnel-ended vessel), with a plot by a French Egyptologist, a libretto written, in French, by Camille de Locle, and then the whole thing translated into Italian by fellow librettist Antonio Ghislanzoni, and the odd 'crossing-out' by Mr Verdi himself. The whole thing was then shipped out to Egypt – composer not included – along with scenery and costumes, ordered from Paris, all to be then held up in the Siege of Paris.

Eventually, it was premiered, though, and it – *Aïda* – became one of the most successful operas in history. Again, if you get a chance, go and see it live, because it really is worth it. Try one of those huge, popular productions, with a cast of thousands, performed in the round, at the Millennium Stadium, or somewhere like. It really is a fantastic spectacle.

Verdi himself refused to attend the premiere. Refused point blank. Said he didn't like all the glitz and glamour, and was not fond of sea travel: and besides, he couldn't do a thing with his hair. He did, however, receive a telegram from the Khedive (literally, a mollusc of the species *Phylum mollusca*) to say that *Aïda* had gone down a storm.

Fascinating, huh?

This was all happening around the same time that Wagner was preparing a Christmas present to his new wife, Cosima – the daughter of Franz Liszt and previous wife of his 'dear friend', Hans von Bulow. Prior to marriage, Wagner had been conducting an open affair with Cosima for some years.♬ As much by way of relief from his *Ring*, he rearranged as a love token some of the tunes from his opera, *Siegfried*, into a cute little piece called the *Siegfried Idyll*, and had it played to her outside her bedroom, with a bunch of musicians squeezed on to the landing. Awwww. Now that's what I call High Romantic, Volume 7! (Not a huge-selling album.) So that's that. Cosima has her *Idyll*, the Khedive had his opera. Actually, let me quickly look up the word 'khedive' while you wait. Key, khaki, khalifa, khamsin, khan……khidmutgar. Mmm. No 'khedive'. Mm. Sorry, can't tell you what it means. I can tell you, however, that, according to my dictionary, a 'khilifat' is 'a caliphate'. Very useful.

I ♥ 1874

1874. Not a bad year, I suggest. And imagine, if you did one of those ubiquitous seven-hour-long schedule-filler TV programmes recalling the year, with various talking heads popping up (the same ones who popped up last week, and seemed to have exactly the same opinion of a completely different year) and full of clips of music, and items you'd forgotten from the year – well, how would it sound? Nothing like the following, I can guarantee.

First up in the clips stakes is Verdi's *Requiem*. This is one truly amazing work – not an opera, obviously, and yet very operatic in style. In fact it was labelled, by conductor Hans von Bulow – he of the flighty baton and even flightier wife – as 'an opera in church vestments'. And you can see what he meant – this is very much a Requiem in the line of Berlioz rather than Bach or Mozart. It's a *very* theatrical, dramatic piece. More importantly, though, it was to Verdi what *William Tell* was to Rossini. By that I don't mean it cost a fortune in

♬ *It's amazing that despite Wagner and Cosima's infedelities, von Bulow remained a dedicated Wagner fan all his life.*

apples – I mean it was the last piece he wrote before retiring for a while. In Verdi's case, it wasn't the full, 'Rossinian' thirty-four years, but he did shut up shop for the next thirteen. Thirteen years! A long time for the people of Italy, no doubt. He just... moved to the country. Wrote nothing, 'Do not Disturb' sign up, everything. (Wipes tear from eye.)

So that was Verdi and his 'operatic' style of 1874. His Italian sound is very different, too, to the German operatic sound of Wagner. It's not just that you don't have to shave twice and bring a change of clothes to get through an Italian opera, it was just, well, different. Very different. Italian opera and German opera had taken different turns on the road, and were travelling different paths. Verdi's stuff was still pushing at the limits, somewhat – I mean, just listen to *Aïda* and *La Forza del Destino*: these were both really stretching it compared with where Verdi started in *Nabucco*, for instance. And so it would be – the two were nearly thirty years apart. And thirty years, musically, in that – and this – day and age means a hell of a lot.

Anyway, that's Verdi's Italy, and Wagner's Germany, but where is France? And who *is* France, as it were? Well, come with me, to the next line but one, and I'll tell you. But bring your hankies – it's a weepy.

THE BIDET BELONGING TO GEORGE

To the composer Georges Bizet, now, whom my computer spell-check wants to call George's bidet. No lie – honest. But don't worry – we have people to check for that sort of thing.

George's bidet was born in 1838 in Paris and was every bit the classic child prodigy composer. He was already enrolled at the Paris Conservatoire by the age of nine and had won Paris's biggest composition prize by the age of nineteen. His compositions were STAGGERINGLY mature and it soon became apparent that the name bidet was going to live forever. But then things took a turn for the worse.

Bidet's situation was, I've always thought, not unlike that of some actors today. I'm thinking about the ones who sample early success. What often happens is that offers flood in and it becomes very hard to separate the wheat from the chaff. This seems to have happened to George's and soon, well, it looked like bidet had hit the bottom, all washed up.

But things did get better. Bidet married the daughter of his composition professor and life began to inspire him more. Due to the high regard in which his earlier works were held, he won a commission for a new opera – an opera that was to be staged in the March of 1875.

If you were to ask anyone to name a piece by Bizet, they would probably say... well, actually, let's find out what they'd say. You there!

Yes, you. The one reading this. Name a piece by Bizet.

Good, yes, *Carmen*. Exactly my point. But then if you ask them to name any other piece by Bizet, you're likely to get no answer, becau—

Right. OK. *The Pearl Fishers*, yes, that's true. Well done. OK. Well, ask them to name another after that and you really get an embarrassing si—

Yes, all right, all right, *L'Arlésienne*, yes. Look, no one likes a smart arse. *L'Arlésienne*, yes. But ask anyone to name a fourth and—

OK, OK, *The Fair Maid of Perth*. But ask absolutely anyone to name a fifth—

...?

...?

...?

HAH! THOUGHT SO! RIGHT. Good. Right, let me start that again. Ask anybody to name just FIVE pieces by Bizet, and you'd probably draw a blank. And, well, it might come as a bit of a shock, then – although not to some of you bloody clever clogs – that he actually wrote, what, 150 piano pieces, alone. He'd won the coveted Prix de Rome composition prize in 1857 – but was never, as far as I can gather, tempted to dress up as a French maid and run after a soprano – and then went on, over the next few years, to write suites, overtures, even the odd symphony. But it was OPERA that he really wanted to crack.

Bizet was said to have a fantastic ear for a tune and an awful eye for a libretto. Take *The Pearl Fishers* – despite its famous 'Au fond du temple saint' (literally 'I'm *fond* of Simon *Templar*'☺) it's pretty ropey as far as the words go. With his 1866 attempt, *The Fair Maid of Perth* (literally, 'the fair *maid* of *Perth*') well, he would have probably been better setting the original book by Sir Walter Scott, so bad was the adaptation. BUT THEN… THEN, IN 1872, HE WROTE THE OPERA *DJAMILEH*!

This, too, was an unmitigated pile of pants. Well, actually, that's not totally fair – there were some great tunes in it. I forget their names, now, but, well, Mahler liked it. Having said that, Mahler was only twelve, so he was probably very easily pleased at the time. Anyhow, some three years later – 1875 – he had a minor triumph with *The Old Woman of Arles*. That's not a bit of gossip, it's the title of the opera – *The Old Woman of Arles*, or *L'Arlésienne*, as he, himself, would have said.

Buoyed somewhat by this, he set to work on a new commission from the Paris 'Opéra-Comique'. He chose a book by Prosper Mérimée (you'd think someone with his track record in librettos would stay well away from someone with a name like that, wouldn't you?). It was a story of depraved young girls, gypsies, thieves and cigarette makers – I think there's even the odd estate agent. Sadly, Paris opera goers found it all a little hard to take, and, on the night of the thirty-first performance, having himself pronounced it a failure, Bizet died of cancer of the throat, at the age of thirty-six. If he had lasted just a few performances more? Well, he would have lived to see his new work declared a masterpiece, and hailed as a total work of genius. Nowadays? Well, nowadays, it's probably the most famous, most popular opera EVER. It is, of course, *Carmen*.

For the life of me, I can't see how it wasn't an immediate success. It has fantastic, immediate tunes; gripping, almost '3D' scoring, and it just grabs you between the earlobes and shouts 'LOVE ME!' Er, as it were. And yet they didn't like it. Well, at first. Poor George. Poor 'his bidet'.

Still, life must go on, though, as artists say, so let's forge ahead. And if Bruckner was the 'sleeping giant' of the 1860s, prepare to meet the 'sleeping giant' of the 1870s.

GESELLESCHAFTED!

OK. Imagine, if you will, that it's **1876**. Are you there? Good. Right. OK. Alexander Graham Bell has just, one moment ago, invented the telephone. In fact, as far as I know, he's still on hold to Directory Enquiries. Heinrich Schliemann has excavated Mycenae, Disraeli has been made Earl of Beaconsfield and, most importantly, London has a sewerage system. Also, in 1876, another pseudonym has shuffled off. Amandine Aurora, or should I say George Sand. Or should I say Lucie Dupin, Baronne Dedevant, if you know what I mean?

Over in Bavaria, Wagner has opened his huge cathedral of opera, the Bayreuth Festspielhaus – an amazing place, built exactly to the composer's own specifications (is there nothing this man can't turn his hand to? Did he grout his own bathroom?), with no visible orchestra or conductor. It also has no side boxes or galleries and no prompter's box. Most importantly of all, what it has got, though, is it has an acoustic to die for. If you look at a picture of it – because, let's face it, most people are unlikely ever to go there, unless they take a serious wrong turn driving down to Tuscany – it's not unlike seeing an opera 'in widescreen'. Your entire attention is focused on the 'band' of drama in front of you. Hence the reason for no prompter's box and no visible musicians or conductor – there are no distractions, nothing to put you off concentrating on the music drama unfolding in front of you. There is, though, a perfect sound coming from... well, that's the point. You're never quite sure. In fact, the more I think of it, the more it is like a good, modern TV. You know how, in some movies done in Dolby stereo, you sometimes hear a background noise or effect that seems to come from almost behind you, or to the side? Well, it's a bit like that in Wagner's Bayreuth. With the orchestra totally hidden, and the conductor too, you sometimes get a sense of the music simply enveloping you, coming from everywhere and nowhere at the same time. Remarkable place. Regardless of any personal view of Wagner, he achieved something special with Bayreuth.

Over in Austria, though, a forty-three-year-old Johannes Brahms was, much like Bruckner had not long before him, wrestling to overcome a personal hurdle. Having made Vienna his home some four years ago, he had taken on the job of Conductor at the very well-thought-of Gesellschaft der Musikfreunde in Vienna – literally the 'company of friends of music', a sort of Royal Philharmonic Society, only with the ability to lead in a waltz – and in 1875, he resigned the job. The reason? Not enough time to compose. So he gave it all up and started to concentrate on the dots. The composer version of an MP's 'spending more time with his family'. Thankfully, it paid off. Refreshed, rejuvenated and refocused,♬ he came up with a whole series of major works, including, eventually, the absolutely yumerous *Academic Festival Overture*. He wrote it for the University of Bremen, who were cute enough to give him an honorary degree. As a result, he worked some college songs into the score and it's said that there was general uproar and throwing-in-the-air-of-hats♬♬ when the orchestra got to the bit which had a grand, triumphal arrangement of 'Gaudeamus Igitur'. It was also, in this 'roll', as it were, that he wrote both the *Tragic Overture* AND...

...and something a whole lot more interesting. You see, not only did he have ample time, now, to compose, he probably also had time to sort something out in his head. He was, as I mentioned earlier,♬♬♬ another one of those composers who felt forever in the shadow of Beethoven, certainly as far as the symphony was concerned. Let's face it, he's forty-three, and hasn't produced one yet – and if anyone was destined to, it was him. So, maybe the release from the nine-to-five of the Gesellschaft meant that he could finally get a grip on all that. Because, only one year later, the musical stork arrived *chez* Brahms, and he found himself the proud father of a finished manuscript – 'It's a symphony!' he cried. And it was: big and bouncing and weighing in at four movements.

When you hear it live for the first time, there's always that bit in the

♬ *Which the more astute among you will know is the title of an early, ultimately discarded draft of a Richard Rodgers song.*☺

♬♬ *Again, the more astute of you will recognize the ancient quote here: 'And there was much wailing and gnashing of teeth and tearing out of hair, verily much in contrast to thine earlier throwing in the air of hats! And they were sore. Not sore afraid, just sore!' from the obscure* The Song of Wensleydale, *Chapter 7, Verses 9–21. Out of print.*☺

♬♬♬ *I refer the honourable gentleman to the section headed 'Brahms and THE MAN' on page 185 of this very publication.*

last movement when you think, 'Is that… it is, isn't it?', because there's a bit in the finale where the composer, probably quite deliberately, writes a tune which is reminiscent of Beethoven's *Ninth.* In fact, Brahms himself was said to get rather prickly if anyone pointed it out, and so, no doubt, had done it deliberately. Odd decision, if I might quote from *Four Weddings and a Funeral* – to feel forever in the shade of someone else when it comes to symphonic writing, and to then almost put a quote in your first piece from the very same, said composer. It was no doubt the final link that that would lead critics for years after to dub the work 'Beethoven's Tenth'. Still. At least he's got number one under his belt. What next? Well, the world's his lobster.

SAX AND VIOLINS

Time now to grab **1878** with both hands, turn it upside-down, give it a good shake and see what falls out of the pockets. Let me talk you through the contents.

First up is an obituary of Victor Emmanuel II of Italy, who passed control of the country to his son, Humbert. There's also a now rather knackered old piece of Karl Benz's new motorized tricycle, which was capable of some rather hair-raising speeds, for 1878: 0–7 miles per hour in only ten minutes. This odd, Elgar-shaped object is actually a bike handlebar – A. A. Pope having just begun manufacturing the first bicycles in Britain. Also, London had just had brand-new electric street lighting put in. What else is here? There's a copy of the new Thomas Hardy novel, *The Return of the Native,* and there's George Grove's *Dictionary of Music and Musicians* – how did people survive before it was published? – as well as Rodin's *The Age of Bronze* and this. A birth certificate. For one Herman Hesse. From last year. And that appears to be it.

Oh, apart from one little thing. Well, I say 'little', it's actually something that luvvies like myself would not be able to live without. Because, would you believe it, in 1878, David Hughes invented the microphone. Amazing – 126 years ago! I'd always just presumed it was much more recent than that, don't know why. And 'David

Hughes'? Who he? Ed., as it were. You can't move for microphones, in some shape or form, these days, but has anyone ever heard of David Hughes? No. Well, not as far as I can tell, or to any great extent. There's certainly no 'David Hughes Sunday' falling on the third Sunday in April, upon which children give themselves candy microphones and everyone has a communal 'loudhail' at precisely midday. No! I think someone should do something about it. Anyway, back down from my box, before Matron sees me, and back to the reason we're here – the music.

THE DAVID HUGHES MEMORIAL PARAGRAPHS

(A small gesture, I know, but every movement has to start somewhere!)

Before we close on 1878, a quick profile of the many-headed beast that is music in the latter half of the nineteenth century. And to get such a profile, we need to answer the following questions.

(a) Where is the Church as a musical influence?

(b) What is the latest 'technology', musically speaking?

(c) How does your skin stay looking so young, Mummy?

Let me have a go at all three.

If you imagine music as being like a polo game, only with more breaks, then we are nearing the end of the romantic chukka. 1878 – it's not far from the end for this luvvie, emotional lot. Coming through now, or soon at least, are what many people have termed the 'neo-romantics' or new romantics. People like Mahler, Scriabin, the later Bruckner – people who wrung the last drops of heart-wrenching angst from their compositional sponges, as well as wearing strange ruffs round their necks and humming along to Antmusic. From then on, after that, where would people go? It's a bit like saying, 'What do you give the man who has everything?' What do you do, if you're a composer, and everything feels like it's been done?

As for the Church, well, other than in the odd corner of Europe, it casts no shadow across all music, any longer. Those composers who do write religious music – and, indeed, many still use the idioms and structures – do so out of a personal devotion or, as in the case of Verdi and his *Requiem*, are inspired directly by events or people.

And the instruments of the romantics? Well, they are pretty much stabilizing from here on in. Berlioz and Meyerbeer had more or less used everything at their disposal and, apart from the addition of the odd flash of colour – like when Adolphe Sax invented his saxophone some thirty-odd years previously, or even people such as Wagner, who invented himself a specially designed tuba so he could write more notes for his brass players in *The Ring* – then that was mainly that.

Oh, and lastly, it's because I have a solid daily moisturising regime. Glad to have cleared that up.

The main 'players' in this world are Brahms, then, and Tchaikovsky. Both late romantics, but very different types. Mr T was a real lush tune addict – he loved a big tune – even at the expense, occasionally, of the development of the music around it. HUGE TUNES, he had, and no doubt that's the main reason for his success. Rule 1 – everyone likes a nice tune, even the ones who say they don't. Brahms, too, could write a tune that you found yourself humming even before it had finished, but he was still a very, shall we say, conservative romantic. Actually, no, that's not quite right. He was, to be fair, a real, dyed-in-the-wool Romantic, but well, that's as far as it went. He didn't move things on at all. He was more than happy to find his own voice – in fact, he was probably overjoyed, considering how long it had taken – and from then on in, stick with it – permanently. Wagner? Well, he simply didn't appeal to Brahms. Brahms's favourite composer was, wait for it, Strauss II. Johann Strauss II. And he made no apologies for it.

'I let the world go the way it pleases!' he once said, and he too went his. Interestingly enough, just as Brahms had no time for Wagner, so Tchaikovsky had no time for Brahms, either. 'What a giftless bastard,' Tchaikovsky once wrote of JB. And there's not much to say about that. Call me a fence-sitter if you like but, personally, I've got time for them all. I mean, compare their violin concertos, Brahms and Tchaikovsky's, both of which were from this very year, 1878.

Both violin concertos are now firmly a part of the Fantastic Four – the big four concertos that have become the first call of violin virtuosi the world over: the Brahms, the Tchaikovsky, the Mendelssohn and the

Beethoven. But, from there on in, the similarities more or less end. Brahms's was more of a symphony with a great solo violin part, and it is well known that the first-night audience were more than a little disappointed by the fact that it was not a big virtuoso warhorse for its first soloist, the famous fiddler Joseph Joachim. The Tchaikovsky, on the other hand, was immediately declared 'unplayable' by the soloist who was meant to premiere it – Leopold Auer – and is generally considered a bit more of a test than the Brahms. But both did eventually catch on, and are now the romantic violin equivalent of jazz standards, each year seeing another crop of recordings. Again, *excusez-moi pendant je m'assieds sur le fence, mais* I love them both to death. You can call me many-sided, you can call me easy to please, you can even wrap me up in clingfilm and call me Muriel. I don't mind.

Nationalism, too, is still running deep, and, just as we edge into **1879**, a word about Smetana. Bedrich Smetana – again, can't fault him on the name front, he simply had to be a composer with that one – was a native of what is now called the Czech Republic, formerly Czechoslovakia, and, in Bedrich's day, the *much* more romantic – no pun intended – Bohemia, a part of the Austrian empire. Smetana was, like many a composer of the day, as we've seen, a bit of a patriot. He'd been there on the front line during the Prague Uprising of 1848 and, after a spell in Sweden, had gone on to become the music director of the Prague Provisional Theatre. It was from here on in, and under a much more favourable political climate than a few years previously, that Smetana would develop not only his, but more or less Bohemia's, musical voice. In doing so, he would also pave the way for people like Dvořák and Janáček, later on.

And so it was, in 1879, as Tchaikovsky was putting the finishing touches to *Eugene Onegin* and Brahms finds himself on a 'symphony' roll – he was working on a third – that Smetana pressed his blotter a final time on the still wet ink of an epic cycle of Czech tone poems.♬ He called it *Má Vlast* or 'My Country'. In effect, it was six tone poems in one: 'Blanik' (the mountain), 'Tabor' (the city), 'From Bohemia's

♬ *A tone poem, or symphonic poem as it's sometimes called, is simply a big orchestral piece of programme music – music that tells a story or describes a particular scene or person or feeling.*

Fields and Groves', 'Sarka' (a sort of Czech Amazon), 'Vysehrad' (the citadel of Prague) and, probably the most well known, 'Vltava', which tells the musical story of the river running from its very source, gaining in speed and size, through Prague – even past a dancing wedding party, camped out on the bank – till it flows majestically into the sea. This particular piece was clearly designed to leave not a Bohemian eye unmoistened, despite the fact that its central tune is not native at all, but Swedish, no doubt from his spell in the land of Konungariket Sverige, as they say in Stockholm.

MISS BRAHMS AND MISS OUT!

Ah, the days of *Are You Being Served?* What heady times. But less of that and more of the man of the moment, Eduard Marxsen. How so? Bear with me a moment.

Marxsen was a pianist, organist, teacher and minor composer born in Nienstädten in Germany to musical parents. From an early age, he helped his dad out on the organ at the same time as learning to play it, alongside the piano. I don't mean he would only play the organ if it was *situated* alongside the piano, I mean merely it was just one of the strings to his bow. He then settled – actually, he didn't play the violin, nor indeed any stringed instrument, so far as I know, so I wouldn't want the 'strings' and 'bow' reference to imply that he did, sorry – he settled in Hamburg as a teacher. It was here – AND FINALLY WE GET TO THE POINT – that one of his pupils was a little boy called Jo.

Jo was a good pupil. So good, that when Mendelssohn died in 1847, Mr Marxsen was moved to say, and I quote, 'A master of the art is gone. A greater one arises in...' ... Little Jo. OK, so he didn't say Little Jo – that's just me, trying to keep you in suspense. He actually said, a full twenty-nine years before Little Jo had written his first symphony, '... a greater one arises in Brahms'. Well, wasn't he a clever little sausage? There can't be many people who can spot a genius that far in advance, and be prepared to go public with it.

So what was Brahms doing to justify the faith that had been placed in him by his former teacher? As we know, he's now given up work at the Gesellschaft der Musikfreunde – presumably because he hadn't sold a single gazelle. The plan had been that he would compose full time, and, to be fair, so far it's all been going swimmingly. He spends most summers at Clara Schumann's place in Baden Baden.♪ In fact, some people were even saying that Little Jo was in love with Robert's widow, but, well, I don't think that's strictly true. And even if he was, there's no evidence to suggest that anything ever happened. In fact, I don't think he even managed to cop a feel.♪♪ They just seem to write to each other a lot, spend lovely summers together, and that's about it. Brahms also does a lot of writing at Ishcl, scene of the Great Vowel Robbery, where Johann Strauss II (just when you thought it was safe to step on the dancefloor) had a villa. What with that and a love affair with Italy, which results in him going back as often as he could, well, it's not long before a very, very happy Johannes Brahms has another masterpiece on his hands. I say not long – **1882**, to be precise – and it's another piano concerto, one of the hardest in the concert pianist's repertoire. And, so very cutely, Brahms decides to dedicate it to who else but…?

Clara? No.

Johann Strauss II? No.

He dedicates it to his one-time teacher and lifelong friend, Eduard Marxsen. HOW CUTE IS THAT? What a cuddly, larger than life-size bear of a man he was.

TWELVE MINUTES PAST SIX. TIME FOR AN OVERTURE

♪ *I heard you the first time.*

♪♪ *The publishers would like to apologize for the coarseness of this line, especially applied, as it is, to one of the world's great composers. They in no way would like it to be inferred that either Brahms or Mrs Schumann were, in any way, the sort of composers to ever try and 'cop a feel'. Indeed, some of the publishers' best friends are composers, and only a small percentage – certainly under 10 – have ever tried to 'cop a feel' with the said publishers. Thank you.*

So, 1882 was proving to be, all in all, not a bad year, really. Brahms unveiled his forty-five-minute-long finger-crunching piano concerto, Mr and Mrs Stravinsky gave birth to a bouncing baby boy, Igor – whose first words were no doubt a wisecrack about how awful the music was on his wind-up toy – and Gilbert and Sullivan produced *Iolanthe* in London. OK, two out of three isn't bad.♬ But let's not forget, also in 1882, that a fresh-faced, twenty-year-old Debussy produced one of his earliest works, the aptly entitled *Spring*.

Just to digress for a moment, in 1882 Debussy had a job teaching piano to the children of a wealthy woman of some standing, not to mention a fair amount of sitting down. He had been hired to play four-hand piano with them and tutor them, as well as going on holiday with them and generally being their musical 'man about the house!' But here's the thing.

THE THING

Told you. The woman in question, who was paying Debussy a tidy sum to play chopsticks with her kids every Sunday, was…? None other than Nadezhda von Meck. And if that name seems familiar, it's probably because she was the woman who was bankrolling Tchaikovsky, but would never allow the two of them to meet. And if the name seems *un*familiar, well, she was still the woman who was bankrolling Tchaikovsky, but would never allow the two of them to meet. In fact, come to think of it, maybe that's why she wouldn't have him round to hers – because she was embarrassed about having old Debussy in the back room, knocking out *Marche Militaire* with her ten-year-old. Then they might have to have that awkward, subdued conversation, 'So… you're patronising other men, are you?' 'Peter, I tried to tell you, in the middle of a 13/8 bar, but… well, it was never a good time.' In fact, who knows, if Tchaikovsky had opened the cupboard under the stairs, for all I know Grieg or Bizet might have

♬ *Apologies, apologies – that was an awful, cheap wisecrack about the music of G and S, and I take it back. But only in the small print.*

fallen out – now that would have been a little tricky to explain to the vicar over barm cakes. Still. That's only a personal theory, so let's not go spreading it beyond these four page-walls.

Back to 1882, now. World-wise, as it were, there's a very cosy Triple Alliance going on between Italy, Austria and Germany; the British have occupied Cairo – with a wordsearch, I think – and Edison has opened the first ever hydro-electric plant. The big book of the year is *Treasure Island* – actually, just think, for a moment, if that book had come out today. The merchandising and marketing men would have a field day – toy island, interactive treasure games on X-Box, everything. The big *picture* of the year is Manet's *Bar aux Folies Bergère* and the big *deal* of the year is that Queen Victoria has given Epping Forest to the nation. How jolly kind, ma'am. Maybe she got wind of the Central Line opening up. Otherwise, Longfellow, Trollope and Rossetti have all died, and Charles Darwin has simply stopped evolving. Musically speaking – or singing, to give it its proper name – Wagner conducts the first performance of his newly revised 'stage-consecrating festival play', *Parsifal.* Of course, if you are a member of Planet Earth, you may prefer to say 'opera'. And last, but by no means least, Tchaikovsky comes up with a little something.

In fact, let me write in hushed tones, because Tchaikovsky has come up with a reserved little number to consecrate the Temple of Christ the Redeemer in Moscow, a very evocative, holy place – still and calm, even. Can you imagine, then, the first performance, back in 1882? In the temple, the crowd, still hushed, are, at first, moved, not just by Tchaikovsky's introduction but by the general atmosphere of candles, semi-darkness and incense, but also by the fact that he has incorporated an old Russian hymn, 'God, preserve thy people', into the music. Lovely. One craggy-faced elderly woman, dressed in black, turns to her neighbour – a craggy-faced elderly woman, dressed in black – and smiles a half-smile in approval. Lovely. And doesn't the temple look nice? Just as the congregation are settling into their seats, Tchaikovsky decides to, how shall I put it? Well, he paints a musical picture of **THE BATTLE OF BLOODY BORODINO!** Complete with the 'Marseillaise' and 'God save the Tsar' fighting with each other for the Tackiest Sequence in Music award. In fact, just when our two old ladies think it's safe, he goes and wheels out the bloody cannons! Just quite *what* was he thinking of?

Actually, stepping back for a moment, can you honestly imagine it? Gargantuan sounds and breathtaking cannons, all set in a first performance at the Temple of Christ the Redeemer. Personally, if I listen to it on CD, I always try to crack open a packet of sparklers at the appropriate moment, in an attempt to do it justice.

THE BIZARRE AND CHARMING TASTE OF A PINK SWEET STUFFED WITH SNOW

Odd title but, still – bear with me.

1883, then. What's... 'goin' down', as they say in the trendy world of dropped letters? Well, I'll tell you what's 'goin' down'. Skyscrapers, that's what's goin' down. Or up, should I say. In Chicago, to be precise. The first ever. Not exactly huge by today's standards, but still, there it was, up there, and, well, doing what skyscrapers do, just... scraping the sky. Well. Good.

Also, Paul Kruger has become President of South Africa; the Orient Express has had its first run – Paris to Istanbul: slight delays in Strasbourg – seasonal manpower shortages, but otherwise a cracking start. What else 'gives', in 1883? Well, Nietszche writes *Also Sprach Zarathustra*, no doubt giving the then nineteen-year-old Richard Strauss something to think about; Renoir paints *Les Parapluies*, and, to be honest, we lose a bunch of heavyweights. Turgenev, Manet, Karl Marx and, saddest of all, just one year after *Parsifal*, Wagner.

One minute's silence, please. 1 2 3 4 5 6 7 8 9 10 11 12 13 14 15 16 17 18 19 20 21 22 23 24 25 26 27 28 29 30 31 32 33 34 35 36 37 38 39 40 41 42 43 44 45 46 47 48 49 50 51 52 53 54 55 56 57 58 59 60.

At the risk of going immediately from the sublime to the ridiculous, 1883 is also the year that the Comte de Chambord died – wait for this one! It's a belter. Here goes. 'That's God proving that, while he may be omnipotent and all powerful, he is a little impolite because...'

...it's coming, it's coming...

'...because HE TOOK THE LAST BOURBON!'

Oh, come on, it wasn't that bad.

RINGFLUENTIAL

So, the world MINUS the Wagmeister. What sort of an effect will that have on the price of eggs? Well, let me come up to the surface somewhere in 1883. The year that the Metropolitan Opera House opened in New York, and, more pertinently to us, here and now, it's the year that Léo Delibes had an unexpected hit on his hands.

Apart from *Coppélia*, Delibes has been more or less dining out on his only other great success, the ballet music to *Sylvia*.

Delibes was another child prodigy, born in 1836 at St Germain-du-Val, midway between Angers and Le Mans. He attended grown-up Conservatoire from the age of twelve – a little late by prodigy standards (remember, Bizet was there by nine) – but struggled to find any real success with his work. Then, when he was thirty, the Paris Opera put on his ballet, *La Source*, a work that was to start his composition career in earnest. *Coppélia* followed soon, a work still very much in the repertoire of ballet companies today. Opera-wise, though, he had lesser success.

Then all of a sudden, just eight years before he's due to pop his pointe shoes, he comes up with the music to an opera with so breathtakingly ludicrous a plot that even Barbara Cartland would have put it back in her bottom drawer. Yet, as so often happens, Delibes is virtually libretto-blind, and he somehow came up with the score to save it. *Lakme* – the world's favourite opera, if you like, considering it contains the delicious 'Flower Duet', beloved of British Airways ads, but nonetheless beautiful for it – thus giving the cue for a *further* fifteen minutes of fame and a few more suppers where he can turn to the woman on his right and start with the line, 'Haven't you seen me somewhere before?'

Not a million miles away, in Troldhaugen, the composer Edvard Grieg is also allowing himself to enjoy life a little more. He's currently at work on a tribute to one of the founders of Danish literature, one Ludvig Holberg. In 1883, Grieg was forty and had the benefit of a Norwegian government annuity to keep him comfortable. So he was able to take it all a little easier, something which might account for why he had done almost all his best work by the time he was thirty-three. Still, he duly finished his suite of pieces for piano, which he called, not surprisingly, the *Holberg Suite*. Then, no doubt, he made himself a cup of coffee. Then, maybe, stared out of the window for a few moments. Maybe he would go down and lean on his gate later that afternoon. He took another sip of his coffee. Maybe he'd look out of the window again. Or should he save that for later, after 'the gate'? So he looked down at his new piano suite.

'I could always… what… transcribe it for strings?' And so he did.

It was this latter piece, by EG, that Debussy called 'the bizarre and charming taste of a pink sweet stuffed with snow'. Right. Yes. Not quite sure I know what he's on about, there, but still. (I'd take him out, Matron, he's almost ready!)

Now, a brief insight into the heady twelve months that liked to call itself **1884** – or 'Toby' to its friends.

TO TOBY!

Ah yes, Toby. What a great year. But what is there to say? Well, I could tell you that some lucky people have been digging in the Transvaal aand haave now got raather a lot of gold in their haands. Not quite so glamorous, some other people have been digging in the middle of London, and have come up with the Bakerloo Line. In Paris, *Le Matin*, issue one, appears, possibly containing an article on the new work by local boy Auguste Rodin, called *The Burghers of Calais*. It might also have had a leader column on the pointless pointillism of

Georges Seurat, as his latest, *Une Baignade Asnières*, was giving people cricked necks the same year. In Britain, George Bernard Shaw joined the small but perfectly formed Fabian Society, while in the good old U S of A *Huckleberry Finn* was a bestseller for Mark Twain.

Back in Vienna, Brahms has swept aside all thoughts now of Beethoven, with his brand-new symphony, which many consider his greatest. Well, at least he thought he had. Sad to say, some critics immediately start calling it 'his *Eroica*'. AAAgghhh! Don't you just hate it when that happens? CRITICS! They can never examine a new work without feeling they have to point out any similarities it bears to things they can vaguely make out themselves. 'Ooh, didn't that bit sound a bit like the first bar of "Oh I do like to be beside the seaside"? It did, didn't it! Pretty sure it did!' – cue article in paper next day: 'This is quite clearly HIS "Oh I do like to be beside the seaside". Patently!' AAAGGHH!

Anyway. I should stop there. Suffice to say, Brahms's *Third Symphony is* Brahms's *Third Symphony is* Brahms's *Third Symphony*. It's wonderful, and that's all there is to it.

THREE FAT LADIES. ER, AND A RATHER THIN GIRL (WITH A FUNNY HEAD)

1888. It was a *very* good year. Let's just focus, gradually, on what was hap— actually, 'and flat feet'. That title should read 'with flat feet'. Can we correct that?

THREE FAT LADIES AND A RATHER THIN GIRL (WITH A FUNNY HEAD) AND FLAT FEET

Lovely. Sorry, but Neville is in the Retail, as they say. 1888, then. A very good year. And to focus in, as I said, well, there was rather a lot going on.

Germany gets through two bosses: William I dies, as does his successor, Fred III. Fred III's place is taken by William II – sounds like a very odd game of chess, doesn't it? William II, of course, is now more commonly known as The Kaiser or Kaiser Bill, Kaiser being simply a Germanic version of the original for emperor, Caesar, much like the Russian word Tsar. In London, Jack the Ripper has started his reign of terror, the Football League has been founded and the *FT* has commenced publication. It would be only a matter of time before someone cracks one of my favourite jokes: What's pink and hard in the morning?♬ Lovely. Only last year, '87, LL Zamenhof had devised Esperanto, the international language, and supposedly '*estras tre facile lernabla lingvo.*' And if you understood that sentence, then it must be true. Back to '88, and Emile Zola publishes *La Terre*, not in Esperanto, but in French, while Oscar Wilde brings forth *The Happy Prince, and other tales.* Elsewhere, the twenty-eight-year-old Mahler becomes Music Director of the Budapest Opera; Kipling writes *Plain Tales from the Hills*, and Van Gogh paints *The Yellow Chair* – nothing like a spot of DIY, is there?

Focusing in a little further still, on Russia, in fact, we find Peter Tchaikovsky, writing up his diary. He has had to go to some rather elaborate lengths to hide his sexuality, although some say his periods of heavy drinking were more simply symptomatic of a generally tormented soul. His journals contain many cryptic references to something he terms 'Sensation Z' – his homosexuality – so, set in the Russia of the 1880s, it's not surprising that his inspiration had, for most of the last seven years, all but dried up. 1888, then, must have seemed like a fantastic year for Tchaik – no doubt he underlined it in red and looked back on it with a smile. It was the year he got back on course. It was the year of his *Fifth Symphony.*

There's something about fifth symphonies, don't you think? Mahler. Beethoven. Shostakovich? And, here and now, or rather there and then, Tchaikovsky. To me, this beautiful 'Circle of Fifths', to purloin a phrase, is more than enough to keep me going on a desert island. While I would miss other music if I didn't have it, to have this

♬ *Answer: the* Financial Times *crossword.*

happy band of brothers would certainly fill a mass of different spots, musically speaking.

Tchaikovsky's is probably the easiest, in a way, out of the bunch. It has one minor problem attached to it, though. Someone, somewhere – own up, whoever it was – once taught me slightly rude words to virtually every movement and, ever since, I haven't been able to get them out of my head. Occasionally, if you can't shake them, it can get the better of you and spoil the entire thing. I remember sitting in on an open rehearsal of it once, and fully expecting the conductor, when he stopped and started the band, to say things like, 'OK, let's go from three bars after the Key to the Shithouse… everybody got three bars after "Shithouse"? Good. AND…' Strangely enough, he didn't.

Tchaik 5 – as I'm reliably told it is known in music orchestral circles – is, to me, absolutely glorious. Of course, if you were the critic of the *Musical Courier* at the British premiere, it was 'a disappointment… a farce… musical padding… commonplace to a degree!' I think he also went on to add that the Beatles were crap, too. Still – you can't win them all. Now, though, let me leave 'Tchaik 5' behind, and, by way of a quick aside, have a look at what it means to be 'romantic' in 1888. What I mean is, what is everybody writing? What does it all sound like? Does it all add up? Well? Follow me as I take a quick cross-section of the Romantic tree in 1888.

A QUICK CROSS-SECTION OF THE ROMANTIC TREE IN 1888

Sorry if that title looks poncy – and it does – but all I mean is, Romanticism – is it something that you can hear? Is everyone doing the same thing, more or less, give or take the odd smoking jacket? Well, the quick answer is…

… 'No.'

Wow, pretty easy, this musicology lark, isn't it? Right. Move on, I think.

OK, go on then. Let me go into a bit more detail.

A QUICK CROSS-SECTION OF THE ROMANTIC TREE IN 1888 – IN A BIT MORE DETAIL

To be honest, romanticism is like that bit just before the end of a Spike Milligan sketch from his *Q* series. You know the bit? The bit – and he used to do it virtually *every* week – the bit where it has all got gradually sillier and sillier? The bit just before the bit where everybody started edging forwards, chanting, 'What are we gonna do now? What are we gonna do now?' Not the 'What are we gonna do now?' bit, the bit before. Am I making myself clear? Well, that bit, THAT'S the Romantic period in 1888.

Why?

Well, because everyone is doing their own thing. Just as the Spike scene got sillier and sillier, so the period was getting 'romanticer and romanticer' and there are about thirty different recognizable versions of 'romantic' going on at once. It's fast approaching the point at which people, real composers, will start edging forwards, saying, 'What are we gonna do now? What are we gonna do now?' They'd call it the 'modern' period for two reasons: (a) it sounded a whole lot better than the 'What are we gonna do now?' period, and (b) Spike hadn't been invented yet. So they plumped for 'modern' instead. For now, though, it's 'very late on romantic', a sort of trad jazz 'last time round', with everyone doing their own thing, but more or less within the same guidelines.

A quick glance around and there really is a lot to take in. Erik Satie was twenty-eight in 1888, having been born into a composing family in Honfleur. As a composer, he is probably the most apt person to be mentioned in the following breath to Spike Milligan, in that his portfolio of pieces on his death would include works such as *Three Pieces in the Shape of a Pear* and *Limp Preludes for a Dog*. He was a piano player in the smoky cafés of Montmartre, who would go on, via his friendship with Debussy, to become a classic, idiosyncratic French composer, but in 1888, he stumped up his *Trois Gymnopédies*, three delightful pieces which seem to have a certain Mona Lisa smile about them.

Equally French, but nowhere near as barking as Satie, was Gabriel Fauré, then forty-three. Fauré is more or less the complete opposite of

Satie – if you can have an opposite to someone – in that his music was refined, finished, not at all light (in the sense of 'pear-shaped pieces') – and had a somewhat 'classical' air about it, although he is definitely a romantic, when all's said and done. He had been taught by the composer Saint-Saëns for the last seventeen years and had held a long succession of small organist posts for most of his working life – a pattern that would continue until he got the 'top gig' at La Madeleine in 1896. In 1888, though, he came up with his *Requiem.* It is not a Requiem in the way Verdi wrote a Requiem, or Berlioz wrote a Requiem – it's more... more a 'Requiem that would suit Betty's Tea Rooms in Harrogate'. It's a Requiem with its little finger raised, politely. Occasionally, it does try and summon up some of the darkness of its subject matter, but always does it very cordially, as if it had been impeccably brought up. Musically, it even tries to apologize afterwards. That said, it is still a small, chocolatey chunk of heaven, and is one of my favourite works. Fauré is often referred to as a 'French Elgar', and, while I think that's complete bollocks, I can see why people say it. The *Requiem*'s appearance, in 1888, coincided, sadly, with the death of Fauré's mother.

Turning back to Russia, 1888 also yielded a piece called *Schéhérazade* by the forty-four-year-old Rimsky 'If you're not going to finish that, can I have it?' Korsakov. An ex-naval officer, he was brought up in the country, basted in folk songs. He wrote his first symphony while still in the navy, before going on to be one-fifth of the Mighty Handful, or Mighty Five, a group of ardently nationalist Russian composers. His major work of 1888 was his symphonic poem, based on tales from *The Arabian Nights.* It's a beautiful piece, full of stories and people, with both the Sultan and Schéhérazade herself being portrayed as themes in the music.

So, look at that for a year. 1888 – the ever-colourful Rimsky-Korsakov, the ever-understated Fauré, and the ever-bonkers Satie. Romantics one and all, yet as different as the day is long.

And if it's differences you want, then no quick glance around the music scene would be *in*complete without a musical butcher's♬ at

♬ *What a great idea – a musical butcher. I can just picture him – a rotund, ruddy old cove in a stripy apron, singing Tavener's 'The Lamb' or Mendelssohn's 'Oh for the spicy hot wings of a dove'.*

another trio of heart-throbs from around the same time: Mascagni, Debussy and Borodin.

THE NAME'S CLASSICAL. NEO-CLASSICAL

To put these three into context, we need that musical butcher's at **1890**. Yes, it's 1890. THE NINETIES! The Naughty Nineties! Ooh! The 'end of days'. The 'fin-de-siècle'. The 'ooh, it'll soon be the 1900s' days. I wonder if it was anything like the 1990s? Maybe it was eerily similar – nothing but covers in the charts, sleaze in high office, but at least ponytails had died out – who knows? I can only surmise on that issue, but there are some things that I know for certain.

Imperialism, colonialism – call it what you will – was a bit of a buzz word. In some ways, it put romanticism in the shade – it played bigger venues, sold more records, everything! Colonialism was HUGE – it was *the* 'ism' for the 1890s. Everybody who was anybody was into colonialism. To give but one example, and, indeed, to give a feeling of everything that was wrong with it, take Heligoland. Where the Heligoland is that, you might be doubly forgiven for thinking, once for the thought, once for the bloody awful wordplay. Well, wherever it is, in 1890, Britain gave it to Germany. Simply *gave* it to them. In exchange for something, of course, namely Zanzibar and Pemba. I mean, imagine waking up, today, and having a leaf through the morning paper, and turning to the person at the table next to you, saying, 'I see Yorkshire beat Nottinghamshire, yesterday... oh, and we've been given to Swaziland, in a some sort of swap arrangement. Pass the toast, will you?' Staggering, isn't it? National sovereignty in 1890, then, was a pink form in a civil servant's bottom drawer, a few thousand miles away. I don't know.

Elsewherenessly, Luxembourg split from the Netherlands, both Eisenhower and de Gaulle were born, and England becomes a bit less of a 'Barnum and Bailey world' as TP Barnum's famous Circus departs town, after a tremendously long run at London's Olympia. Over in France, Alexander Gustave Eiffel's 320-metre-high tower has kept its place on the Paris skyline, despite the fact that the World Exhibition had now gone, and Oscar Wilde has published *The Picture of Dorian Gray*. There's also a new craze going round. It's called 'coming down with flu'. Indeed, flu is getting as big as Gilbert and Sullivan.

On a music tip – gosh, how trendy am I? – Rimsky-Korsakov has finished off yet more work by another composer, this time Borodin. R-K and fellow Russian Alexander Glazunov polished up his opera, *Prince Igor*, which had been left incomplete at his death three years previously. (What's wrong with a work that's Incomplete, that's what I say!) *Prince Igor* is a wonderfully exotic work, a great spectacle. I can't help thinking, perhaps unfairly, that the blend of Borodin's original vision plus R-K's – and Glazunov's to be fair – extra, colourful orchestration have, in the end, produced a work that is better, dare I say it, than Borodin would have produced had he completed it on his own. I once saw a performance of it, at the Royal Opera House in the late '80s (19, not 1880s) where the central bass role was taken by a man called Paata Burchuladze. I had never heard of him before the performance, and had been tipped off to expect a truly MASSIVE bass voice. All through the first scenes, I was sat there, admittedly enjoying the music, but, equally, thinking, 'Well, I haven't heard any particularly *massive* bass voice yet. Maybe they were exaggerating?' when suddenly this short, round man entered, stage left, sweeping on as if secretly propelled, like The Penguin in the *Blues Brothers*. He got to centre stage, stopped, and, suddenly, out came this STONKING bass voice. The biggest, richest, most sonorous I think I have ever heard. Stunning. It felt like a tube train was passing under the theatre every time he sang a note. I'll never forget it. If you see the name on a Royal Opera House poster any time, then seriously consider remortgaging to afford the entrance fee.

Also, within *Prince Igor* are the beautiful and striking 'Polovtsian Dances', which come complete with dancing girls and act as a sort of *Surprise Symphony* chord for the people in the corporate boxes, who only turned up because someone in the office had tickets. Gravadlax has, on occasion, been known to fly off the ledges, like a fishy projectile vomit.

In la belle France, they have le beau Debussy.

Follow the Seine west out of Paris and you will come to St Germain-en-Laye. Most tourists who venture there now are either going for the two fantastic chateaux, which afford gorgeous views across Paris, or they're heading for 33, Rue au Pain, the Museum of Claude Debussy. Back in 1862, though, the museum was a lowly shop, Debussy's dad's shop, to be precise, above which the composer was born on the 22nd of August. After a classic 'prodigy/conservatoire/composition lessons' upbringing, he became a sort of live-in musician for the wealthy Nadezhda von Meck (see Tchaikovsky), before winning the Prix de Rome like many before him, and hot-footing it to Rome, as part of his prize. When he returned he was no longer in the service of Tchaikovsky's patron. Probably a good thing – all that skulking around in wardrobes for fear of being found out was not doing his chords any good. Now twenty-eight, he's also shaken off a temporary fascination with the late Wagner and is trying his hand at a sort of early neo-classicism. He's just finished the *Suite Bergamasque* for piano, complete with 'Prelude', 'Menuet', 'Passepied' and the simply heartbreaking 'Clair de Lune'. He was attempting to emulate the stylish reserve of the clavecin (old-style French harpsichord) players from the seventeenth century, and probably found the suite's name in Paul Verlaine's poem, 'Clair de Lune, '...*masques et bergamasques*'. If you've never stepped beyond the threshold of 'Clair de Lune', then you still have a treat owing to you.

Finally, in Italy, there's Pietro Mascagni. Before we look at him properly, can I just say that the one fact I can't get out of my mind is that Mascagni was born in Leghorn. I think I read that somewhere when I was about fourteen, and it's stayed with me ever since. I imagine the minute I found out, no doubt in a school music lesson, I probably broke into a bad Foghorn Leghorn impression, 'Boy, ah say BOY...' etc, and, like most things that make me laugh, it has stuck. Anyway, just wanted to get it off my chest. Mascagni was a year younger than Debussy and, for him, 1890 would prove a bittersweet year. Having discarded the 'over-academic' teaching at the Milan conservatory, he'd spent a fair amount of time on the road, as conductor to a travelling opera company. Having settled down and married, 1890 saw him come up with his hit opera, *Cavalleria Rusticana* –

which loosely translates as 'Rustic Chivalry'. It was probably a hit for three reasons. Firstly, it's got some hit tunes embedded in a taut and concise plot. (It's short enough to be staged, almost without exception, alongside the equally well-trimmed *I Pagliacci*.) Secondly, it was not another 'Wagner pastiche' from yet another Wagner disciple. But, most importantly, it was probably the first example of 'realism' in opera. They called it '*verismo*', and a *verismo* opera would probably not have wild, showpiece, *coloratura* arias, just for the sake of it. It would, though, have realistic, everyday storylines, or themes from real life, and would have lots more recitative – the bits where singers 'sing the plot', as it were. They're not set pieces, like arias, but, having previously been used as brief links, or introductions to great arias, they became elevated in *verismo* operas, so that audiences felt that they were in a slightly less removed world than previously. I mean, to be fair, opera is still, even today, a bizarre, fake world, but post-1890 it became a little less bizarre and fake. For Mascagni, it proved to be a big hit, the only problem being that he spent the next fifty-five years trying to repeat his success, without joy. Fifty-five years trying to write the hit follow-up but never getting further than 'some esteem' or 'enthusiastically received'. How sad.

Without wishing to disseminate hearsay or gossip, I was once told that Mascagni ended his years at the end of the Second World War, in a hotel room in Rome which had been recently liberated by the Allies. Having been stripped of all his honours due to his following of Mussolini and the Fascists, he was reduced to walking from GI camp to GI camp, begging for money, desperately telling people, 'You know that great tune, that tune that everybody loves – I wrote that. Honest!' If true, the tune he was talking about was the famous Intermezzo from *Cavalleria Rusticana*, which still reels in the money for tissues and triple CDs and what have you, but which left the man from Leghorn penniless. Absolutely pen- ah say, penniless.♫

1891. Well, here we are. Out of cigarettes. Holding hands and yawning. See how late it gets. More importantly, haven't we come a long way in just, what, 233 pages. Heck of a long way. In fact, I feel

♫ *Sorry. Couldn't resist.*

we know each other well enough now, so... why not call me Stephen. And I'll call you... *you*. Good. Feels better already. Now, back to business. The business of 1891, and there's lots going on, as ever. Just as Kaiser Bill visited London, the Triple Alliance, clearly getting on like a scouse on fire, have signed up for another twelve years, with an option to buy. The Prince of Wales is the talk of the town not for talking to plants, but because of a recent libel case. In the course of the case, which involved cheating at cards, it came out that he had been throwing a fair bit of money at the old baccarat. *And we're not talking Burt!* Also, Rimbaud has died, but at least his legacy lives on in Blackpool (in the form of Les Illuminations). The artist Gaugin has nipped off to Tahiti, while in the literary vein English folk seem to be taken with the new stories from the *Strand* magazine, by Arthur Conan Doyle, featuring my favourite detective, Sherlock Holmes. Just to round off, Henri Toulouse-Lautrec has started designing music hall posters, Seurat has gone to meet his maker – possibly to be told 'It's rude to point' – and the fifty-one-year-old Thomas Hardy writes *Tess of the d'Urbervilles*.

Now to a name that is, just like Wagner, only six letters long but, in the history of music, is colossal. MAHLER. Mm. Lovely. Engaging name! It's one of those names that makes me think... *surround sound* or... the music of *fresh* country air, or... a sort of all-enveloping *musical bath*. It's a very *brown* name, I've always thought, MAHLER. Yes, definitely brown – just like Mozart's *29th Symphony*. Mahler, you see, is more or less The Next Big Thing in 1891. After a rather sad, not to say tragic, early life, with siblings dropping like flies all around him, Mahler managed to get on the musical ladder and put himself through conservatory. He *knows* he's going to be a great composer and so, being a bit of a Captain Sensible, he makes himself take up conducting. This would allow him to pay the bills, immerse himself in a sea of other scores, and generally get by financially, in a way that composing doesn't always allow. That's why, when he completed his *First Symphony*, he was Director of the Royal Opera House in Budapest, as I mentioned earlier. By the time of the premiere, he was beginning to get a name for himself as one of the great interpreter–conductors of the day. Indeed, Tchaikovsky called him 'a man of genius'. That was back in 1879, though, and it would be a good fifty years or so before his symphonies were accepted as some of the finest in history. In 1891, he was hard at work on his '*Resurrection*' *Symphony*, something which had been occupying him for the last three years, on and off. It was to be the sequel to *The Titan*, and, for it, he'd set a poem by the German poet Klopstock♫, called 'Auferstehung', or the 'Resurrection' of the title, and this would eventually form a huge, earth-shattering finale for soprano, chorus and orchestra. As I said, it goes by the mighty name of the '*Resurrection*' *Symphony*.

But I prefer to think of it as Keith.

THE SLEDGEHAMMER AND THE NUT

Despite the fact that William Ewart Gladstone is elected as Liberal PM, for the fourth time, in **1892**, the year is more famous for giving the original spin to the words New Labour. Keir Hardie becomes the first Labour MP ever, timing his arrival in Parliament more or less to coincide with Mr Diesel patenting his internal combustion engine. In the twilight world of the arts, it seems that if you have a woman in the title, you flourish. Grievous Bodily Shaw follows up *Cashel Byron's Profession* with this year's *Mrs Warren's Profession*, while Oscar Wilde comes up with the evergreen *Lady Windermere's Fan*. Elsewhere, Monet has started a series of pictures of Rouen Cathedral while Toulouse-Lautrec has focused his attention on the Moulin Rouge. The newspaper obit columns record the deaths of Walt 'Don't Call Me Slim' Whitman and Alfred 'Do Call Me Lord' Tennyson, whereas the foreign news pages mention that fifty-one-year-old Antonin Dvořák has been appointed Director of the New York Conservatory of Music – for full story, see arts pages.

If the same arts pages had featured a brief résumé of the life and career of Dvořák, it might have read something like the following.

♫ *He of the two smoking barrels.*

> Dvořák was born in the fairly humble village of Nelahozeves, just north of Prague. His dad was the village innkeeper as well as the butcher, and any music that he heard early on must have been fairly simple stuff – folk music, mainly. At the age of sixteen, he was sent to organ college, which, to be fair, is an awful thing to do to anyone. He went on to learn violin, though, as well as viola, and eventually ended up playing in the band of the Czech National Theatre, where his musical director was none other than Smetana. At the age of thirty-two, he married, and, at thirty-three, won an Austrian composing competition. This was the big break, albeit, by great composers' standards, a little late. On the board of the composition prize jury sat Brahms, who was clearly impressed with Dvořák's work. The two became firm friends, and Brahms introduced the younger composer to his publisher, an important step on the road to becoming musically solvent. From here on in, things fell into place for Dvořák. It wasn't long before he had been made Professor of Music at the Prague Conservatoire, and, to bring us up to date, director of the new music school in New York.

In the further worldlymode of musibold, as Lord Stanley of Unwin might have said, deep joy.

Tchaikovsky – a year older than Dvořák – has managed to brush aside his melancholia. He'd been touring America and had been cheered to be regaled as something of a living legend. In the end, though, he would miss Russia too much, and end up going home. The short-lived mood of optimism, though, led to a light, frisky new ballet score. It was based on a little fairy story by Estimated Time of Arrival Hoffman, and was packed to bursting with cute, fluffy tunes that make your teeth 'PING' with brilliance and your Christmas jumper GLOW with fuzziness. Luckily for us, the scenery for this little bundle of joy – *The Nutcracker* – is pulled out of the stores every year around Christmas and New Year, and its joy seems as if it will never stop. Of course, sadly for Tchaikovsky, its jolliness was but a brief respite from his tortured and morbid depression, and his friends began to wonder how long he would be able to survive.

In Vienna, the same year, the cognoscenti are all awhirl over the premiere of Bruckner's new symphony, his eighth. Ironically, despite his age – he's now nearly seventy – it's only been since his seventh that he's been considered a true master. Sadly, too, he's only got four years left. His *Eighth* is, as those in the know had now come to expect, a mammoth work, running to nearly an hour and a half unless the conductor has somewhere to get to. Coming after the slow movement of his *Seventh*, written in honour of his late idol, Wagner, the *Eighth* still shows Bruckner as a huge disciple, with its quartet of Wagner tubas and a scherzo that is virtually perfection.

Stand the two pieces back to back, and they are chalk and cheese; north and south; hairy and smooth (not sure about that one, but still) – the Bruckner a mighty sledgehammer of a piece, with the Tchaikovsky the nut. As concert-going spectacles go, they need a different frame of mind. The *Nutcracker* is a tight, pleasure cruiser of a piece, a sort of hop-on, hop-off of perfect little tunes, while Bruckner Eight is more an ocean-going liner – once you're on board, you're on board. There's no getting off for quite a while, but there's plenty of luxurious, sophisticated entertainment to keep you ecstatically happy all the way. My word, don't I talk bollocks? But you know what I mean.

1893 IN THE STYLE OF THE ELEVEN-YEAR-OLD JAMES JOYCE. ONLY WORSE

'Eighteenninetythreesome of independentlylaboured with Kiermosthardie aswellasthe dual-duel-jewelaffordedby franc(incensed?)russian and now trulyallied. Cheerfor Hansel greetall by humperdinck, englebert – names alongsidedly decidedly HenryBenzKarlaFord and backagain. Oh, moveover newartnouveau-ver, the tolling bellextolling 'gone Gounod, hear Coalport, gone petrilichtchaikovskyite'. Man reaches Manchester-le streets run with watercanal, while materialmatters in matabele materialize in rabelaisian rebellion. A lady, Margaret Scottfree is a woman with little importance-or-less, at once the same time.'

Good. Clear as a bell. Actually, let me just pick one partially concealed item from that litany of nonsense, namely 'gone Gounod, hear Coalport, gone petrilichtchaikovskyite'. That was meant to be something like 'Gounod♬ dies (in 1893), but Cole Porter is born, whereas Peter Ilyich Tchaikovsky dies.' True enough. In exchange for one of the greatest songwriters ever, we had to part with Gounod and Tchaikovsky in **1893**.

Earlier in the year, Tchaik had travelled to Cambridge to receive an Honorary Doctorate of Music from the university, and, not long after, conducted the premiere of his new symphony, the *Sixth*, presumably with one hand firmly on his crown so as to spare the people in the front row the distasteful spectacle of his head falling into their laps. (Well, it would be awful, wouldn't it? I mean, just think of the dry-cleaning bills, alone.) He'd labelled his *Sixth Symphony* the 'Pathétique', and its first night audience would prove to be more than a little unimpressed. But let's not get on to that.

Cut now, instead, to Ellis Island, where Dvořák had recently landed – not long after Tchaikovsky had left – with the firm intention of making America his home. Spookily, he, too, had an Honorary Doctorate in Music from the University of Cambridge in his case.

So. It's 1893 – I know, I know, I keep saying that – and two very different composers have come up with two very different symphonies. I mentioned chalk and cheese earlier, and here it is again: these two symphonies, heads firmly above the parapet, as if to prove not only quite what a melting pot of different styles and sounds 'late romantic' really was, but also quite what a different hand life had dealt their two creators. On the one hand, you have Tchaikovsky's *Sixth*, the 'Pathétique', complete with a quote from the Russian Requiem

♬ *Gounod, Charles: French composer, mainly remembered today for his reworking of Bach's* First Prelude *to make the 'Ave Maria'. In his time, he thought he might turn out to be a priest, but, eventually, composing got the upper hand. He won the obligatory Prix de Rome (didn't they all) and even spent five years in London, where he went on to found what is now the Royal Choral Society. Sorry to put Gounod in a footnote, but, well, space* is *at a premium.*

service and described variously as one of the greatest of the genre, 'a homosexual tragedy', and 'the most pessimistic utterance in all music'. On the other hand you have Dvořák's *Symphony No 9*, 'From the New World', complete with quotes from Negro spirituals and Native American tunes, and so full of optimistic exuberance for a new beginning. 'Pathétique', and 'From the New World' – just their titles say it all. Within months, the depressed composer of the 'Pathétique' would, some say deliberately, help himself to a glass of cholera-infected water and die. Within years, the optimistic composer of 'From the New World' would return to Prague, become boss of the Conservatory, and be made a life peer in the Austrian House of Lords. Two symphonies, two composers, two vastly different outcomes; but both high romantics at the height of their powers, producing simply fantastic works. Incompletely and utterly yumerouslyness.

SEAL OF THE CENTURY

Wow, this seems like a huge leap, but, well, I refer the honourable gentleman to the title on the front of the book cover that I gave, a few moments ago. *IN*complete! *IN*complete! OK? Good. Now, I want to cut, mercilessly, to **1897**, so let me lift up the edge of the carpet and show you a few years that I swept underneath.

I've got to mention **1896**, without whom this film would never have been made. Sorry, I was reading from the wrong set of notes, there. I've got to mention 1896, because of Richard Strauss, and a piece of music he composed therein. It's more or less a symphony – a three-movement symphonic poem, to be precise – the first two minutes of which are a sort of 'The Big Bang for orchestra', and make one of the best uses, ever, of the organ as an orchestral instrument. It was called, after the Nietszche book, *Also Sprach Zarathustra*, and part of it went on to fame and probably no fortune when it was featured in the Stanley Kubrick film *2001: A Space Odyssey*. It was also the year that gave us the last Gilbert and Sullivan operetta, as well as a whole lot of stuff going on in South Africa – far too complicated to get into one line. It is, of course, also the year that a host of countries unite in the first modern Olympic Games. All that and one of the greatest, most romantic (in the 'slush' use of the word, I mean) operas ever written. The thing of beauty that is… *La Bohème.* (Wipes tear from eye.) But, sadly, we haven't got time for that right now – maybe later. We've got to crack on and seal the century.

Yes, it's **1897** – what about that for sleight of hand? – and we really are skating. Very soon, there would be a new century, and then where would we be, eh? Indeed. But for now, it's '*fin de siècle*', as they say in Leeds – the nineteenth-century's autumn years. Queen Vic was having her Diamond Jubilee and HG Wells is the author of the moment. This year, he had startled everyone with *The Invisible Man* and, a couple of years back, it was *The Time Machine* – he's on a roll. Also, JJ Thomson has discovered the electron. In fact, I have a transcript, here, of the precise moment he did:

'…Bloody hell, that's small!'

Wow. It's as if you were there, isn't it? Added to that, there was a famine in India, the remains of a Gold Rush in Canada's Klondyke, and, well, you can almost feel the new century approaching. The art world, too, is really pulling into another interesting period. Just as Sir Henry Tate donates an art gallery to the British people, figures such as Matisse and Pissarro are really beginning to produce amazing work. This year, it's *The Dinner Table* from Matisse, and the *Boulevard des Italiens* from Pissarro. Rodin is also still knocking 'em out – a bronze of Victor Hugo in 1897. In music, sadly Brahms has died, and Mahler has taken over as MD of the Vienna Opera House. Good and bad, I suppose, depending on your point of view. Yes, he did produce wonderful things with the Viennese Opera, but it is said that he didn't suffer fools gladly – a bit of an acid tongue, old Gus, by all accounts.

Of music in general, though, in 1897? Well, it's still such a mix! It's not just a mix of styles now, either, it's a mix of out and out languages too. That Spike Milligan bit I was talking about. It's not that people don't agree on the *styles* of the sounds to make any more, or on the *feel* of the music. No. Very soon, if not already, they will start to disagree on the very ESSENCE of music – the syntaxes, the languages, the rules on what even *constitutes* music. In much the same way as it happens in literature and in art, music will look in on itself and say, 'Well, no, actually – I don't take that as understood at all. I want to go right back to the basics and question how we think of, and what we think of as, music.' And let's face it, once you start doing that, there's no stopping.

But for now, we're safe. No one has split the atom, no one has split the tone. Er, as it were. Indeed, if you wanted to be assured that 'music' is still intact, so to speak, and that it would always be there if everything went wrong, then you need look no further than what John Philip Sousa was putting out in 1897.

It was called *The Stars and Stripes Forever*, and it felt like pure, bottled Uncle Sam, scored for military band. It would do Sousa's bank balance no harm at all, with the royalties making him better off to the tune of some 300 grand, during his lifetime alone. The clever little sausage. For now, though, let's nip back to Blighty, with a stop-off in Paris.

1 ACROSS: CONFUSING GAME IN MUSIC FROM 1899 (6)

Before we get to 1899, a stop-off, as promised, in the Paris of 1897. Paul Dukas was Paris born and bred. He lived in Paris, studied at the Paris Conservatoire and, indeed, would end up teaching composition there before his death, in Paris, at the age of sixty-nine. He was one of a number of young chaps who were very fond of the music of Lille-born composer Edouard Lalo. By 1897, though, Lalo was dead, and Dukas was working on a symphonic poem – wasn't everybody? – which he hoped would make his name as a thirty-two-year-old composer with his very *own* voice. Sadly, in the incomplete and utter scheme of things, we haven't really got too much space to devote to M. Dukas, let alone Edouard Lalo (I hope against hope that he had two children called Leila and Lulu but I can find no evidence for it), except to mention two things. Firstly, in 1897, Dukas did, in fact, come up with a piece that established his own voice, namely *The Sorcerer's Apprentice*, beloved of Disney fans everywhere and originally written as a musical depiction of Goethe's story 'Der Zauberlerhling'. 'The Sorcerer's Apprentice' is one of those titles that is equally poetic in all three languages – in English, it certainly has a certain style and shape; in German it is impressively declamatory, and in French, it's simply sumptuous: *L'Apprenti Sorcier*! Mmm. Gorgeous.) Secondly, the tragic thing about Dukas is that, some ten years or so after having found his voice, he lost it again – that is to say, when he was in his forties, he burned almost all the works he'd written since the age of twenty. Tragic. He's also one of those people who, when you discover their dates, seem to be in the wrong time. Before I knew anything about him, I had always put him in my mind next to Brahms or Mendelssohn. To find out he was still alive in 1935 came as a complete shock. Paul Dukas and, say... Churchill, sharing breathing space. Doesn't seem right, does it? But it is.

1899 is right on the edge. We are teetering not only over the vast unknown of a new century but also over the gaping chasm of a new era. A new *musical* era, that is. They would eventually call it MODERN – the Modern Era – which is a bit daft, if you ask me, because, well, of course it's modern, it was 'today'. What else would it be? And what do you call the period after that, then, eh, when you've burnt your bridges with 'modern'? The VERY modern era? The BLOODY modern era? The 'Ooh, it's so modern, it hurts' era? Exactly! Where will we be then, eh? Well, that remains to be seen. For now, let me tick off my eras, otherwise the time and motion people will have me up on one:

☑ Early
☑ Medieval
☑ Renaissance
☑ Baroque
☑ Classical
☑ Early Romantic
and
☑ Late Romantic (it always helps, having a sibling in an older year)

Good, and any minute now, I'll have Modern. Marvellous, the complete set. I haven't felt this happy since I got my full series of original GWR rolling stock pictures, signed by the drivers. Priceless! Enough of that, though, because I wanted to zoom in on England, as I said, and, in particular, on Malvern in Worcestershire. Bit of a giveaway, really, for yes, I am heading for the home of England's finest, one Eddie 'The Eagle' Elgar.

Yes, the man in the handlebar moustache – or, as someone once said, 'Not so much a handlebar, more the whole bike!' – is the saviour of English music, Elgar. But where is he? Not geographically, I mean, but in 'the great scheme of things', as they say on a monsters' housing estate. It may help, actually, if we try one of those either/or sets of questions on him, the sort of the thing that have become very popular as small space-fillers in the Saturday and Sunday papers. Try this:

Beatles or Rolling Stones?
Oh, Beatles, I think!
Big or small?
Big.
Roger Moore or Sean Connery?
Mmm, Roger Moore, I suppose. (In fact, I think he'd look good with handlebar eyebrows.)
Brahms or Wagner?
Definitely Brahms.
Upstairs or downstairs? *Again, definitely DOWNstairs. Er, but never BELOW stairs!*
What was your most embarrassing experience?
I once passed the port to the left!
Where or when were you at your happiest?
With my wife, Alice, walking in Malvern.
How would you like to be remembered?
As the man who wrote the gentle 'Sospiri'. Definitely not the guy with the complicated moustache on the back of a £20 note.

Has that helped? No? Sorry. Worth a try.

Elgar was the first *important* English composer, at least on the world stage, since Purcell back in 1695. In fact, England, in between these two giants, was dubbed 'the land without music'. But Elgar changed all that. Elgar was the first British composer in years who was not only recognized as 'great', but whose music could be traced back to its land of origin. It didn't *sound* like any other country – not colourful and vibrant Russian, not delicate, pointillist French, not even severe, iron-clad German. It sounded ENGLISH. Not surprising, really, when you look at Elgar himself.

In 1899, Elgar was forty-two. He was born in Broadheath, near Worcester, the son of the local organist and music shopkeeper, a man very much at the centre of musical life in the town. 'A stream of music flowed through our house and the shop and I was all the time bathing in it,' he once said. His early hits were cantatas – *The Light of Life*, *King Olaf* and *Caractacus.* They were delightful, 'of their period' choral works, but destined to be eclipsed by what came in 1899 and beyond. It was in this year that he put together a set of pieces based on a single, short theme. He called them the *Variations on an Original Theme – the Enigma*, or *The Enigma Variations* for short.

To be fair, there were two enigmas involved. The first was that each piece was a musical picture of one of Elgar's friends but bore only the initials or the nickname of that friend. So 1899 society had to work out who it was being portrayed in each movement. So, for example, the most famous movement, 'Nimrod', could be worked back to Elgar's publisher. How? Nimrod was 'the mighty hunter' in the Bible – the German for hunter is *jaeger* – August Jaeger was Elgar's publisher. See? It's not quite Araucaria, but it was good enough. But it's the second enigma which is possibly more interesting and it is simply this: what was the theme? Was it just a totally original theme, written by Elgar – end of story? Or was it, as rumour came to have it, hiding another well-known tune? Some say it *is* totally original, some say it is 'Auld Lang Syne' – messed around a bit – while others say it is 'Rule Britannia' or the theme to *Are You Being Served?*♬ ☺ There is even one school of

♬ *To be fair, that's actually my own personal theory.*

thought – yes, this has, over the years, occupied many waking thoughts of the musical cognoscenti (or should we say in this case *in*-cognoscenti?) – that the theme isn't the theme at all, and that it is merely a tune that 'fits round' another tune, this second tune left unplayed. Are you with me? No? Never mind. It doesn't really matter. As for Elgar himself, well, in true English schoolboy style, when asked to reveal the theme, he more or less replied 'Shan't! Can't make me!' Sorry, let me rephrase that: he retained an impressive level of decorum by maintaining a healthy silence on the matter all his life, eventually taking the secret of the *Enigma* to his grave. *The Enigma Variations*, though, thankfully will remain with us for ever.

1899 was also the year that the young Viennese composer S———g wrote his work for string orchestra, *Verklärte Nacht*. Sorry about disguising the man's name, but I don't want to frighten the horses. It's a name that can discomfort people, you see, and often necessitates the use of a supporting helpline, to run during the credits.♬ His full name is printed in the footnote at the bottom of this page.

S———g would have been twenty when Elgar wrote his *Enigma Variations* and he, too, was a shopkeeper's son – a shoe shop, though, not a music shop. His dad died when he was sixteen, and he immediately went out to earn money to support his family – often walking a fine line between living and barely just existing. As a result, he had virtually no proper musical training, although he had already, by then, taken up violin and cello. He put his innate musical talents to good use, though, by conducting theatre orchestras and taking in other people's music, which he would orchestrate for money. His early

♬ *Arnold Schoenberg was the first great exponent of a style of music known as 'twelve-tone', or, if you're writing a posh academic paper, dodecaphony. It sounds complex but it's really quite simple. If you look at a piano keyboard, you will notice that there are twelve different notes between any two notes of the same name. So, between middle C and the C above, there are twelve notes; between D and the D above, twelve again, and so on. Basically, the whole of music is made up of twelve notes repeated over and over again at different registers. All Schoenberg did was invent a set of rules that said you couldn't play any one note again... until you had played all the remaining eleven first. Does that make sense? So, if you wrote an E, say, you couldn't just write another E straight after it. You had to wait till you'd played each of the other eleven notes – (C, C#, D, E♭, F, F#, G, A♭, A, B♭ and B, in this instance) before the E could sound again. Of course, most people think this somewhat arbitrary rule results in music that sounds like the devil clearing out his garage. It is for this reason that I will spare you the name Schoenberg except in small print.*

music, such as the aforementioned *Verklärte Nacht*, is very much in the style of Wagner or even Richard Strauss, so, if you see it on the bill of a concert, the composer's name alone should not make you run for the hills. It was only after this, and, to be fair, after the epic *Gurrelieder* (the 'Songs of Gurre', the Danish castle, home to the song-cycle's hero, King Waldemar), that someone accidentally left S——g out in an overheated room, and he, sadly, detuned himself. Schoecking, but true.♬☺

PC WORLD

Would you believe we're up to **1901**? It only seems like yesterday that it was the day before. We are well and truly nearing our completeness, not to mention our… our… utterance. As it were. So, while I'm here, let me take in the sights and sounds of MCMI.

Actually, just looking back over my shoulder and peering into last year, I can see the unlikely debut pairing of *Uncle Vanya* and *Lord Jim*, as well as Cézanne's superbly titled *Still Life with Onions*. Also, following last year's relief of Ladysmith and Mafeking, Britain has now annexed the Orange Free State and the Transvaal. The Man with the Huge Handlebar Moustache – Elgar – revealed his *Dream of Gerontius*, something about which Sigmund Freud would no doubt have had something to say in his big book of last year, *The Interpretation of Dreams*. Elsewhere, The Man with the Huge Handlebar Moustache – WG Grace – has retired, having scored around 55,000 runs in a career spanning forty-five years. As for The Man with the Huge Handlebar Moustache – Sir Arthur Sullivan – er, well, he has died. Oh dear. Jolly popular things, these 'handlebar moustache' thingies. But anyway, back to 1901.

The big news of 1901, of course, was that Queen Victoria died. Yes, the Woman with the Huge Handlebar… actually, no, I'd better not. Just in case. The longest reigning British monarch has finally

♬ *OK, so not true. In fact, a cheap shot. Schoenberg is, clearly, hard to listen to, but it can be very rewarding. There's a choral work, just to take one example, called* Friede auf Erden *– Peace on Earth – which is just too beautiful for words. That's odd, really, considering it's full of them.*

gone to be with her consort, and is succeeded by her son, Edward VII. In other news, the Peace of Peking ends the Boxer Uprising, Theodore Roosevelt succeeds the assassinated William McKinley, and the building of the Panama Canal is finally agreed and sealed into a treaty. Great things, treaties. I have this idea that they were the historical version of the office sales conference. I can just imagine people talking about them, in much the same way:

> 'Hey, *I went on a great treaty last month!*'
> '*Yeah? Where?*'
> '*Oh, only Frankfurt.*' *Sighs.* '*Yeah, last year it was Washington!*'
> '*Fantastic!*'
> '*It wasn't half. You should have seen the boss signing! It was awful!*'
> '*No-o-o!*'
> '*Oh, yeah!*' *Pause.* '*Mm. Hoping to get 'em to stump up for Versailles, next time.*'
> '*Nice!*'

What else? Well, on the whole, much as we passed – officially at least – from the late romantic to the modern age, well so we have passed from the century of steam to the century of electricity. I mean, more or less. In fact, it's a good way of highlighting the 'music' thing – as well as this 'age' thing – because these labels, 'late romantic' and 'modern', or whatever – well, they are just that. Labels. Nothing more. And, just as nobody changed from the century of steam to the century of electricity *overnight*, so nobody downed romantic tools and took up modern ones. Quite the opposite, in fact. The Romantics would continue *being* romantic for a good few years yet. In fact, you could argue that they never died out, but we'll get on to that later.

Back in 1901, as ragtime becomes the big thing in the US, over in Paris, Picasso has got the blues – big-time, and he would stay 'blue' for the next four years. (Obviously didn't know about St John's wort back then.) Over in Italy, Verdi has died and left much of Italy heartbroken. Hundreds of thousands turn out to see him to his final resting place in the grounds of the home for retired musicians in Milan – a home he himself founded with the proceeds from his many successful operas. Dvořák is still doing well, though, coming up with many beautiful works from the comfort of an old age where he was celebrated as a living legend. In 1901, he gave us the opera *Rusalka*, with its stunning aria, 'Song to the Moon'. It's inspired a lot of good music, the moon, when you think – Dvořák, Debussy, sort of Beethoven (even though it wasn't his title). Over in Russia, though, it was doing nothing to inspire the twenty-eight-year-old Sergei Rachmaninov.

1901 was a turning-point year for Rach. He was, generally, doing well. He'd got one piano concerto under his belt, as well as his opera, *Aleko*, and the ubiquitous 'Prelude in C sharp minor'. The latter was already becoming a bit of a millstone round his neck, and, while he still thought it was a great piece, he resented being asked to play it absolutely everywhere he went. What he needed was another PC. But there was a problem.

To be fair, it was a little cocktail of a problem, one part the critics and public to four parts the composer Glazunov. Glazunov had been entrusted with the premiere of Rach's *First Symphony*, but had not really done the composer any favours. The performance was an unmitigated disaster, with many people saying that Glazunov was three sheets to the wind. The critics and public slated it, and a sensitive Sergei went into emotional meltdown. He burned the score of the offending symphony – possibly something of a luvvie gesture, as the orchestral parts survived – and suffered a crisis of self-confidence and depression. The answer was a much-documented series of consultations with a hypnotherapist, Dr Nikolai Dahl, or 'Tarka'☺ to his friends. Some say it was 'positive suggestion', or the hypnotherapy, which brought back his muse, some say it had only been a temporary writer's block anyway, and it would always have cleared with a man like Rachmaninov. Whatever the method, the result was, in 1901, his most enduring work, even now, and it bore the dedication 'To Monsieur N. Dahl'. It was, of course, his *Second Piano Concerto*.

For me, the PC2, and indeed, to be fair, most of the Rachmaninov oeuvre, is a taste I have only relatively recently acquired. My innate, immediate reaction to such PURE romanticism was always to put the defences up. I like less 'over the top' works, so I thought, music that didn't give you a piggy-back as it waded through treacle and delighted in its own slush. This was the case right up until my late twenties, when, all of a sudden, I just fell into it, in much the same way as some people inadvertently fall into an entire career. I let myself go, let down my guard, first with Puccini, who we'll come on to soon, and then with Mr Rachmaninov himself. Now, of course, I couldn't live without him, just as I couldn't live without virtually any of my favourite composers you'd care to mention. To me, listening to Rachmaninov is like filling a bath with rich, warm, chocolate sauce and allowing yourself to bathe in it, drink it in, lie in it and lick it all off afterwards. Something I do fairly regularly, now. Musically speaking, of course.

Rachmaninov's *Second Piano Concerto* illustrates perfectly what I was banging on about earlier – about the 'periods' or 'eras' being just labels. It was 1901 when he wrote it, a full year after the bell for the so-called Modern Period had gone, and there he was, gaily writing the full-monty, 100 per cent luvvie, romantic gush, and so he would continue to do. Three cheers for him.

Incidentally, while we're on the subject of former East German goalkeepers – in my head, at least, I was – let's just try and plot the size of Rachmaninov's hands. To get some idea of the size of those famous paws, try this. Draw a line 10 inches long. Better still, allow me. Now put dots at either end. That's how far his left hand could span, from thumb to little finger. Fair enough, you might say. But now, put dots at 1, 3 and 6 inches along the line. These were the points where his fourth, third and second fingers could go. (Or Ruby Ring, Toby Tall and Peter Pointer, as Rachmaninov used to say.) That changes things a little, doesn't it? And remember, this wasn't just something he could stretch, at pain. This was the kind of chord he could throw in IN PASSING in the middle of pieces. And his right hand? Well, that's on the next page. Look at that.

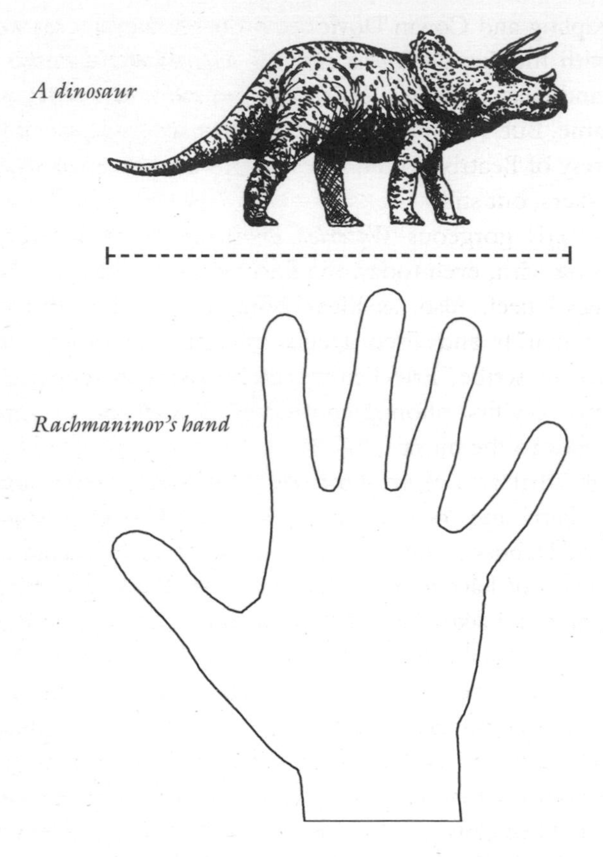

PARIS AND VIENNA – A TWO-CENTRE BREAK

1902. The Boer War had just ended. With a treaty, of course. Everyone took themselves off to, let's see... Vereeniging. Not too bad, I suppose. It certainly could have been worse – Hunstanton was available due to a late cancellation, I understand. The final casualty statistics were something like Boers 4,000, Brits 5,800, which says it all, really. Other stuff? The Aswan Dam opens, Portugal is declared bankrupt – it only finds out when its card is refused at the supermarket, which is embarrassing – and Charles Richet, the French physician, discovers the whole scenario of anaphylaxis (extreme allergic reaction to antigens).

In the arts, Kipling and Conan Doyle are probably the biggest writers of the year with the *Just So Stories* and *The Hound of the Baskervilles* respectively, and, alas, *zut alors, bof et honi soit qui mal y pense*, we've lost Zola. Shame. But, looking on the bright side, we have gained Peter Rabbit, courtesy of Beatrix Potter. Not sure it's entirely a fair swap, O great-one-upstairs, but still.

Monet's utterly gorgeous *Waterloo Bridge* captures, forever, the Thames crossing with, even today, the finest views in the capital, give or take a huge wheel. Also, as Elgar works on his first *Pomp and Circumstance* march and Fred Delius dictates the notes of his *Appalachia* to his scribe, Eric Fenby, the heart-throb tenor Enrico Caruso cuts his very first phonograph record. Which sort of reminds me, let's get back to the music.

Let me take that two-centre break, as it were, and see what was happening in Paris and Vienna. In Paris, first, there's Thoroughly Modern Claude Debussy. This frisky forty-year-old was someone who, no doubt, would not have minded the label 'modern' in the slightest. He found Brahms, Tchaikovsky and Beethoven simply dull, and wanted his music to follow a totally different route. Living in Paris, the centre of the visual art world at the time, he was probably more up to date than most with new forms and ideas. He'd even been able to hear things like the sounds of a gamelan♪ orchestra He'd come across them at one of the grand exhibitions that were so popular around the turn of the century, and he'd been awestruck. It must have sounded different from any other music he'd ever heard and he wanted *his* music to be different – to *sound* different. A few years back, he'd managed to get tongues wagging with his *Prélude à l'Après-midi d'un faune*, in which he'd tried to soften the focus of his music, if you know what I mean. What I'm trying to say is that he'd tried to do exactly what seemed to be happening in painting at the time. In a Monet picture, you often see a subject in soft focus, as it were, and not sharp and photographic like the artists

♪ *If you, like me, thought that 'gamelan' was a song by the Bay City Rollers, then you should try and get to experience them. They are little Javanese percussion instruments, tuned and varying in size, which make one of the most delirious sounds imaginable. London's Royal Festival Hall used to – think it may still – have a gamelan room so, if you're ever in town, pop in. Loosen your tie, leave your brain at the door, and visit a parallel musical universe.*

of old. Debussy had done more or less the same with *PAL'AD'UF.*♪ Now he wanted to go a step further. So he wrote an opera, ironically a variation of the Tristan and Isolde story, and he did it in a pretty new and different way. There was no huge, big-tune aria; there was no real dramatic role for the orchestra; and there were almost *natural* speech rhythms for the voices. It would probably have sounded 'not right' to the opera-going public of 1902 – not worthy of a riot, as such, but, well, simply 'not right'. Dull, even, forgive me for saying so. They maybe wouldn't have got it. They could have been shouting for the big tunes, but wouldn't have really been disgusted by what was on offer. I'd love to have been there, just to see, for sure, what the reactions were. I get the feeling it would have been a case of a short, polite silence, followed by the word '*Et...?*'

As for Vienna, well, Mahler's new symphony would probably have got more or less the same reaction, even though it was completely different. Since we last came across Mahler, he's converted to Catholicism, chiefly to become boss of music at the Vienna Opera House. In 1902, some five years into his tenure, he'd managed to finish his latest symphony. And here's where we put him up against Debussy.

Mahler and Debussy in 1902. Two very, very different composers indeed. Mahler was no innovator, really. He was a symphonist. Despite the work of Beethoven, Brahms and Bruckner, he felt that he could take the symphony further – and he was right. He wanted to take the symphony to its height, a sort of 'Romantic Symphony, the Final Reductions, EVERYTHING MUST GO', as it were. He'd gone down a totally different avenue from that trodden by Debussy and, not surprisingly – and sorry to state the obvious, but I have to – he'd ended up somewhere totally different. Both works are masterpieces with the Mahler maybe giving up its treasures a little easier than the Debussy – and it's not often you hear that said about old Gustav. Mahler's *Fifth Symphony* – for it is he! – centred on the majestic *Adagietto*, is a brown, autumnal, rolling sea of a piece, whereas Debussy's *Pélleas et Mélisande* is a fine, idyllic work which somehow steals from bar to bar like a ballerina on pointe.

♪ *What a great acronym – Debussy's* Paladuf. *Love it.*

A 'MUSIC IN FINLAND' ~~EXTRAVAGANZA~~ PARAGRAPH

We get to Finland just in time for the New Year. Of **1903**, that is, and, as the famous Lord Monty of Python so rightly sang, 'Finland, Finland, Finland, the country where I quite want to be, eating breakfast or dinner, or snack lunch in the hall!' Ah yes, true words. Words of wisdom. And as they went on to say, so sadly neglected, and often ignored. Well, back in 1903, a man called Jean was going some way to repairing that.

Back then, the words 'Finland' and 'music' were beginning to be used together, most commonly, to talk about the man called Jean. He was once called Johann, but, by 1903, he'd long since changed his name.

People were now (then) saying that Jean Sibelius WAS Finnish music. To be fair, it's pretty much the same today, for most people anyway. Finnish music was and still is Johann Julius Christian Sibelius. By 1903, aged thirty-eight, he was a bit of a local, national and, pretty much, international hero. His work, *Kullervo*, had made him a bit of a celeb, some twelve years ago, and *The Swan of Tuonela*, *En Saga* and his *First Symphony* had done nothing to dent his reputation. He was the saviour of Finland's national music. In 1899, he'd produced his tone poem, or symphonic poem, call it what you will, *Finlandia*. I get the impression that *Finlandia* more or less sealed the triumphant fate of Sibelius, in 1894, in that, from that moment on, he could do no wrong in his own country. Had he filled his time with nothing more than whittling wood and 'mowing the old lawn' from that point on, he would still have spent his years having his drinks bought, turning down offers from blondes to have his children and seeing his face appear on stamps. Actually, that last bit's true – he did appear on Finnish stamps.

So, if life was so good, what was eating old Jean, because something was? I'll tell you. By 1903, he still hadn't achieved his boyhood dream. In fact, to be fair, he never would. You see, as recently as 1891, Sibelius had still been applying to the Vienna Philharmonic to be a VIOLIN PLAYER. Not a conductor or composer, but a FIDDLER. He'd *always* wanted to be a fiddler, from as far back as he could remember. He was good, too, but, sadly, not great, and he would never make it. So. How to come to terms with the fact that he was never going to be the greatest concert violin virtuoso the world had ever heard? Apart from consoling himself with fine cognac and great cigars, he did the next best thing. He wrote, arguably, the greatest violin virtuoso *concerto* the world had ever heard. In 1903.

It's a concerto that takes your breath away. Fierce. Urgent. Celestial. Angry, even, and not surprisingly. The last movement seems to transcend just a concert piece to become a ten minutes or so of music theatre. I have no real practical knowledge of the violin – unless you count picking one up from the transport lost property office, having left it on countless buses while still at school – but I always imagine that you can really attack the last movement of the Sibelius *Violin Concerto*. It's so aggressive, so 'and furthermore...', it's the violin giving an Arthur Scargill speech, complete with jousting finger. Marvellous work.

'I ~~DON'T~~ DO WANT TO CHANGE THE WORLD, I'M ~~NOT~~ LOOKING FOR...'

Are you sitting comfortably? Then I'll begin. Once upon a time, in a land far, far away, there was an awful lot of war going on, and thousands of people were being killed. No, not exactly a fairy story is it? Descriptive enough of **1904**, though. Russia and Japan were the main ones, *this* year, to be fair, with Port Arthur besieged, Seoul occupied and what have you. In the field of science, Rutherford and Soddy had just postulated their general theory of relativity, the first ultraviolet lamps had appeared, and – well I imagine it counts as science – Rolls-Royce had been founded. Also, Freud had published a little light bedtime reading in the form of *The Psychopathology of Everyday Life*. Lovely! Bet it was flying off the shelves as people read it with their cocoa, the world over. What else? Jean Jaures issued the Socialist paper, *L'Humanité*, Helen Keller graduated from Radcliffe College, and the first radio transmission of music occurred in Graz in Austria.

As for Anton Chekhov, well, he's only gone and died, hasn't he! Tch! Not before issuing *The Cherry Orchard*, though. Add to all this Picasso's *Two Sisters*, Rousseau's *The Wedding* and the death of Dvořák, and well, that's nearly the end of 1904.

But not quite! Oh no.

No. Before 1904 can finish, the London Symphony Orchestra give their first ever concert. Still going strong today, despite a close shave in 1912, when they cancelled their crossing to New York aboard the *Titanic*. Lucky, really. Still. All's well that end's well.

Musically, there's such a lot going on, so it might be a good idea if I just illustrated two pieces back to back, by way of saying 'Gosh, weren't there a lot of crazy different styles going on, back then,' and also by way of skipping the rest out. Yes, why don't I do that.

Charles Ives. It's a very nice name, very placid, I always think. But it conceals a wonderful life, that placid name. Mr Ives was originally a Connecticut businessman and a very successful one, too. He made millions. From insurance, would you believe. But when he had to leave his business through ill health, he turned to what had up until then been his hobby – his music. His dad had been a band leader, and I think it's fair to say that he was not a typical late-nineteenth-century example of the species. He'd have his son sing in one key while he played piano in another, just for fun. (This is one area where I feel I'm at a distinct advantage compared to even some of the best musicians in that I've been able to sing in anything BUT the key being played ever since I was little.) With an upbringing like that, something was always going to stick, and Ives went on to experiment with 'bi-tonality' (as they call it in boffinland, literally 'two keys') in his more serious mature pieces. So, in *Three Places in New England*, from 1904, he features two bands playing different music at different speeds. It was said to have been inspired partly, too, by an occasion where he witnessed something similar in the street, with two marching bands approaching the same point, playing different stuff. Great fun.

This was also the Year of the Butterfly for the forty-six-year-old Giacomo Puccini. Puccini was born into a time in Italy when a man with a gift for heartfelt music and a love of opera could only ever do well. By the time Puccini was twenty-six, Verdi had been on a self-imposed musical silence for some eleven years – hadn't produced a note, opera or otherwise. And he wouldn't for a good few years yet. A Verdi-less period, in the end, of some thirteen years! A gap had opened up in Italian opera. Puccini entered a one-act opera, *Le Villi – The Witches*, in a local publisher's opera competition. Totally brushing aside that it was not even mentioned in despatches, he managed to get the work staged and it was a big success. By 1904, Puccini had already written three truly great operas – *Manon Lescaut*, *La Bohème* and *Tosca*, with *La Bohème* entering many folks' books as one of the greatest operas ever written. This year, though, produced what Puccini would go on to call his own favourite from his entire collection of operas. It concerns a young geisha called Cio-Cio San and her tragic love for the BASTARD! US naval officer, Lieutenant Pinkerton. He left the opera with the same title as the original play on which it was based. *Madame Butterfly*.

Puccini opera isn't everybody's cup of tea. Indeed, as I confessed earlier, there was a time when I wouldn't go near it with a bargepole – well, have you ever tried to check a bargepole into the ROH cloakroom? It's lush stuff, it's raw stuff, too, in the sense that Puccini is shameless in using material that other composers might shy away from, for want of being called 'cheesy' or 'louche'. ('Jejune', even.) But Puccini says, no, if that's what tugs at the heartstrings, then that's what I'm going to write – and he does. It's shameless stuff – 'vulgar', I remember being a buzzword, one season, at the Opera House's production of *Turandot* – but it's quite simply FAB. *Un bel di*? You bet it is.

And you see, that's what I love about 'classical' music – how can you ever think you'll tire of it when it can mean Charles Ives's *Three Places in New England*, but it can also mean 'Dolce notte' from Puccini's *Madame Butterfly*? Is there any more varied thing on the planet?

SYMPHONY OF A THOUSAND DAYS

To be strictly accurate, or should that be 'inaccurate', that headline should read Symphony of a Thousand Or So Days, but, well, it didn't read quite as well. The Thousand (Or So) Days are the ones between the dawn of 1907 and the dusk of 1910, and they just happen to be The Thousand (Or So) Days within which Mahler wrote one of his biggies. The one that would send the orchestra manager in Munich apoplectic, with its demands for an extended set of musicians of up to a thousand people. (Poor man, probably had a nervous twitch for the rest of his life, like Herbert Lom in the Pink Panther movies.)

1907, then. The Russo-Japanese war ended with the, wait for it, Treaty of Portsmouth. The Treaty of Portsmouth! Wow, I bet they were all a bit sore about that. Portsmouth! And they'd been hoping to have it in Barbados! Also, Norway has separated from Sweden (Norway got the CDs), the Sinn Fein Party is now founded and Albert Einstein has, by this point:

a) formulated the special theory of relativity,
b) formulated the law of mass energy,
c) created the Brownian theory of motion, and
d) formulated the photon theory of light.

It's no doubt at this point that someone taps him on the shoulder and says, 'Hey, Albert, love. Look, nobody likes a smartarse. OK?' Elsewhere, Oscar Wilde has published *De Profundis* – from the grave, Picasso has moved from blue to a healthy pink, while Cézanne and Ibsen have, in turn, moved from a healthy pink to a less healthy composty brown. Er, that is, they died. Sorry. Tried to break it to you gently. In 1907 too, the recently created Nobel Prize for Literature goes to Kipling, while, in the 'arty' world, Cubism is the big noise, as proven by Pablo 'Pink' Picasso's *Les Demoiselles d'Avignon* – which loosely translates as 'Ooh, I don't fancy yours much!' As for the divine world of music, well it is probably blissfully unaware of the latest trick up Gustav Mahler's sleeve.

Mahler's world had been rocked of late. When one of his daughters died from scarlet fever, he partly blamed himself for having 'tempted fate', as it were, in writing the *Kindertotenlieder* – the 'Songs of the Death of Children'. So, he moved away from Vienna to America, where he would eventually conduct the Rachmaninov I mentioned earlier. So by 1907, he was at the Metropolitan Opera

House, sparring with the conductor Arturo Toscanini and not having too good a time of it. He did, though, find time to finish his *Symphony No 8*, the aforementioned GIGANTIC 'Symphony of a Thousand'. It is in two simply GARGANTUAN sections. When it was finally premiered, in Munich in 1910, it would set its first-night audience alight and the rest of the world would eventually follow on behind, too. It is, in many ways, the ultimate resting place of the symphony. Just as Wagner had shown people the ultimate resting place of opera, so Mahler gives them the direction for 'where symphonies go to die'. It calls for virtually all the forces that Mahler could fit on the page – a double-sized chorus, extra boys' chorus, seven soloists and five times the number of woodwind. What would symphony composers do after this one? Actually, I'll tell you what they'd do. They'd shut up shop and go home. That's what they'd do! Now, let me duck and dive round 1908 and come to rest on 1909 and 1910.

A DUCK AND DIVE ROUND 1908 – COMING TO REST ON 1909/10

Doesn't that typeface make those words look fantastic? I bet it could make any writing look fantastic. As an experiment:

Half a dozen eggs
Carton of semi-skimmed milk
Jar of Marmite (have run out)

See? It even makes my shopping list look great, doesn't it? Great thing, typefaces. Anyway, let me miss out 1908 – apologies, but I've got a book to end – and go straight to **1909**.

In Britain, Asquith is PM and Lloyd George is his Chancellor. Louis Blériot has just made the crossing from Calais to Dover in thirty-seven minutes, and the age of electricity has, sort of, gained a sibling. Following the first ever production of Bakelite, some people are saying the 'plastic age' has started. In London, HG Selfridge sets out his department store – although yes, he doesn't actually sell fridges – while in Vienna, Freud sets out his thoughts on psychoanalysis, and in France,

Diaghilev's Ballet Russe have set out to capture the hearts of Paris. The artist Utrillo sees Picasso's blue and pink periods and raises him a white, and Vassily Kandinsky starts to produce the first truly abstract art. What else? Well, the Girl Guide Association is established, and no doubt lots of the new recruits are simply *desperate* to have the latest 'in' hairstyle – the strange, new *permanent waves*. Oh, darling, it's so YOU!

So there we are: girl guides and perms. That's the important stuff from 1909 covered. But what about 'la musique', as they say in Ilkley and Otley?

Music was busy still figuring out where it wanted to go. Mahler has already written the last romantic symphony, more or less. Yes, Rachmaninov and Puccini will continue writing Rachmaninov and Puccini for as long as they have air left to breathe – nothing would have stopped them, the dyed-in-the-wool romantics. And, of course, there were others. Others like Delius, a sort of English Debussy – in a school of his own, as it were. Whereas someone like Wagner had triggered off a whole religion of disciples, Delius was a one-off. He was a rogue player, following no one and leaving no trail. He eventually found his voice in pieces like *Sea Drift* and *Brigg Fair*, not to mention the breathtaking *A Mass of Life*. *A Mass of Life* is a vast swirl of Nietzsche's words and Delius's dreamlike, soul-stirring music, and is another of those pieces that should be 'experienced' in a live setting. Actually, what am I on about – ALL music should be experienced in a live setting, that's the name of the game. But pieces like *A Mass of Life* can prove simply too big for even the best CD system. If you hear a movement like 'O Mensch, gib acht...' or whatever, for the first time on CD, there's always a chance that you will hear it in the same way you might play a computer game for the first time. You can enjoy it, you can go to lots of places with it, but you might only ever get to the first level. Hear it live, and all sorts of different levels open up, levels you can get on to via doors and nuances you just didn't find the first time. It's obvious, I know, but music IS live. It's written in the small print. It has to be. MLUISVIEC. Look at the word. It's been there all along.

As well as Delius, there were also people like the thirty-eight-year-old Ralph 'Rhymes with Safe' Vaughan Williams and Igor 'Rhymes with Nothing' Stravinsky.

Vaughan Williams was another individual composer, although one who'd had more of a standard schooling than Delius, some of it under Max Bruch and some of it under Maurice Ravel (of whom more later). The combination of Bruch and Ravel teaching and the rarefied Charterhouse–Cambridge–Royal College of Music upbringing produced a unique blend in VW. I'm reminded of that feeling you get when you see a picture of the baby of a couple you know. Often, as obvious as it sounds to say it, the baby does look like a combination of the two parents, only with its own 'new baby' uniqueness. I know, I know, it's obvious, but it's just that it never ceases to amaze me. Well, VW is a bit like that. You can hear the German of Bruch in his music. You can hear the delicate 'français' of Ravel. It all comes out, though, with the particularly conservative Englishness of a Cotswold village. It's delicious, too, a musical creamy tea, only the jam's got schnapps or absinthe in it.

Stravinsky – Russia's finest. Wow, the name alone fires me up. It was one of those names that I had to have opened up for me. I refused to do it myself. Someone had to physically sit me down in front of a crummy school record player, perched precariously on its specially built hardwood ledge in the corner of the room, and force-feed me the early ballets. Even then, I wouldn't ingest it. It took a liquidized *Symphony of Psalms* before my eyes widened and I thought 'OH... MY... GIDDY AUNT!' And that was it. From then on, I listened differently to Igor Stravinsky. Sometimes, he painted pictures for me in his music, sometimes he just gave me a series of building blocks and seemed to be saying, 'Here, you assemble these. Make what you want out of them.' One of the occasions I most remember as being the former was with *The Firebird* – I know, amazing that it wasn't *The Rite of Spring*! Someone played me the Finale from the suite of *The Firebird* and I was just *gone*. It seemed to be modern music meets Hollywood ending. I was hearing all sorts of things – I could hear someone splashing bucket after bucket of paint everywhere across a wall-sized canvas, as if they were creating a Pollock-type painting. I know, I know – mixing my eras, but that's what the music seemed to be saying. But the overriding image that stuck in my head was when the orchestra settle in to those last chords. The J. Arthur Rank-type procession has finished, and these oscillating chords start, the beginning of the end. Every time – EVERY TIME – I hear a magic carpet. EVERY TIME. As soon as they start, I'm on this flat, exotic magic carpet, and we're levitating a little, then a little more, then we reach out the height of a tall room: then we descend a little, then a little more, until finally we touch down again. We haven't gone on a trip anywhere – even though it may sound like I have! – we've just... tried it out. Levitated on the spot, gone up, gone up again, then lowered, lowered again and then finally come to rest. That is exactly what is happening for me towards the end of the finale of the *Firebird* suite. One day, I'll go and see a performance and see just exactly what DOES happen at this point in the ballet.

Igor Fyodorovich Stravinsky was born at the right time and in the right place. After a fairly musical upbringing at the hands of his father – a bass in the Imperial Opera – he was lucky enough to meet Rimsky-Korsakov. He was just twenty-one at the time while Rimsky, at fifty-nine, was very much the grand ageing, if not old, man of Russian music. Stravinsky played through some of his early pieces to R-K and, just three years later, became a fully fledged pupil. The two became good friends, with Stravinsky going on to provide both music for Rimsky's daughter's wedding, and, eventually, a death chant for his own funeral. It wasn't long before he came to the attention of the big thing in ballet choreography at the time, Serge Diaghilev, and, before long, he would be shocking the music world with his dance music. But more of that in a moment.

THE TIME OF THE KINGFISHER

The time of the kingfisher or, put another way, the halcyon time. The golden years, that 'oooh' bit in history – call it what you will, just don't call it Keith. It's the time after which things would never be the same again. I prefer to label them '1911 to 1914'. So come with me, if you would, and we will walk through the halcyon years together.

In **1911**, Stravinsky was stirring it up again with his music to the ballet *Petrushka*. It was strong stuff, too. I know everyone goes on about the riots at the first night of *The Rite of Spring*, but just take a listen to *Petrushka* some time. It's amazing, and it must have sounded so *weird* in 1911. If you know it, think of the Russian Dance from *Petrushka*. Got it in your head? Now think of 1911. It's the year King George V was crowned. Now think back to that music – does that sound like the music? Now King George V, again. Now the music. Honestly, does that music sound like King George V? No! And I bet it sounded even less like King George V back then, too. Am I making sense? What I mean is that they don't seem to go together, do they? And that's the point. Stravinsky was...

CLICHÉ ALERT ! CLICHÉ ALERT ! CLICHÉ ALERT ! CLICHÉ ALERT !

...'writing out of his time'. Sorry about that, but it's true. *Petrushka* was arguably more out of its time than *The Rite of Spring*, but it was the *Rite* that caused a riot and, as a result, gets the billing above the title.

1911, by the way, is the year that the Kaiser was speaking, rather ominously, about Germany's 'place in the sun' – the same year, thank goodness, that thirty-seven-year-old Winston Churchill became First Lord of the Admiralty. In China, the Manchu dynasty fell, having been in power since 1644. WOW and then some. 1644. You see?! You see?! Yes, *things always change*, yes, agreed. (Have you still got *Petrushka* in your head?) But around this time they seemed to be changing in giant leaps, sea-changing, so to speak. Aircraft were used in a war offensive for the first time in 1911, the Italy–Turkey war, in fact. Sounds sort of 'Mmm' now, a bit 'Oh, really?' now. But think back to then. Aircraft in war must have seemed like something from another world – it must have been so frightening, so different, so weird. THIS is the world Stravinsky was reflecting, not the 'little-finger-poised-with-cucumber-sandwich-and-George-V' world. That doesn't fit Stravinsky and his *Petrushka* at all. No. He's writing music that can see through that to beyond. He's writing music that says...well, it says Braques, the cubist painter. Its says....Paul Klee, it says Jacob Epstein – all of whom were producing great stuff in 1911: Braques and his *Man with a Guitar*, Klee with his *Self Portrait* and Epstein with his tomb of Oscar Wilde, actually. And if you think back, one final time, to the Russian Dance, from *Petrushka*, then it might also be saying... 'Mahler is dead!' And, indeed, both symbolically and physically, he was.

OR WAS HE?
Mmmm?
Eh???
Mmmm???

Well, yes, actually, of course he was: died 18th May 1911, if you want the exact date. So, very dead. A lot dead. Dead dead. Dead to the power of dead. He'd 'come over all dead'. (That's enough 'deads', I think. Just wanted to make my point.)

So the answer is 'Yes', obviously he is. I just said he was.

But if Mahler is dead, who is it that's writing the lush, romantic music in 1911? Who is it that is not quite writing 'the music of change', à la Stravinsky? Indeed, Stravinsky, himself, called this composer 'cheap and poor'. Well, step forward, with score in hand, one Richard Strauss. The score in question was that of his opera, *Der Rosenkavalier*. To put it back into context, it was the music of change for Strauss – it was very much *his* way of going forward.

Richard Strauss had been born into a very musical family – his father being a very famous horn player, who played in orchestras conducted by Wagner. Having shown a ridiculously early and well-formed talent for composing – his *Festival March* is from when he was ten – he studied at university in Munich, before becoming an assistant conductor to Hans von Bulow. Looking back, he's rather like one of those people who wrap cars up in clingfilm and save them, in pristine condition, in a garage, for years. Then, they bring them out, aeons later and unwrap them. While they appear bright and shiny, they don't really appear *new*, if you know what I mean. They have all the *trappings* of new, but they're *not*... new. In addition, you have to take everything Stravinsky says with a pinch of salt, too. Given time, 'Rudd' Igor would often change his mind on most subjects, eventually going on to give you a quote that *totally* contradicted everything he'd previously said on a given subject. Nevertheless, Stravinsky's *bons mots* notwithstanding, whichever way you look at it, Strauss was holding on for dear life to an era and style that all around him were saying was dead.

HEAR THE WORLD UNRAVEL

One year later, **1912**, and Maurice Ravel would have been thirty-seven – a great age for a composer, I would imagine, if you had your health and a good twenty-five years left in you. And this seems true of Ravel, who did his first work for Diaghilev's Ballet Russe company in 1912, thus highlighting a pattern. Diaghilev's company is a rather forward-looking dance troupe, working out of Paris, and counting the great Nijinsky – the dancer, not the horse – among their number. It was the same company who had inspired Stravinsky to greatness a year earlier. This is one of the most gratifying parts of the entire 'great' artistic process – generally speaking, greatness breeds greatness. Up until his ballet music, Stravinsky had produced nothing more interesting than the *Symphony in E flat* – a good piece, but not monumental. The combination of Diaghilev, Nijinsky, the Ballet Russe *and*, it must be said, Paris itself – the capital of the Modernist movement – and, well, it seemed to make people raise their game. Certainly it did with Ravel. Despite having some great work under his belt already – *Pavane pour une Infante défunte*, *Jeux d'eau* and *Shéhérazade* – in 1912 he produced what a lot of people see as his greatest work, *Daphnis and Chloe*. Oddly enough, Diaghilev hated it. And, indeed, the first-night audience hated it. No change there, then.

Imagine you were playing 'May I?'. You know, the game where you are given an instruction and you have to say 'May I' before you do it. Only, in this instance, you're playing it in 1912. You're given the instruction, 'Take two cavernous nostril breaths.' So, you clear the lungs, and breathe in, through your nose, two massive cavernous nostril breaths. What would you scent? Well, I'm getting … hints of… Lenin and Stalin in *Pravda*: I'm smelling Woolworths opening… I'm… I'm getting a rumour of… the first parachute jump… yes, and I'm getting… is that Picasso's *The Violin*? I think it is. There's also a frisson of Modigliani… maybe the *Stone Head*… or is it *Woman with Long Neck*? No, it's definitely *Stone Head*. Mmm, I'm also getting… what is that? A strange… afterscent… it's… oh, it's the *Titanic*. Sinking. My word, what a year. That really was something. All that and Delius comes up with *On Hearing the First Cuckoo in Spring*, an orchestral tone poem which seems to capture the essence of this period – a dusky, deliquescent time, when God was in his heaven and all was still right with the world. Of course, if you were playing 'May I?' then you would just have had to go right back to the start, because you didn't say 'May I'.

Ah, to be young again. For now, though, let's see in the new year of **1913**.

Can you imagine it? The countdown – 10, 9, 8, 7, 6, 5, 4, 3, 2, 1… at which point the band break into those cataclysmic bars from Stravinsky's *The Rite of Spring*. People look up nervously from their merry, cross-arm clinches. A couple try to form some kind of dance steps around the those chords that sound like the warning of the end of the world. Amazing, not so much off-beat chords as no-beat chords, each one like nail in the coffin of the halcyon years. Nobody was expecting that. That's not exactly the music of party hats and Snowballs, is it? But, to be fair, Stravinsky is really only reflecting what's going on. Two Balkan wars, Gandhi arrested, *Sons and Lovers* by DH Lawrence, *Death in Venice* from Thomas Mann, but, possibly most fittingly, *Du Côté de chez Swann*, the first part of *A la Recherche du temps perdu* by Proust, written from within the cosy silence of his cork-lined Paris flat.

Elsewhere in 1913, the first Charlie Chaplin movies are beginning to appear and Benjamin Britten was born. In perhaps the most jarring juxtaposition, though, the hit song of the year becomes 'It's a Long Way to Tipperary'. So, on the one hand, you have *The Rite of Spring*, on the other 'It's a Long Way to Tipperary'. Fab. I guess that would make for a pretty difficult round of 'Singing the words of one song to the tune of another'. Bags not me, Humph.

You'd be forgiven for thinking, considering the big music of 1913 – *The Rite of Spring*, that is, not 'Tipperary' – that when war did finally break out a year later, the heady, noisy world of music would get even headier and noisier. Well, as I say, you're forgiven for thinking that. **1914** goes on to produce two of the softest, sweetest moments in all this music we call classical – *The Banks of Green Willow* and *The Lark Ascending*, both pieces that could only have been written by Englishmen.

Both pieces are very much products of their time. Vaughan Williams's *The Lark Ascending* is a glorious piece of picture painting, with a solo violin taking the part of the eponymous bird, swooping, soaring and hovering, yet all time preserving the inner integrity of the music. *The Banks of Green Willow* was the product of VW's friend, George Butterworth, and, indirectly, the product of Eton, Oxford and the Royal College of Music. George Sainton Kaye Butterworth, to give him his glorious full name, was twenty-nine when he wrote his most famous piece. At the outbreak of the war, he immediately signed up. Almost as soon as he got to the front, he was decorated for bravery, but was then killed on the Somme. He received his Military Cross posthumously. The age of innocence is over. Let's get to **1915**.

OH, WHAT A LOVELY...

Obviously, in terms of context, war dominates. Last year, battle-wise, it was Menur, Mons, Tanneburg, Marne and the first battle of Ypres. This year, again, it's Ypres, the four battles of Isonzo, the landings at Gallipoli, the first zeppelin attacks on London and the submarine attack on Le Havre. Keeping people sane or occupied or both were films like *The Lamb* with Douglas Fairbanks, *The Tramp* with Charlie Chaplin and even *Birth of a Nation* by DW Griffith. Ivor Novello does his bit with the hit song 'Keep the Home Fires Burning', while the big books of '15 are John Buchan's *The Thirty-Nine Steps* and Somerset Maugham's *Of Human Bondage*. In art, Raoul Dufy paints his *Homage to Mozart*, Chagall paints *The Birthday*, and Marcel Duchamp comes up with the first canvases of what comes to be called Dada. In fact, just to digress for a moment,

[Editor's warning – joke approaching:]

...I've always felt that...

[Yes, definitely joke on way]

...if I were ever to paint...

[locked on...]

...I'd be like Duchamp...

[ramming speed]

...because...because...

[going into cinema slow-mo]

...because...MY ART BELONGS TO DADA!

[there she blows]

Sorry, I'm OK now. One final thing, though, on 1915. Actually a couple of things. First, Einstein publishes his General Theory of Relativity. This isn't the cute one, the $E = mc^2$ one. This one is a twist on the concept of space-time, as it were. If I could explain briefly – ad libbing wildly here – you see, he basically said that, well, its geometrical properties were to be conceived as modified locally by the presence of a body...WITH MASS. Yeah? And that a planet's orbit round the sun, as observed in three-dimensional space, arises from its natural trajectory in modified time (obviously!) and that there is no need – NO NEED – to invoke gravity. Er, as Newton did. From the sun. Acting on a planet. Simple really, huh? And worth every penny of *Einstein for Dummies*.

Secondly, though, and perhaps more pertinently to this book, the other big thing about 1915 comes from Finland. Here, a fifty-year-old Sibelius is struggling to overcome his creative block. The war has stopped him travelling – he'd been touring Europe and America – and it appears also to have stopped him composing. Well, a little. He would eventually finish only one piece during the whole of the First World War. But then again... what a piece!

People who love their labels have called it 'his *Eroica*'. (As I've said before, why does everybody have to have an *Eroica*? Which reminds me, I must write mine.) The final movement is simply majestic. In fact, forgive me for going all American on you here but the final movement is awesome. Just, like, kinda, you know – awesome. Not just that intractable tune, but also that ending. That Victor Meldrew of an ending, so mind-boggling it makes me short of breath, clipping the words '*I don't believe it*' even on the umpteenth hearing. The ending has been called 'Thor swinging his hammer'. It has also been called 'frigging difficult to get everyone playing together' by many a fledgling conductor, but best not get into that. This whole symphony is resolute, staunch, unbending, inexorable and ultimately fine, in the best sense of the word.

But where to from 1915? Well, **1916** would seem like the most obvious place. I would concur, and posit that there is no better place to start than with Parry. If you get my thrust.

I think it's fair to say that Hubert Parry had the big hit of 1916, unless you count *Chu Chin Chow*, and, I have to say, I don't. Parry was a Professor of Music at Oxford when he came up with what is somewhat unfairly interpreted as his 'one hit', 'Jerusalem'. I mean, have people simply forgotten the incidental music to Ogilvy's *Hypatia*? Well, yes, frankly, they have. Despite the fact that our Hubert went on to complete a massive range of songs, cantatas and even symphonies, today he seems to be judged on just 'Jerusalem' and the occasional choral concert outing of 'I Was Glad' or 'Blessed Pair of Sirens' (known when I was a lad as 'Blessed Pair of Nylons', I don't know if it still is). True, 'Dear Lord and Father of Mankind' is still sung on Sundays, but lots of people don't even know it's him. It's a crying shame, and one which I insist on doing something about RIGHT NOW.

OK, maybe later.

Sorry. That's life. Haven't got time to sit around feeling sorry for a Victorian country gent. Besides, give it a couple of years – to 1918, in fact – and the 'Votes for Women' campaign takes rather a shine to old 'Jerusalem'. It's hardly surprising, considering Mrs Parry was one of the campaign's leading lights. Give it a few decades, and you'll have every Women's Institute using it as their very own 'music to get your kit off to' as they try to whip up interest in their glossy calendars and broccoli lectures.

Back to the war, and it's getting hard to keep up. There was Verdun, the Somme, and – over and over again – Isonzo. The war just keeps on keeping on, and, along with it, the first theories of the idea of 'shell shock', postulated by FW Mott. Elsewhere, James Joyce has published the semi-autobiographical *Portrait of the Artist as a Young Man*, Dada is now HUGE – particularly in Zurich – and jazz has broken free of New Orleans and is sweeping the USA. All that and Yehudi Menuhin was born. It's said the doctor slapped him on the backside and he didn't cry – he just asked for an A.

1917, now, and let's go to the twenty-six-year-old composer who appears to have looked like a goldfish. Er, smoking a cigar. True, honest! Take a look at a picture.

They say he forgot what music he was writing every three and a half seconds. (OK, so that's not true.) The man in question is Sergei Prokofiev, and this year, 1917, he produced his first big work, confusingly called the *Classical Symphony*. This delicately drawn piece was, despite its reflective nature, the music of revolution – the October Revolution, to be precise. Actually, to be more precise, I should say the November Revolution, because the October Revolution happened in November, the 7th, in fact. The reason it was called the October Revolution was that, by the terms of the *old* Russian calendar, it was still only October 26th. (Is that perfectly clear?)

What else from the year of revolution? War, of course, raged on, with the US having entered the fray. As the English royals renounce their German names, the battles of Passchendaele and Cambrai take their toll, and it must have become very hard to link this Cambrai with the Cambrai that was once the centre of the musical universe. Away from the sword, the pen of Siegfried Sassoon is busy adding the final flourish to 'The Old Huntsman' and Jung has completed his *Psychology of the Unconscious*. In Paris, Picasso has gone all surreal when asked to come up with the set designs for the Erik Satie–Jean Cocteau–That Man Diaghilev ballet, *Parade*. To be fair, Picasso is probably only mirroring Satie's somewhat individual score. If you are mainly used to the calming Satie tones of a *Gymnopédie* or a *Gnossienne*, then a healthy blast of *Parade* would certainly show you a different if related side to this most idiosyncratic of composers. The score calls for some very odd instruments indeed, namely a gun, a typewriter and, of course, a police siren.♫ So nothing out of the ordinary there, then. Actually, while we're on the subject of Satie, can I call time out, please.

SATIE TIME OUT

This won't take a minute. I just want to say, while we're on the subject of Loopy Erik, I think it's fair to say that Satie was keeping up his reputation for coming up with the best titles EVER for pieces of music. The man who would have given his publishers sleepless nights because of his tendency to write his scores in red ink without bar lines was also the man who came up with some names for classical music pieces that just haven't been bettered. I've mentioned *Limp Preludes for a Dog*, for example, but there's also *The Bureaucratic Sonata* and, my personal favourite, *Trois Pieces in the Shape of a Pear*. Delicious. Just what the doctor ordered. Right, time in again.

1917 TIME IN

1917 was an up and down sort of year for art. The Old Guard were doing what the Old Guard did best, namely dying. Rodin, Degas, both of them gone in 1917. (Special mention to Hilaire Germain Edgar Degas, one of the best names in French art. Lovely.) At the same time, though, the new lot were really enjoying being a part of one of the golden periods in art: Modigliani's *Crouching Female Nude*

♫ *In fact, it is largely unknown that Mozart's* Musical Joke *calls for a police siren in the score, although it is always played at a section when the horns are playing too loud for it to be heard. As I say, this is largely unknown, because it is largely untrue.*

was from 1917. So was Pierre Bonnard's *Nude at the Fireplace* as well as the lithographs by Georg Grosz, *The Face of the Ruling Classes.* Good year, huh?

Puccini came up with a little corker in **1918**, an aria called 'O mio babbino caro'. Gorgeous stuff. To be fair, it is more or less the highlight of three one-act operas called *The Triptych*, or *Il Trittico* – just to prove that the Italians can make anything sound fantastic. 'O mio babbino caro' – or 'O my beloved Daddy', to give it its proper translation – is from the third of the operas, *Gianni Schicchi*, with the other two, *The Cloak* and *Sister Angelica*, barely ever getting a look in. In March 1918, the world lost Debussy, too. Sadly, I imagine it had more pressing things on its mind, at the time, because the West was still firmly in the grip of world war. But, following the second battle of Marne, the German retreat to their own territory, the conference of Versailles and the declaration of a German republic, the world witnesses the Armistice of November 11th.

IF YOU WANT TO GET A THREE-CORNERED HEAD...

1919 and here comes that man again. No, not him. Our man in the tight pants, Diaghilev. Turning out to be quite an important bloke, this Diaghilev – constantly coming up with requests for his Ballet Russe that resulted in some of the best work being drawn out of his coterie of composer friends. He's just commissioned the sound of 1919, the music for a ballet called *The Three-Cornered Hat*, from Manuel de Falla – or to give it its far superior authentic title, *El Sombrero de tres picos.* FANTASTIC! De Falla had been one of the troupe of artisans all living in Paris at this fantastic time, but had now gone back to his native Spain, where he'd produced what were to be the three big works of his life: another ballet, *Love the Magician* ('Oh, darling, love the magician! Mwah, mwah!'), the exotic piano and orchestra piece *Nights in the Gardens of Spain*, and, of course, this year's *Hatty Town Suite.*

Haven't got time to dwell on him, though. I have to keep moving because it's a really big year. Teddy Roosevelt has died – probably a blessing, really, because he had one eye missing, his fur was worn and his stuffing was coming out. It's the year of the League of Nations in Paris, of the Hapsburgs in exile, and of the Red Army in the Crimea. Jan Smuts has been made PM in South Africa and Lady Astor has been made MP in Britain. All fairly crucial stuff, in one way or another. The Bauhaus, too, has been founded and built – in that order – by Walter Gropius. Kandinksy, Picasso and Klee are producing simply stunning, world-class stuff, and, instead of a novel, this year, Thomas Hardy has opted to publish his *Collected Poems.* Oh, and in the US, Mr AD Juillard has left a cool $20 million to found a new music school which would not only eventually bear his name but also give rise to the rather unfortunate TV series, *Fame*, in the mid-80s. Good on him. So, on to **1920**, and... do I hear *La Valse*?

THE DARK SIDE OF THE TUNE

The answer is probably no, you don't hear *La Valse*, unless, of course, you're one of those ... 'special people'. Hmm? No, of course you're not. Anyway, *La Valse*, by Ravel. Again, a commission from that man Diaghilev. SEE! Clever little sausage, our Serge. Still getting the best out of people. In this instance, he got Ravel while it was still good to get Ravel. You see, Maurice Ravel had been, for much of the previous four years, an ambulance driver on the Front. Verdun, mainly. I know – it seems odd to think of someone like Ravel, out there on the Front, ferrying the sick and wounded. The war had really knocked the stuffing out of him, as you might imagine it would do to a seven-stone, sensitive soul like him. The conflict is said to have virtually broken him, and he ended up retiring, shattered both physically and emotionally, and suffering from insomnia and bad nerves. Afterwards, he went into more or less complete seclusion in his beloved home, thirty miles outside Paris. He did continue to produce great music – *La Valse* being a case in point – but, with his nervous problems and his awful memories, the inspiration came far less often. It also can't have helped that Diaghilev didn't like the final score to *La Valse*, either, and his refusal to use it must have come as a bit of a blow to a man just two years out of battle.

No such problems seemed to be afflicting Theodore Gustavus von Holst, who, by now – 1920 – had changed his name to simply Gustav Holst, to lessen suspicions of German sympathies. In 1920, he suddenly found himself with a hit on his hands, when he gave the first performance of the piece he'd been writing during the war, namely *The Planets*. This mild-mannered, Cheltenham-born teacher would never better this work, and so the wait of six years or so to hear it premiered was well worth it.

Now, bless me, Father, for I'm skipping forty-eight months to get to Gershwin's blue period.

BLUE IS THE COLOUR...

Rhapsody in Blue, I mean, because... well, it's important, isn't it. The first really successful attempt to take the new music, jazz, into the classical concert hall. And there's that word again. Classical. Still sticking as the name for this sort of music despite the fact that it really means the music of the time from 1750 to around 1820. Never mind. If that's the biggest of our worries, then we're doing well. But of course... it isn't. Let me mention some of the other things that are bothering me about music right now, if I may.

A LITTLE CHAT

You see, I've got a friend who has got themselves into a spot of bother. Yes. I know. But, you see... this friend is called... *music*. Mm. I know, I know... no, I know it's not the first time, but... look, just hear me out, will you?

Thank you. You see, the way I see it, it's something like this. You remember when I expressed my feelings about Mozart and, well, I said that dog years are ment to be like human years, only times seven. Something like that. So, you give a small child a puppy, and what happens? Of course, in seven years' time the small child has progressed by, yes, well done, seven years, but the dog? Well, officially, the dog is now about fifty. And, well, a fifty-year-old and a seven-year-old sometimes don't have a lot in common, do they?

Yes, yes, I'm coming to the point, right now. My point is... my point is... well, forget Mozart, now. I think MODERN MUSIC is the puppy. The small child? Well, the small child is the AUDIENCE. The two don't proceed at the same pace. Not at all. That's why, in **1925**, composers like Alban Berg (a follower of S——g) can put out pieces like *Wozzeck* – don't know if you've ever heard it? It's a tough if hugely rewarding piece – when probably what the mass audience could take was no more than, say, Lehar's operetta *Paganini* or at best, maybe, the more verdant shifting sounds of something from the sixty-year-old Great Dane, Carl Nielsen – maybe a symphony, like the *Sinfonia Semplice*, from the same year, 1925. But, that's the problem, really. Music was never going to go backwards. Not since S——g left the transfigured night behind and found the moonlight. The moonlight from the puppet, I mean.

By golly, that sounds clever, doesn't it? All I'm saying – in this poncy, roundabout way – is that when S——g ditched any attempt at hummability, which he still had in buckets in his piece for string orchestra, *Transfigured Night* (1899), in favour of the 'It's music, Jim, but not as we know it' atonality of his song cycle, *Pierrot Lunaire* ('the moonlight from the puppet') – in which he tipped over the edge, musically, into what to a layman would seem like total cacophony – then, well, music was never going to be the same again.

Composers had, since the death of Wagner, been looking for the next place to go, the next not so much 'style' of music, but 'music' itself. They'd been looking for the next 'music', the new music that would be the next homeland, the next '–ism' if you like, that would come after Classicism and Romanticism. But, well, it never came. Not as far as the audience was concerned, at any rate. And this is the child and the puppy, back again, growing at different rates. The composers were becoming more and more intellectually stimulated by new methods – new methods that sounded, to the untrained audience's ear, like... well, like they were *wrong*. Music that wasn't right. I mean, when Berg's opera *Wozzeck* was premiered, it was greeted with utter disbelief by the German critics. As the *Deutsche Zeitung* put it:

I HAD THE SENSATION OF NOT BEING IN A PUBLIC THEATRE AT ALL, BUT IN AN INSANE ASYLUM. ON THE STAGE, IN THE ORCHESTRA AND IN THE STALLS – PLAIN MADMEN!

See? They don't like it up 'em, Mr Mainwaring. And they would go on not liking it up 'em for quite some time, in fact. Even now, although *Wozzeck* gets a public airing quite a lot – for modern music, at least – it is still an no-go area for a huge majority of people calling themselves *music fans*. Personally, I can only recommend, till I'm blue in the face, that you go to see a *great* production of it – it really can leave you breathless, just so long as it's done right. Give it a try. As Mrs Doyle would say:

'Go on, go on, go on, go on, go on, go on, go on, go on, go on...'
'Ah, you will, you will, you will, you will, you will, you will...'

Oh, look – I'm blue in the face.

While I recover, let me break this to you gently. I'm skipping on a year. Sorry. Maybe if I point to something behind you and shout, 'Ooh, look at that!' you won't notice.

'Oooh, look at that!'

TWENTIETH CENTURY ROCKS

The sun has risen on a slightly damp, overcast morning in **1926**. The last four years? Forget them. They were just a dream and they're gone. It is **1926** and let me take a quick cross-section of the musical year. Three pieces from the twelve-month period that brought us Hemingway's *The Sun Also Rises*, Fritz Lang's *Metropolis* and, of course, not forgetting the ever popular hit song, 'I found a millionaire baby in the 5 and 10 cent store.' (Ahhh, they're playing our somewhat unmemorable song again.) From the new Hungary came the forty-four-year-old Zoltán 'Best first name in all music' Kodály and his *Háry János Suite* – I wouldn't like to tell you what we used to call it at school. I have a certain soft spot for this piece, it being all about one of the biggest liars on the earth, and me having written a book called *The Liar*. The suite that was formed from Kodály's opera is a real corker, packed with great tunes as well as some beautiful soundworlds – the sound of the cembalo and the musical portrayal of a ginormous sneeze. In England, the twenty-three- year-old William Walton is premiering his suite, *Façade*, complete with the grand and slightly intimidating Edith Sitwell projecting her poems from behind a curtain. The score comes complete with musical quotes from some diverse sources – there's a bit of Rossini's *William Tell* in there, and even a bit of 'Oh I Do Like

To Be Beside the Seaside!'♫ Finally, from Poland, 1926 gives birth to the often neglected, yet often staggeringly beautiful, music of Szymanowski, and his setting of the *Stabat Mater*. Szymanowski came from the disappearing background of Poland's landed gentry, although, when his family estate was ransacked in 1917, he devoted himself to finding the voice of contemporary Polish music. Take a listen to his *Stabat Mater*, one day, because he succeeded.

Three cheers for twentieth-century music. 'Hip hip'...

I said 'Hip hip'...?

Grumpy sods.

RAVEL'S DENOUEMENT

It's **1928** – look, it's my book, if I say it's 1928, it's 1928 – otherwise I'm taking my ball back – and Ravel is puzzling over a piece of music. He's just received a commission from a dancer for a piece of orchestral music, and it has made him reach for the scraps of manuscript he started some time back. They were all about one simple short tune, repeated over and over again. In the same key. He got them out and looked over them again. Could you really sustain an entire fifteen-minute-long piece with absolutely no 'development' of the tune, and staying in just one key? The answer?

No, 'course you couldn't – OR THEN AGAIN, COULD YOU?

It would be the supreme test of a supreme orchestrator, because, to be fair, few other composers knew what sounds an orchestra could and couldn't make the way Ravel did. And furthermore, he proved it in 1928, with his *Boléro*.

OK, so it does go into another key, just a little way from the end, but to brilliant effect, it's got to be said. Nowadays, of course, some say it is tarnished, somehow, by associations with Torvill and Dean. Well, to that 'some', I say 'TOSH and POPPYCOCK!' It's still the

♫ *I know I've said this before, but, on this occasion, it's true. Honest.*

same stunning piece of music. So! Get real. It's allowed. You CAN think of Torvill and Dean when you hear it, this is a musical snob-free zone, here. Don't you worry. You can even think of lovely Dudley and his rather tall, blonde leading lady, with the... beads. Makes no difference. The music still sounds the same. And again, yes, it is one of those pieces that is played a heck of a lot, these days, now that it has become so popular. But, well, you can't ruin it. It's the sign of a great piece, maybe. Can't sit here hypothesizing, though. Got to get on. Got nearly forty years to cover in the next few paragraphs. Good job I brought a packed lunch.

FROM BEGGARS' OPERA TO COMMON MAN

Yes, the year that produced the *Boléro* also produced a new style of opera in Berlin. The words were by Bertolt Brecht, after the eighteenth-century John Gay (yes I know John Gay didn't get into this book in his own right, so to speak, but I'm afraid his century was full. I mean it was standing room only and he fell out the back.) And the music was from Kurt Weill, who, despite coming next to Anton Webern♬ in many of the music books, thought that music should be readily appreciable by the people. None of the boffin-type, system music for him – he thought that his audience should be humming his tunes before they left the theatre. Of course, he couldn't resist giving it a boffin name, could he – 'Zeitkunst' or 'contemporary art', really. I don't know, they just can't help themselves, can they? What's wrong with MUSIC, for goodness' sake?

Anyway, if he was the people end of things, and S——g, Webern and Berg were the other end, then skipping backwards and forwards in the middle was the wonderful, slightly dotty character of the forty-six-year-old Stravinsky. He was virtually a portfolio of ALL the different schools of modern music in one. Never stuck to one thing for too long. Much as in life, he was a series of not-so-much contradictions, as, well,

♬ *Another follower of Schoenberg.*

U-turns, I suppose. He went from block to block, in a sense, as if he was on stepping stones. One minute, he's just MODERN – although Stravinsky himself once famously said that he didn't *write* modern music, he just wrote *good* music – anyway, one minute he's modern, then he's using the S——g rules of harmony, and then the next minute he's almost 'classical' – or neo-classical, as the boffins like to say. From the Greek 'neo' meaning new, so not the original classical music, but the twentieth century's revisited version of it. So in **1930**, he came up with one of my most favourite pieces, ever – the *Symphony of Psalms.*

It's extraordinary stuff – a spooky-sounding cantata for chorus and orchestra, which can leave you in tears one minute then have you thinking of horror movies the next. It was just every bit as good as that other great hit from 1930, Hoagy Carmichael's 'Georgia on My Mind'. Ah, a belter. And, who knows, maybe playing in the background when CW Tombaugh discovered Pluto. 1930, you see. A good year. But roll on **1934**.

RACH-ING IT IN

At the beginning of 1934, Rachmaninov was, like Holst, Elgar and Delius, still going strong. However, unlike Elgar, Holst and Delius, Rach was still going very strong when 1934 came to an end. By this point, he had already toured America a few times – as a pianist, that is – before eventually making it his permanent home. If you compare his 1934 effort with Stravinsky's of 1930 – both Russian, both settled in America – then you get two very different pieces. Totally different. And why? Well, probably because of the audience thing, again. Stravinsky was, more or less, writing for the history books. Rachmaninov was writing for the audience. And I don't mean that as a put-down. I mean, well, he just was. He was by now in America with a place in Switzerland, and touring to make money. And, of course, being a pianist–composer, when he needed a new piece, he simply wrote one. As in 1934. Just think. The German president, Hindenburg, has just died, and Hitler has proclaimed himself Fuhrer: the democrats are forced out in Austria, following the revolution; and the thirty-year-old Salvador Dalí paints the surrealist *William Tell*. Now, listen to the lush, gush and dangerous to hush tunes of Rachmaninov's *Rhapsody on a Theme of Paganini*. Does it really seem to match? I'll leave that to you.

Just one year later now, and the Nazis repudiate the Treaty of Versailles, Mussolini invades Abyssinia, and Hitler establishes the Luftwaffe. In a speech to Parliament, Churchill warns of the German menace in the air. Now, imagine a Prokofiev ballet of the same year, *Romeo and Juliet*. In one scene, his music is set alongside some stunning choreography, which pits the Montagues against the Capulets. If you haven't seen a production, do go. For now, though, can you bring up the sound of the Montagues and Capulets in your head? Have you got it? Keep it going as you read. The Kenneth Macmillan version has the two opposing sides lined across the stage. They strut, arms alternately outstretched, left, right, left, right – they're strutting so arrogantly, left, right. And then you realize. They're goose-stepping. Left, right. Rachmaninov may not have captured 1934, but Prokofiev has certainly captured **1935**.

And then there's the small question of Shostakovich. It's scandalous I've let myself get this far, without really mentioning Dmitri Shostakovich. One year after Prokofiev unleashes *Romeo and Juliet*, Shostakovich is meant to be coming up with a new symphony. By now, he's only twenty-nine, and he is constrained by the Soviet authorities, who monitor and vet his every note.

Many composers in Russia suffered at the hands of the strict Soviet regime. The Communist Party had a very clear idea of exactly which type of music was good for the people and if they didn't hear it in your music, you were in trouble. Shostakovich had had problems with an opera of his, *Lady Macbeth of Mtzensk*, which the official state newspaper, *Pravda*, had labelled 'chaos instead of music.' His *Fourth Symphony* had, more or less, been stopped at the rehearsal stage, and had not even premiered. He was under massive pressure to come up with music that fitted in with the order of the day – 'socialist realism', as they called it. So, in **1937**, he unveils his *Fifth Symphony*, bearing the now infamous subtitle 'A Soviet Artist's Response to Just Criticism'. It was a massive hit – thank goodness for that. It is, regardless of what anybody might say about its inception, a wondrous piece, with a slow movement to end all slow movements. If, after listening to it, it doesn't make you want to just pack it all in, give up your job and take up composition, then I... ? No?... It doesn't? Well... flower pressing, then?

No? OK, try this.

If, after listening to it, it doesn't make you want just to pack it all in, give up your job and... and... and run your own grouting and repointing business, from home, then I don't know what will? Hmm? Eh? I've hit the nail on the head, haven't I? Hah! Thought so.

That was from 1937. Let me take you by the hand and lead you through the streets of 1938. I'll show you something that'll make you change your dentist.

Nearly forgot, though. Carl Orff, our man in Munich. He's 1937, actually. Now where does he fit in the scheme of modern music? I mean, think of the music from the Old Spice ad. The same one that is used in the *Omen* films. Have you got it? Well, I mean... *quite*. Eh? QUITE! It doesn't sound like 1937 at all, does it?

It turns out Orff, who was by then aged forty-two, had set some rather bawdy words written by some rather bawdy monks in thirteenth-century Bavaria – the more astute among you might have jotted down a little note, perhaps on a post-it or something, to remind yourself that I mentioned this on page 25. Orff set them to some distinctly bawdy sounding music and immediately found himself with a hit on his hands. His one hit, too, to be fair. In fact he lived until 1982, which, by my reckoning, means he almost certainly saw his music on TV, advertising Old Spice. Weird. Wonder if he used it himself. Sad thing was, upon the success of *Carmina Burana* – for it is he – he ordered his publisher to pulp all his previous works! AAAAGGGHHHHHHH! Don't you just hate it when that happens? Anyway, I digress.

1938. By now, we've had a quick game of royal chess – E7 to G5... check... G5 to E8... check... E8 to G6... check: and now G6 can mate. Er, as it were. Anyway, what I'm trying to say is that George VI has been crowned. Also, Chamberlain is now PM, and Hitler is being 'appeased', but to no avail. In 1938, he makes himself 'war minister' and marches into Austria as the pogroms sweep through Germany itself. It's also the year Orson Welles created a bit of a panic with his radio production of HG Wells's *War of the Worlds.* There were some people ringing the station in panic, others ringing to say they were being invaded and even more ringing to say they didn't get the answer to last week's mystery voice. The power of sound, eh? Also, *The Lady Vanishes* is Hitchcock's big film, Len Hutton scores 364 at the Oval against Australia, Christopher Isherwood says *Goodbye to Berlin* and, over in America, the twenty-eight-year-old Samuel Barber has come up with a little *String Quartet.*

By chance, it's heard by the great conductor Arturo Toscanini, who suggests that the slow movement might benefit from being re-scored for full string orchestra. Barber obliges and Toscanini premieres the piece in the November of '38. Again, a bit like Carl Orff and his *Carmina B*, while it could only have been written in the twentieth century, its language is that of another time, with just a sheen of the 1930s. In Barber's case, it sounds like late Mahler more than anything else. Of course, the public loved it. Still do, in fact. It's known simply as Barber's *Adagio.*

1939. Taken on its own, Rodrigo's *Concierto de Aranjuez* – particularly the slow movement – seems to be simply evoking memories of a small Spanish town, and, indeed, it was meant to do precisely that. But when you take into account not only the fact that the thirty-eight-year-old Joaquín Rodrigo had been blind since the age of three, but also the year in which it was written, the melancholia of the slow movement seems to blend in well with events. Rodrigo's *Concierto* WAS written at the onset of war, but was a personal tribute to the Spain to which he had just returned, from Paris. Delightful. But now, as the saying has it… 'Time and Tide are a jolly good read and a now outdated form of soap powder'. So let's kick on.

Of course, to be fair, the first thing that people bring to mind when you say 1939 is not Rodrigo and his concerto. Hitler's determined efforts to unite much of the world in war have finally come to fruition. There is, indeed, a war on. Musically speaking, the war will play its part, takes its toll, as it were. This will particularly be the case when composers come to reckon up the emotional effects of six years of battle. But also I'm thinking in particular, here, first of the French composer, Olivier Messiaen, who had enlisted in the French Army when war broke out. Born in Avignon in 1908, and tutored early on by Paul Dukas, he was then thirty-one and was soon captured and sent to a German prison camp at Görlitz, in Silesia. It was here that he wrote what is often referred to as the greatest quartet of the twentieth century. He called it, not surprisingly, considering the view he must have had from his writing desk, the *Quatuor pour la fin du temps* – the 'quartet for the end of time'.

Luckily for Messiaen, he was repatriated in 1942 and went back to his job as organist of Trinity Church, Paris, a post he held until his death in 1992. Also writing through the war was Shostakovich. He was in the fire brigade at first, in Leningrad. Bad eyesight had kept him from active service, but he was soon moved to the then Soviet capital, Kuibishev, where he put some of his experiences into a new work, his *Seventh Symphony*. To quote the composer himself, 'Neither savage raids, German planes nor the grim atmosphere of the beleaguered city could hinder the flow of ideas'. It's known as the '*Leningrad*' *Symphony* and, once again, Marquess of Fry rules apply – go hear it live to get a better idea of how impressive it is.

Over in the US, two important composers were brushing shoulders. Aaron Copland had, by **1942**, found his voice, as they say in composerland. He *had* been through a period of experimentation but, at the age of forty-two, was now at home with some of the more Native American folk sounds that found their way into music. He had also done the double – that is, achieved that rare thing of critical acclaim and popular acclaim. In addition, he had also pointed the way for film composers for years to come, who would imitate his 'grand canyon' chords and soaring tunes – more of this later.

Just leaving America in 1942, after a stay of a few years, was twenty-nine-year-old Benjamin Britten, who had gone back to face the Tribunal for Conscientious Objectors and do his part in the war effort – by taking part in official concerts. This he did and, not long after his return, he had come up with one of his most beautiful pieces to date, the *Serenade for Tenor, Horn and Strings*. It is, in effect, a song cycle setting a selection of poems by, among others, Blake, Keats and Tennyson to sometimes sublime, sometimes searing Britten music. It is also, in a way, war music.

I never forget a quote I heard about the great jazz trombonist, Jack Teagarden. It was basically along the lines of how he was able to play the tune of virtually any jazz standard and make it sound like it was the way the composer had intended it should be played. I often think of this when I hear Copland's *Appalachian Spring*. It isn't so much that it sounds the way the composer intended – for that we have recordings conducted by the man himself. No, it's more that *Appalachian Spring* sounds as if it has been around for ever, a bit like the way I've heard Sir Paul McCartney talk about his song 'Yesterday'. It's said he dreamt the tune one night, and, when he woke the next day, he wandered round with it in his head. Occasionally, he would ask someone, 'Have you heard of this tune?' and hum a few bars. No one he asked seemed to know the tune. After a while, and somewhat reluctantly, he came to realize that the tune was his, and that it had come to him in a dream. Again, forgive me for harping on, but various parts of *Appalachian Spring* seem like that. Yes, I know it has a Shaker tune – or the 'Lord of the Dance', as we used to call it – in the middle, but it's not that. It just feels like Copland almost wrote down the notes to a great piece, that somehow gives the impression it has been around for centuries.

He did all this, of course, in **1944**. Yes, I really have hopped, skipped, jumped and taken away the first number I thought of and, well, jumped on ahead.

It's the year of the D-Day landings, the Battle of the Bulge and the V1 flying bombs in London. It's also the year Maréchal Pétain is imprisoned at Belfort, and Hitler's generals try, but fail, to assassinate him. Elsewhere, there's TS Eliot's *Four Quartets*, *The Glass Menagerie* by Tennessee Williams, and *No Exit* by Jean-Paul Sartre. And, briefly, in the art world, there's the loss of Mondrian and Kandinsky, but Picasso and Braque have gone all, well, organic, I suppose, as they produce *The Tomato Plant* and *The Slice of Pumpkin*, respectively. Sod the Turner Prize, just enter them for Best in Show (Section 1, small garden produce).

Now, I really need to take a leap, here, so stay with me, if you will.

I want to end up in 1957, so I'm going to have to take you on something of a magical mystery tour.

FRY'S TOURS: INAUGURAL JOURNEY

Move in, down the bus, please. Fill all the seats. Thank you. A few rules first: no food or drink, please – this is a bus, not a refectory. No standing in the aisles, no talking to the driver – that's me – and no sticking your tongue out at the composers. In fact, no rude gestures of any kind. OK, there'll be a whipround for the driver – that's me – at the end, large notes only, please.

OK, we're off.

Over to your left , way over to your left, in fact, is Benjamin Britten in **1945**. He's busy on his opera – are you hearing me at the back? – on his opera *Peter Grimes.* Also, you may notice Evelyn Waugh, just behind him, waving a copy of *Brideshead Revisited* – don't wave back, please, it only encourages them – as well as Frank Lloyd Wright's new Guggenheim Museum. If you're thinking it's a bit peaceful, then well done. Yes, the war *has* ended.

On your right, in **1946** – please don't get out of your seats – you'll see David Lean filming *Great Expectations*, Eugene O'Neill signing copies of *The Iceman Cometh* – available from the driver at the end of your journey – as well as what appears to be the sleeping figure of John Logie Baird. In fact, he is... dead. Any minute now, wait a mo— yes, there he is. Benjamin Britten again – gosh, he is busy, isn't he, ladies and gentlemen. Obviously hit a purple patch – and this year he's finishing off *The Young Person's Guide to the Orchestra*, using a little tune by our old friend, the composer Henry Purcell. Keith, can you not do that with the skylights, you wouldn't do it at home! I know you don't have skylights at home, but stop it anyway.

Straight ahead of me, you should be able to see the smiling face of John Cage. Can you all see him? It's **1952**, you see, and if I just stop speaking for a moment, and let you...

...did you hear that?

That was nothing. *Niente*, as they say in Dewsbury. Bugger all. *Pas une sausage*. Odd one, really. John Cage, the forty-year-old modern composer, decides that music is all around us. You know. The birds, the trees, the traffic, even. So he writes a piece – IN THREE MOVEMENTS – which has directions to remain 'Tacet'. Silent. So, if you can imagine the first 'performance', in inverted commas: someone came out on to a concert platform – pianist I think it was, complete with page turner, and proceeded to play nothing. For 4 minutes 33 seconds. Of course, Cage has had the windows opened, so that you can hear the noise from outside, everything. THAT's the MUSIC, in the eyes of John Cage. What goes on around you. I believe the music on the first night consisted of a fair few fortissimo 'You've got to be jokings' and the odd largo hand clap. Even a sforzando cry of 'CRAP!' And do you want to know the best bit? People record it! They do. In fact, I can recommend the Frank Zappa version. I don't know what it is, there's just something about the performance.

On your left again is **1953** – Coronation Year. The music you can hear is William Walton's *Orb and Sceptre*, written especially. The couple outside are still *Waiting for Godot* – have been since last year. Please don't throw them food. The gravestone on my left is that of Dylan Thomas, who died this year, although it is partially obscured by the sculpture in the foreground, which is entitled *King and Queen* by Henry Moore. Sorry? Yes, Janice, the curvy bit of rock with the hole in the middle. Yes, it is finished.

Just passing out of view, behind us, there is a Spanish-looking gentleman in safari shorts with a net. That is Joseph Canteloube. He's very much the Gallic version of Vaughan Williams. He collects French folk tunes the way you and I might collect famous people's mortuary photographs. Or is that just me? Anyway, Mr Canteloube is very happy this year because his new piece, *Songs of the Auvergne*, is a big hit. It contains tunes he collected on his travels up and down the volcanic peaks of the Auvergne – surprisingly enough. On the wall behind him, you can see a poster for one of the big movies of this year – **1955** – *The Seven Year Itch.*

Putting music into contect can really throw up seeming anomolies, like *The Seven Year Itch* and *Songs of the Auvergne*, which just don't seem to gel. On the other hand, it can shed more light on certain pieces too. Take the next year, **1956**. If you can look to your right, you might catch the Catherine Wheel hips of Elvis Presley, only partly obscured by Leonard Bernstein's operetta, *Candide*, which is situated to the rear of the year. A far more fitting pair, Elvis and Leonard, I think. *Candide* has suffered somewhat from having a showstopping overture. As a result, a lot of people don't ever get to hear the rest of it.

Finally, we are now just pulling into **1957**, so can I just answer two questions I had earlier: yes, this is the place for a loo break, and yes, Eden has indeed given way to Macmillan. Behind Mr Macmillan, who is sat on the park bench, are representatives of The Six, the six countries who sign the Treaty of Rome, and thus start us on the inexorable trail to the prosecution of people selling bananas by the pound. The beginnings of the Common Market, in other words. There are desegregation riots in America – in Arkansas the paras are called in – and Jack Kerouac coins the phrase 'beat' or 'beatnik' in the cult book from '57, *On the Road.* All that, plus *The King and I*! What more could you want? As it is now 6.30, some of you may want to take a wash in your rooms, before going on to the concert of two new works from 1957 – Shostakovich's *Second Piano Concerto* and Bernstein's new one. I'm reliably informed they are both lovely, although my mum did tell me you might want to bring a book, or at least a good magazine, for the Shostakovich outer movements.

Actually, tour Time Out. Thanks. A quick Bernstein moment, if you will.

Bernstein was born in 1918 in Lawrence, Massachusetts, but of Russian descent. After studying piano and composition at Harvard, he pursued a career in conducting, first as assistant to the legendary Serge Koussevitzky at Boston, and then, in his own right, with the New York Philharmonic. In much the same way as Mahler before him, the conducting was just one side of the coin for Bernstein, allowing him, as it did, to compose at the same time. Thus it was that in 1957 he got together with Stephen Sondheim to write his biggest hit. Based on Shakespeare's *Romeo and Juliet – West Side Story.* It is still, today, a totally exuberant score, with – quite simply – some fantastic tunes. Well, it's got to be said.

OK. Your Time In.

And that just about brings us to the end of my very first tour. Thank you for travelling with Fry's Tours. I would remind you that there is a collection for the driver – that's me – on the way out, and, also, could someone remember to take with them the sickbag that's on the back seat. Thank you.

THE YOUNG ONES

If I could be so rude, could I just ask you to put a bookmark in this page for just a moment. Remember which line you're on, if you would, close the book, and look at the front cover.

Are you back? Right, well you will have noticed that the words on the front said 'Stephen Fry's INCOMPLETE and utter history of classical music'. And, in my view, incomplete is such a beautiful word, isn't it? It's a perfect dectet of letters, a divine decimal delight which deliciously describes the nature of the next section. In... complete. Innnnnn... complete. Gorgeous, isn't it? Makes me want to jump on a chair and sing it to the tune of *Fingerbobs.* 'In... complete... In complete...' Stunning, isn't it?

I guess what I'm trying to say in the previous paragraph is that we are about to zoom, lickety-spit, through a full three decades, not even stopping to spare the horses. So do forgive me. Here we go.

With the possible exception of Cliff and the Shadows, the other young ones of **1962** were Benjamin Britten and the *Sunday Times* Colour Supplement. (OK, so Benjamin Britten was forty-nine, which is stretching it a little to call him a young one, but the *Sunday Times* Colour Supplement was brand new this year.) Britten's incredibly moving *War Requiem* is a moving mixture of Latin Mass and the poems of Wilfred Owen. Well, I did say some of the effect of the war would take a while in coming. It was premiered just a year after the Bay of Pigs became the temporary centre of the world, and the same year that 3,000 US soldiers and marshals had to accompany James Meredith on his first day at college, to stop riots happening round him. Why? Simply because he was black.

Two years later and possibly one of the most famous 'What Were You Doing When…' events, ever. The year will forever be etched in the brain to many – certainly for me, I know – mainly for the question: **'Do you remember what you were doing the day…** the day Deryke Cooke thwarted Mahler's ambition to write the same number of symphonies as Beethoven?' At least, that's how I remember it. Yes, it's amazing, isn't it? Some musicologist finds Mahler's last sketches, and just goes and finishes them off. So you have… Mahler Ten. In **1964**. Very odd. Someone would eventually do it to Beethoven, too, but not for a good twenty-four years yet. What else has happened? Well, **'65** saw Bernstein's *Chichester Psalms*, commissioned by the Dean of Chichester, oddly enough, and premiered the same year as Lyndon B. Johnson was. Well, to be accurate, he wasn't premiered, he was presidented, I suppose. Still. Onward. No time to lose.

1967 becomes the year of Jeremy Thorpe leading the Liberal Party; of the Six Day War; of Martin Luther King leading marches against Vietnam; and of both the US and Soviet space programmes in crisis following deaths on launch and re-entry, respectively. Elsewhere, at Cape Town's Grooote Schuur Hospital, Christiaan Barnard performed the world's first heart transplant. Oh, and here's a fine couple of statistics to put alongside 1967 in your brain's filing system:

IN 1967, 5.3 BILLION CANS OF SOFT DRINKS WERE SOLD IN THE US ALONE. (5.3 BILLION!!!)

Also, do you remember that quote from Alexander Graham Bell, about his telephone – 'I firmly believe that, one day, every city will have a telephone!' Well, according to statistics from 1967, there were already, by then, 100 million telephones in the US alone. Would you Adam and Eve it. All that and we lost Dorothy Parker. 'This is not a novel to be tossed aside lightly. It should be thrown with great force.' Marvellous, but I don't know. Does it all fit with this music from 1967? I mean, Aram Khachaturian, the Armenian composer who was by then well into his sixties, brought out *Spartacus* in '67. Play the Love Theme from *Spartacus and Phrygia* in your head – or *The Onedin Line*, if you prefer – and tell me if it fits 1967. I'm not sure.

Not quite finished with the Swinging Sixties. I need to just mention that in **1969**, while Neil Armstrong was misquoting himself, Karlheinz 'No, but I've trodden in some' Stockhausen was in the middle of the first performance of his vocal classic, *Stimmung*. Now, call me odd, but I've got a recording of *Stimmung* – on vinyl, if you will! – and I think it's absolutely fab. Perfect music for putting on when you've had more than the odd glass of Chateau Margaux and someone is passing something round. OK, that's enough of that. Thank you.

Agenda Item 17: Any other business?

Shostakovich is now up to fifteen. Symphonies, that is. By **1972** – yes I said 1972 – he has premiered Number 15 which seems to get past the Communist Party unamended. That's more than could be said for 13. Communist leader Krushchev made him change the words. It seems a world away now, the old Soviet regime, doesn't it, and yet you have to remind yourself, it wasn't long ago, was it? 1972, I mean. Flares, *Last Tango in Paris*, an Oscar for Liza Minelli in *Cabaret* – and, just to forever help you to place it, Shostakovich's *Fifteenth Symphony*. Wow. There was also the death of Picasso, the death of WH Auden, and, one year later, Britten's *Death in Venice*.

Britten premiered his latest opera, *Death in Venice*, at his still-thriving festival in beautiful Aldeburgh. Sadly, it was around this time that the composer's health reduced him to doing very little composing at all.

1974. Just to place it for you, it was also the year Harold Wilson became PM again, the year Grenada won its independence, and the year Lord Lucan disappeared after the murder of his children's nanny. No, I haven't seen him. After that, well, musically, the '70s became more of a graveyard than anything else. By the time Thatcher came to power in **'79**, we had already lost Milhaud in '74, Shostakovich in '75, Britten in '76 and Khachaturian in '78. Add to that the loss in '77 of two of the world's greatest singers – Maria Callas and Elvis Presley – and you might be forgiven for retiring to your room to wrap yourself in your beloved vinyl collection.

True, the Polish composer Górecki – pronounced Goretski, apparently – had come up with a new symphony just as Concorde came in to service in 1976, but more about that later. The Górecki, that is, not Concorde. Although, having said that, let me find some time for the Italian composer Luciano Berio. Apart from writing all sorts of weird and wonderful stuff for his wife, the singer Cathy Berberian, and a bunch of solo stamina tests for different instruments, called 'Sequenza's, he also found time in the '70s to revisit a set of folk songs he'd arranged in 1964. He repolished them in '73, and, by the mid to late '70s, they were getting more than a few performances around the world. The reason? Well, probably because they didn't sound like someone tuning a shortwave radio. If you are one of those people who feel they can't really listen to twentieth-century music, then try these, because they are a very easy way in, albeit via some cute old tunes. I may be wrong, but I believe the score calls for two rather large car suspension springs to be struck at various points. Don't let that put you off, though – the Berio *Folk Songs* are lovely. Anyway. Off we go. Let me nip on to **1980**.

To Hoy, in fact, in the Orkney Islands. Very beautiful little place, I'm led to believe, and, by 1980, it had been the home of the English composer Peter, now Sir Peter, Maxwell Davies, for some nine years. He's one of what is often referred to as 'the Manchester group', because they were all making music in Manchester and they no doubt went round in a group. Probably, you know, all chewing gum, wearing shades and looking hard. Maybe not. Anyway, out of a set that included Alexander Goehr and Harrison Birtwistle as well as Elgar Howarth and pianist John Ogdon, Maxwell Davies is probably the one who wrote stuff that you have some vague chance of ever whistling. So, while the SAS stormed the Iranian Embassy on a crisp May morning in 1980, he was peacefully and, I hope, obliviously, putting the final bar line on his new work for solo piano, *Farewell to Stromness*. It is a delightful piece, written as a composer's protest against the imminent threat of uranium mining.

To be fair, it's a world away from things like his *Eight Songs for a Mad King* in the late '60s. Having said that, if you see the *Songs for a Mad King* on the bill anywhere, do try and get along, because they are a great piece of music theatre, if they're done right.

Anyway, let's take a stroll through the, let's face it, awful decade which was the 1980s.♬ Music, maestro, please.

1981 – CLARKE, OF COURSE

Well, so much to tell, so little time. **1981**, and, when Prince Charles marries Lady Diana Spencer, he does so to the strains of Jeremiah Clarke's *The Prince of Denmark's March*, otherwise known as the *Trumpet Voluntary*, at St Paul's Cathedral. The result is a rebirth for this unlikely little tune some 280 years after it was written. Couples across the country were demanding that their local organist draft in a friendly trumpeter so they could 'get married like Lady Di'. Also, the world gets the new work from Karlheinz Stockhausen, the composer who's mad, bad and dangerous to hear. It's called *Donnerstag aus Licht*, one day's worth of a seven-day-long cycle of operas, and the premiere, at La Scala in Milan, featured among other things trumpeters rigged up to loudspeakers, playing from the rooftops across the square in which the opera house stands.

1982, and new concert halls go up in Toronto, Denmark and at the Barbican, in London. It's also the year Carl 'Splash it on all over' Orff dies. Actually, that's Brut, isn't it? Oh, yes, 'the mark of a man', that's it. Ah, the power of advertising. In **'83**, cue the Richard Wagner.

♬ *When I say 'awful' here, I guess I'm not meaning musically, but culturally. Ponytails, Thatcher's children, mobile phones the size of telephone boxes. Red braces. Greed is good. Dreadful.*

No, no, he's not back from the grave. It's just his centenary, that's all. One hundred years since the death of Little Richard, but sadly... NO years since the death of William Walton, who shuffles off just as the Monty Python team are pondering *The Meaning of Life*. It's also the year we first got CDs. Yes, 1983 saw the birth of the compact disc. And the death of the art of great cover design.

Moving on, to **'87** in fact, Margaret Thatcher becomes the first British PM in 160 years to win a third term. And the confirmed incidences of last year's new bovine plague, Mad Cow Disease, are on the increase. Also, in 1987, cue the Wolfgang Amadeus Mozart.

No, no, *he's* not back from the grave. It's just that, in 1987, an original notebook containing symphonies 22 to 30, in his own handwriting, is auctioned for a staggering four million dollars. FOUR MILLION DOLLARS! He could hardly get a few gulden for his manuscripts when he was alive and in debt and now they fetch $4 million! In 1987, the music world lost Jacqueline Du Pré and, in **1988**, cue the Beethoven.

No, no, he's not back from the grave – I must stop doing this – it's just that, in 1988, the Royal Philharmonic Society decides to premiere the work it had originally commissioned from old Ludwig before he died in 1827. All that existed, before 1988, were a few sketches. In 1988, though, a man called Barry Cooper fills in the gaps and – voila – a brand-new movement of a Beethoven symphony. I don't know if you've heard it, but, well, I'm not sure what I think of it. It's odd to hear something which sounds both unfamiliar yet clearly recognizable. Weird, really.

1988 gone. **1989** now. Sir Michael Tippett premiered his new opera, *New Year*, in Houston, Texas; communism more or less collapsed in Eastern Europe; and we lost Vladimir Horowitz and Herbert von Karajan. A year later and America is bereft of two of its greatest twentieth-century composers – Leonard Bernstein and Aaron Copland. Copland, particularly, did more than any other US composer to give America its voice, and he influenced numerous composers who came after him. You can still hear his legacy in the film composers of today – more of which later. Even on TV, you can't go very far among the schedules without hearing someone who couldn't have existed had it not been for the pioneering work of Copland – he really started from scratch and founded the all-American sound so misused today. I can't watch *The West Wing* without being reminded of two things: one is Copland-style harmonies and the expansive sounds of the theme tune, which, I think, unless I dreamt it, is written by somebody called Snuffy Walden. The other is, of course, will Donna ever tell Josh?

'ESSAY QUESTION: MOVIE MUSIC – IS IT THE NEW CLASSICAL MUSIC? DISCUSS.' (NOT MORE THAN 500 WORDS.)

I'd like to start with a quick overview. Where is MUSIC? Where is its audience? Is it in crisis? And... Have I told you lately that I love you?

Well, if you ask me, Classical music is...

HERE..........

and the audience is......HERE.

At the risk of labouring my point, let me go a step further. Look around you. You see that thing you can just see miles away on the horizon? Well, that's the audience, way over there. Classical music has, more or less, with a few notable exceptions, lost sight of them – the audience, that is.

Or has it?

Well, on the one hand, the modern audience for what we have always called classical music is small, elite and, for the most part, made up of the musical cognoscenti – composers themselves, ardent musical followers of composers, people who collect locomotive numbers, academics, etc. I'm talking about the people who listen to what academics would call 'new' classical music. So, people who would turn up for the premiere of a Luigi Nono piece, or buy Pierre Boulez's *Pli Selon Pli*, the revised version, on CD. This is, officially, what the 'serious' set see as modern, newly written classical music. To these, I get the feeling people like Tavener♬ aren't really classical music at all, but mere fripperies.

It's as if classical music completely forgot that, well, it was also, at one time, the popular music of the day. True, there has always been change: startling new pieces – shocking even – that left the audience speechless, wanting to take their ball home. Remember **Wagner**, Beethoven, Bach – they all made audiences reel. Maybe not as often as they made them cheer, but it *has* always happened. What the avant-garde wave of composers did was, well, was to talk in a language that not so much left people shocked, but left them unaware that it was music in the first place and therefore deserving of a shocked reaction. In the same way that people could wander into an art gallery and not so much be startled by, say, a pile of bricks or a light flashing on and off as actually UNAWARE of it. So music, for a time, failed to even engage its audience. Whether it lost the power to shock or whether it was still shocking, but, like the flashing on and off light, no one even realized, well, it's a moot point. What I think *is* certain is that by going the way it did, modern classical music did two things. It paved the way for the obligatory backlash, which we'll come to later, but, and possibly more importantly, it allowed a whole tranche of composers, working in a specific and parallel world, to steal a march: to slip in, unnoticed, and claim the title 'the great composers' of today. More importantly, possibly, it allowed them to slip in unnoticed and *claim the audience*, too.

So, who were these masked men and women?

The Movie Composers. That's who.

So. Let me run through a brief menu of the people who now, I think, hold the title 'People's Composers' – the movie composers. But for now, allow me to sweep up a few of the corkers that came before.

1985, and the man who wrote the accompaniment to the moving gunsight that followed James Bond writes a gorgeous soundtrack to the Meryl Streep/Robert Redford movie, *Out of Africa*. The name?

♬ *John Tavener, a very spiritual British composer, born in 1944, and heavily influenced by Russian Orthodox music. He originally came to prominence on the Beatles' own Apple label. His music is hauntingly beautiful.*

Barry. John Barry. Then, in **1989**... Ennio Morricone adds to his list of great movie scores that include the Oscar-nominated *The Mission* and *Once upon a Time in America* with this year's oh-so-lovely soundtrack to *Cinema Paradiso*.

1990 and John Barry is back again. The year that saw millions watch, on live TV, the release of Nelson Mandela, sees the release of another Barry classic, the delicious *John Dunbar's Theme* for *Dances with Wolves*.

Right, we're up to **1992**, the year the frequencies 100 to 102 opened up with classical music, calling itself Classic FM. Bit of a shock, it's got to be said. The man off 'game for a laugh' telling you to bet on 'Battling Beethoven' in the 2.30 at Sandown. But still, it worked. **1993**, and the score is John Williams 2, Michael Nyman, 1.

John Williams – *Schindler's List*. This one is a corker. John Williams couldn't really have been anything else, really, other than a film composer, could he? He has the amazing knack of being able to write the perfect music to match the film. His music always *sounds like* the film. That may sound obvious, but some composers don't get it, it can just sound grafted on. That's why the theme from *Schindler's List* SOUNDS black and white, somehow. It's a perfect match for Spielberg's film masterpiece, while something like...

John Williams – *Jurassic Park*... well, this may sound daft, but I think it sounds like dinosaurs. It's... towering and lofty and epic, with undertones of 'Don't mess with me!' If you know what I mean!

In sharp contrast to John Williams is Michael Nyman, and *The Piano*. Nyman is a sort of Jack Nicholson of movie composers. By that I don't mean smiling and weird, I mean he always plays himself. A Michael Nyman score is a Michael Nyman score is a Michael Nyman score. As they say in the world of triple-entry book-keeping. As they say in the world of triple entry book-keeping. As they say in the world of triple entry book-keeping.

Ah, now this is a cute one. **1994**. The Channel Tunnel opens, Tony Blair is elected leader of the Labour Party, and playwright/former angry young man John Osborne dies at the age of sixty-five – all as the surprise film hit of the year produces an Oscar for the composer Luis Bacalov, *Il Postino*, or, as it's now known, *Il Consignio*.

1995. An interesting year, I think. Nick Leeson single-handedly brings down Barings Bank, Nelson Mandela becomes president of South Africa, and John Major wins the Tory leadership challenge – 'Oh yes'. I don't know, if only we'd known about Edwina, he might have lasted a lot longer. Also, though, the year of Patrick Doyle, with the Oscar-nominated soundtrack to *Sense and Sensibility*. A gorgeous score. Also in 1995 we got a taste of things to come. I remember it staying in the Classical Charts for what seemed like months. And long after the film died down, the score was still topping the charts. Yes, it was the start of the uileann pipes craze, namely... James Horner – *Braveheart*.

The year after *Braveheart*, as the Globe Theatre is finally opened after some years of campaigning by Sam Wanamaker, there were Oscars for Rachel Portman for *Emma*; and Gabriel Yared for *The English Patient*, which scores a direct hit, particularly with its delightfully ursine title, Rupert Bear. Ahh, bears. Don't you just love 'em? Yummy. Anyway, **1997**. Princess Diana is dead, Hong Kong is returned to China, and the *Titanic* does anything but sink. I always love hearing a composer playing his own music, whether it's Peter Maxwell Davies playing *Farewell to Stromness* – readily available – or even Robert Schumann playing his own 'Traumerei' – a little more rare – there's something about it that makes me listen with fresh ears. James Horner's recordings of some of his own music to the *Titanic* are in this category.

Now, in 1997 Stephen Warbeck had had some success with the music to *Mrs Brown*, but his **1998** offering brought him a nice, shiny, golden Academy Award. And very lovely it is too. Great film. Great score. It is *Shakespeare in Love*. Gorgeous.

Now, skipping on to the year... **2000**. A new millennium. By now, we've had the Clinton–Lewinsky saga, Elgar has got himself on the back of the £20 note – good thing too – and we are in the age of the Euro. All this, and a cult hit for Tan Dun with *Crouching Tiger, Hidden Dragon*. Beautiful yet haunting music it is. To **2001**, though – foot and mouth, 9/11. A testing year. Plagues and terror – it was ever thus. The films of the year, musically speaking, are possibly...

Stephen Warbeck – *Captain Corelli's Mandolin*

Howard Shore – *The Lord of the Rings – The Fellowship of the Ring*
John Williams – *Harry Potter*

Three of the films of 2001 further signalled the rise and rise of movie music. In terms of Oscar honours, while John Williams is the second most nominated and rewarded Oscar composer, with thirty-seven nominations and five awards, it is Canadian Howard Shore who has appeared to come out on top, recently. Shore's scores to both *The Lord of The Rings – The Fellowship of the Ring* and *The Lord of the Rings – The Return of the King* both won him Oscars at the 74th and 76th annual Oscar ceremonies.

Not bad, Fry. 7/10,
PS, you owe me an essay on Keats.

ALL MOD CONS

So, there it is. Some of the film music of the nineties and noughties. Is it the new classical music? Well, it could be. But, as I said a little earlier, there has been the 'obligatory backlash' to the crash-bang-wallop music of the avant garde, the 'what the ***!' music of the arch-modernists. And this, too, has created a whole new, different, more accessible breed of composer. Some of them new, some of them old, but all of them with a different outlook. Film composers? They're done and dusted. Allow me now, if you will, to quickly zip back to 1992. Classical music 'post' Classic FM, if I could be so bold. Where is it going? What's it all about? And so on, and so forth. Well, let's crack on and find out.

Hang on to your G strings and clasp tight your bow – we're off. 1992 was the year Classic FM launched and it didn't take long before the first discernible 'Classic FM hit' was born. And wow, was it a intriguing one.

It actually came in **1993**. Steffi Graf beat Jana Novotna to win her third consecutive Wimbledon title; and Roddy Doyle won the Booker Prize for *Paddy Clarke Ha Ha Ha!* When Gavin Bryars recorded a down and out singing an odd little ditty to the glory of God on the streets of London, he didn't quite know what to do with it. So, he went back to his studio – you see, that's already pretty different to the composers of old, isn't it? – and set about looping it, over and over again, with an increasingly loud and insistent string backing. The result was strangely moving and frequently leaves many people in tears. Again it stayed in the charts, week after week, haunting the airwaves. Sadly, the singer is now dead, but every time we play him, the phone lines light up with people wanting to know who's singing. The name of the piece is the enigmatic *Jesus' Blood Never Failed Me Yet* and I think it is up there on a par with Mozart's *Ave Verum* for sheer beauty.

Still, in 1993, another 'curve ball' here. As I said earlier, the somewhat obscure Polish composer, Górecki, actually wrote this piece in 1976, just as *One Flew over the Cuckoo's Nest* was sweeping the board with five Oscars at the Academy Awards. Then he just put it in his bottom drawer, in his home town not far from Auschwitz, and largely forgot about it. In 1993, however, a new recording was released, featuring the soprano Dawn Upshaw and the London Sinfonietta. This time round, though, it was a different story. The melancholy wailing of this *Symphony of Sorrowful Songs* seemed to strike a chord, and it went on to sell by the million, and become one of *the* music stories of the nineties.

As the tide of classical music began to take a turn for the better, the new year of **1994** dawned: a year in which the World Cup was scheduled for its quadrennial return. High up on the list of many people's concerns was not just 'Will Germany Win it Again?', but also, 'What are we going to do for a theme tune?' Four years earlier, in a stroke of genius, the powers-that-be had decided to ride the wave and harness the surge in popularity of classical music. And so, for their football World Cup theme of 1990, they'd looked to both Giacomo Puccini and Luciano Pavarotti. 'Nessun dorma' might sound like a Japanese people carrier but in 1990 it put Puccini on to the football terraces. I think Giacomo, the people's composer of Italy, would have loved it.

'Nessun dorma' is always a little bit of a problem in the opera house because the cheeky devil Puccini didn't put an end on it – it just scampers hurriedly on to the next bit of the opera. As a result, if you don't know this, and you inadvertently jump to your feet shouting 'Oh I say, that man, bravo, what?', well, then you don't half look a right pillock. That is, if you are even heard, above the deafening carillon of mobile phones that seem to go off more or less everywhere these days. In 1994, the World Cup came from America, and Bernstein's *West Side Story* was commandeered to act as the signature tune, but it didn't quite emulate the success of its Italian counterpart. Now onward.

Another interesting one came along a couple of years later, leaving a very significant marker in the sand, as it were. It was **1996**. Let me help you place it – CJD is identified as the killer of ten people in a macabre link to so-called 'mad cow disease', a Big Mac costs £2.70 and England lose on penalties to Germany. Perhaps that last bit won't help you place it. Anyway, to Karl Jenkins, a larger-than-life walking Welsh moustache with a musicality to kill for but, perhaps more importantly, a one-time member of the electronic rock group Soft Machine. He made a good living out of writing music for adverts. In 1996, though, he struck gold after the music for the Cheltenham and Gloucester Building Society became staggeringly popular. Eventually, it came out on CD as *Adiemus*, infectiously catchy and, again, it was Number One for longer than I care to remember.

And a million miles away from what **1997** was going to produce.

If it's 'Now, that's *NOT* what I call the sound of 1997 VOLUME 26!' that you're looking for, then I think I've got the answer. As it were.

And indeed it most definitely isn't. The music of 1997, that is. It's the work of two people: the first was Sir Edward Elgar, a larger-than-life walking English moustache with a musicologist to die for; the second is the musicologist himself, composer and all-round clever clogs, Anthony Payne. In 1997, Mr Payne unveiled Elgar's completed *Third Symphony*. Completed by Mr Payne, that is, with the permission of the Elgar estate. So, some sixty-three years after he died, Eddie 'The Eagle' Elgar is back in the charts. It's very much like Elvis and 'A Little Less Conversation'. Only without the hips.

The same year, 1997, has a couple of belters up its sleeve. Not only does JK Rowling produce her first Harry Potter, but also composer, former left-handed arthropod and all-round nice guy, Sir Paul McCartney, comes up with his latest and by far the best classical offering to date, 'Standing Stone'. Lovely stuff it is too. But, on to the sad hit of 1997, and it comes from John Tavener. At the funeral of Diana,

Princess of Wales, on September 5th, Lynne Dawson sings from the Verdi *Requiem* and Elton John sings his rewritten 'Candle in the Wind'. But it is an esoteric cantata by the spiritual minimalist John Tavener that soon becomes one of the country's most requested 'classical' works. His 'Song for Athene'.

It may have become popular, in a sense, for all the wrong reasons, but it is nevertheless a simple and beautiful piece of music. And quite typical, in many respects, of the way in which some modern composers have chosen to ignore the shock effects of the avant-garde in favour of a return to a sort of 'new romanticism'. Sorry, labels all over the place, but it's sometimes very hard to put into words. Just like the neo-classicists could never be mistaken for pure 'classicists', so these 'new romantics' are certainly lush and tuneful, but, ditto – you would never mistake them for the original romantics. And sorry if all this talk of new romantics is making you think of Steve Strange – I do apologize.

1998 and it's that man again. James Horner. As we saw in the filmy bit, he's pulled out another plum, called the *Titanic* soundtrack. It's in here again because, well, because it was just SO huge in the classical charts – aeons, it stayed. It's from the year that Sir Michael Tippett – the grand old man of serious English music – died, aged ninety-three. Five operas, four symphonies, five string quartets, four piano sonatas and lots, lots more. Not to mention Dana International, who in 1998 won the Eurovision with the song 'Diva'. Also, this is the year a new talent became popular. His name is Ludovico Einaudi and his particular brand of naive minimalism was to win him many followers, not to mention, no doubt, gold discs. But the big classical hit of 1998 came from an inspired pairing of medieval choral works and modern jazz saxophone. Who would have thought it? Inspired! Absolutely inspired! The Hilliard Ensemble sang the medieval choral stuff, and Jan Garbarek supplied the sax. The resulting music, *Officium*, is just sublime. Utterly beautiful. Medieval choral meets modern jazz. Who would have thought it would work? Indeed, their first idea, early sackbut and krummhorn meets raga, well, that didn't do quite so well. Now, where are we? Oh yes, a 'farewell' which is a million miles from Haydn.

Again, it's another piece that came to prominence solely through people power. The 'Ashokan Farewell', written for the small town of Ashokan in America by Jay Ungar, became popular in the new millennium – **2000** (the year of the Dome, the London Eye and Venus Williams beating Lindsay Davenport in the Ladies' Singles at Wimbledon). It's a quaint little piece that may not have gained in popularity had it not been for the stunning arrangement by Captain John Perkins. But it was movie composer Hans Zimmer who found himself with the most popular score of the year, with his music to the film *Gladiator*. The man whose previous hits had included the theme tune to TV's *Going for Gold* wrote a score that didn't seem to put a foot wrong – every note of it fitted the film to perfection.

What of the last few years, though? Well, it's more artists than composers that dominate. Charlotte Church, Leslie Garrett, the million-selling Russell Watson. But classical music composition is still healthy. Glass, Tavener, Reich– they are all still composing. And 'good old classical music', as it were, has only recently been revived by advertising and sports events – this year looked to both Handel's *Sarabande* to sell its jeans, and the Opera Babes' version of Puccini's 'One Fine Day' to sell the World Cup. And why not? Does no harm. Merely puts good music in the path of more people, doesn't it?

And TV continues to give a helping hand too. As recently as, what, the other day, more or less, a phone company gave John Tavener the call, to seek help selling its wares with his cantata *The Lamb* ringing out its Orange tones up and down the country. John Lewis used the services of Ludovico Einaudi to sell its wares, too, and artists such as Amici Forever and Mylene Klass continue to fight to break down the borders of where classical music stops and another music starts. Then there's Andrea Bocelli, the Italian tenor, who will sell out any huge venue wherever he goes, proving that, if you can just get it right, the audience for classical music is massive. And, of course, there's John Williams and his soundtrack to the latest movie about hirsuit golfers, *Hairy Putter III*, which manages to keep a real, living and breathing classical score at the top of the popular music charts. God bless JW!

And that more or less gets us up to date. I can't quite believe I'm writing this but, well, that's sort of the last piece in the jigsaw that was *Stephen Fry's Incomplete & Utter History of Classical Music*. We started some 302 pages ago with a cave painting in France, and we end, here, with the bats and belfries of the boy spellmeister.

Splendid.

I'm the wonderful wizard of Fry.

Au revoir.